NURTURING FAITH AND HOPE

NURTURING
FAITH&HOPE

Black Worship as a Model for Christian Education

Anne E. Streaty Wimberly

The Pilgrim Press

Cleveland

In gratitude for the nurture of faith and hope
given to me by the congregation of my childhood,
Second Methodist Church, now called New Hope
United Methodist Church, Anderson, Indiana

The Pilgrim Press, 700 Prospect Avenue East
Cleveland, Ohio 44115-1100
www.thepilgrimpress.com

08   07   06   05   04   5   4   3   2   1

Library of Congress Cataloging-in-Publication Data

Wimberly, Anne Streaty, 1936–.
    Nurturing faith & hope : Black worship as a model for Christian education / Anne E.
    Streaty Wimberly.
        p.   cm.
    Includes bibliographical references (p. 199).
    ISBN 0-8298-1568-6 (paperback : alk. paper)
        1. African Americans—Religion.   2. Public worship.   3. Christian education.   I. Title:
    Nurturing faith and hope.   II. Title.

BR563.N4W545 2004
264'.0089'96073—dc22

2004057329

CONTENTS

1044

110892

PREFACE

THE WORSHIPING CONGREGATION is an important place for those who enter it, but what happens there that makes it so? Why do we come to worship? When I have raised the question with individual persons, in small groups, and in my seminary classes, a lively discussion has invariably ensued. In exploring my own answers with others, I found myself revisiting a lifetime of Sundays and other occasions when I was privileged to be part of numerous worshiping congregations, sometimes as a worshiper in the pew and various other times as organist and choir director. I remembered spirited and spiritual "homes" of worship where I sought, met, and communed with God and those with whom I worshiped in ways quite difficult to put into words. The word that kept coming to mind, however, was nurture—the kind of care, of nourishment—from which new meanings, purpose, and strength for Christian living come, not always without a struggle, but come indeed.

Although what we shared differed in some very distinct ways, a common thread seemed to weave through all of our stories. This common thread was the intertwining of praise and thanks to God with the quest to know ever more deeply what it means to be people of faith and to live with hope in the fray of life. Those who shared seemed to say in a unified voice that the quest is for something to happen in heart and mind during the worship experience that brings forth a deepening relationship with God and a genuine embrace of beliefs with which to live as black Christian sojourners in today's world.

The yearning that was voiced in my conversations with others about worship sparked another question: What *is* happening in our worshiping congregations that nurtures us in our search for faith and hope and that does so in ways that evoke *within us* the answers that we seek? I embarked on a journey to discover responses to this question. This book is the result of that journey. As you enter it, I invite you to begin with the two sets of questions I have raised here—the ones posed in the beginning of the preface and the one just stated. Whether you are a worshiper in the pew, an individual person responsible for leading worship, a Christian educator, or another who has interest in worship as nurture, my invitation is for you to dialogue with what is shared herein for ways it reflects or suggests, affirms or prods changes in life in your worshiping congregation. My further invitation is for you to place yourself in the center of your reading with the intent of reflecting critically on your own experiences in worship, and those ways in which you are already being nurtured or would like to be through your experiences in worship.

I have drawn attention to my conversation partners along the way who have provided the impetus for what is written throughout the upcoming pages. There are, however, several persons whose names must be entered here because of extraordinary kinds of assistance they gave without which the work would not have been completed. I am indebted to Dr. James Michael Lee, who some years ago encouraged me to write a book on the gifts of the black church to religious education. Although the purpose and shape of this book is quite different from the one he envisioned, there are throughout it, I think, shining examples of ways of being and doing in worship that are gifts to be savored by black church leaders, laity, and others.

Words are insufficient to express the depth of my gratitude for the time, untiring assistance, processing skills, encouragement, and prayers of Mrs. Pamela Perkins. I count her contribution to the completion of this book as an extraordinary gift. I must add here words of great appreciation to Rev. Dr. Carol Helton who continued to give the clarion call for persistence in getting the work done and to offer assistance in whatever way needed. My seminary classes at Interdenominational Theological Center on the Congregation as Educator and the Church's Educational Ministry have been invaluable in their insights, critique, and suggestions as others have been, including Rev. Tiwirai Kufarimai who read and commented on portions of the manuscript. Most of all, however, my special gratitude and love go to my husband, Dr. Edward Wimberly, who stood by me in the late hours, read and typed numbers of pages, listened to my thinking aloud, affirmed ideas that "made sense" and gave direction for those that did not, and simply showed the depths of his care throughout. I am grateful for the gift that he is to me.

Introduction

BLACK WORSHIP AS NURTURING EXPERIENCE

Make a joyful noise to the LORD, all the earth.
Worship the LORD with gladness;
come into his presence with singing.

—Psalm 100:1–2

A POINT OF DEPARTURE

CHRISTIAN WORSHIP IS WIDELY considered today to be a vital educational ministry event and nourishing resource. It necessarily complements intentionally planned and sustained church school experiences and other related Christian education activities in the life of the church.[1] This view of Christian education is not new. Historically, teaching and learning the Christian story and its meaning for Christian life were central to the worshiping congregation's task of continuing to shape the lives of new believers, who began preparation for it in formal instructional settings.[2] The current renewed emphasis by Christian educators and church leaders focused on the pivotal role of education in and through worship has emerged for at least three primary reasons.

In one respect, the revitalized importance follows the results of research that highlight the diminishing effectiveness of existing instructional forms of church education. Consequently, there is the perceived need for alternative ways of carrying out educational ministry in congregations.[3] Second, connected to this finding is the recognition that worship services continue to be the heart of congregational life. The worshiping congregation is the largest gathering of people with more in attendance than in church school.[4] As such, although it is not a substitute for planned systematic forms of education, worship stands as the primary place in which the congregation comes before God in its own peculiar manner; and in this way, worship discloses to new worshipers and ongoing generations its own understandings of faith and life and its own particular style.

A third reason for the increasing focus on worship as a Christian educational environment is the embrace by many of a holistic orientation to Christian education.[5] In this view, every aspect of ministry including worship contains educational implications. For example, the people of God are fashioned, according to Maria Harris, through every aspect of the church's life including worship.[6] Others focus on the unique contributions of worship to Christian education by describing worship as a distinctive and powerful habitat for integrating the presence of God, the experiences of daily life, and visions of the future.[7] Through the language of ritual and relationships in worship, says Jeff Astley, persons learn "a range of emotions, experiences and attitudes that lie at the heart of Christian spirituality."[8] For Craig Dykstra, the experiences of confessing, repenting, proclaiming, and praying create openings for persons to see and grasp both our own self-destructive patterns of living and the redemptive activity of God.[9]

To some degree, the salience of black worship as educational experience is also being lifted up in black religious circles and by others. Black Christian educator, Ethel Johnson, along with Charles Foster highlight the requirement for the interdependence of worship and teaching.[10] Melva Costen, in her book *African American Christian Worship*, asserts that worship is opportunity for raising hope in the face of adversity,[11] whereas, the position of black pastor and educator Carlyle Fielding Stewart III, is that worship in the black church is a principal educational medium. For Stewart, worship is an informational arena, especially through sermons and songs. This educational environment stands apart from, yet in tandem with, the planned educational program focused on investigating, interpreting, and applying central truths and claims of the gospel.[12]

Stewart identifies worship as a pivotal informational arena because it is needed to respond to the questions that persons bring with them into the worshiping congregation: "So what? What does this mean for my life? Is this something new in the telling of this story? What will this worship service or sermon tell me that I don't already know? What preexistent or new truths borne out by personal experience will be corroborated by the experience of worship?"[13]

In the book *Educating Congregations*, Charles Foster cites the importance of organizing education in congregations around central events of the church that include event of worship. For him, worship embodies event-full education through which "we encounter ourselves, others, and the mystery of God in transformational ways."[14] Of particular interest in Foster's focus on worship as event-full education, though, is his statement that worship in black congregations offers a lively paradigm for today's church's education. Specifically, he reminds us that, in the heritage of our black congregations, Sunday morning worship has tended to embody and reenact the biblical stories that have brought meaning to our lives. Foster emphasizes that "the power of this education cannot be overestimated. It sustained people through unbelievable trouble and tribulation. It maintained community vitality in the face of the forces of marginalization and oppression. It equipped people to live faithfully in a hostile world."[15]

The remarkable power of black worship makes possible our discerning a way through life's opportunities and its darkness by "faith" that "always sees a star of hope."[16] This is the emphasis in this book. However, pivotal to this emphasis is what I see as the distinctive nurturing manner in which the ritual process of the black worshiping congregation mediates this discernment in light of the present stories of black persons.

BLACK WORSHIP AS NURTURE IN RESPONSE TO PRESENT STORIES

My use of the term "nurture" is an intentional one. The term is derived from the Latin verb, *nutrire*, which means "to suckle, nourish, or cultivate." It bears some similarity to education, which builds on the Latin *educare*, which means to "bring up," and on *educere*, meaning "to lead out." However, it is more basic to the vitality of life or to existence itself. That is, without nourishment, life would diminish. We would die. By making nurture central in what I want to share in the chapters of this book, I mean to accent that all who comprise the black worshiping congregation—the pastor, liturgists, musicians, worshipers—serve as communal nurturing agents who make possible our forming and sustaining an alive faith and hope. That is, while the ritual of the black worshiping congregation is the process through which nurture happens, nurture happens through the implementing activity of those who are part of the experience of worship. Moreover, nurture takes place through interactive communication or a "call and response" conversation between worship leaders and congregation and among the worshipers that is to have the effect of enriching nurture by what it evokes, sustains, and deepens in the worshipers.

The image of the worshiping congregation as the "nursing mother" is a fitting one and conveys the idea that persons may be self-educated, but cannot be self-nurtured.[17] At the same time, however, I want to make clear that worshipers are not passive in receiving nurture. Nurture summons something within worshipers. Nurture is evocative. It prompts our dealing with the nourishment that is given to us. To make a difference in our lives, nurture must arouse not just the something, but the "more" that brings an awareness, a discernment, even a struggling with the effects of nurture or what is being cultivated in us. As one worshiper put it:

> I don't come completely empty into worship. I have already within me my own understandings of the Christian faith that have been hewn over time, experience, hard knocks, and study. But, I want more for living, more that deepens my faith and builds my hope, more that activates my own desire to nurture others by what I say and do. I also might have an understanding that doesn't fit with what I am receiving in a sermon, for example. But, I will look for and reach out for what is there in a song or a prayer. For me, the spirit of God's presence that becomes real through the sense of community that comes forth in unrestrained movement or clapping, shouting, or even in moments of silence is beneficial. That's evidence of the reality of God's nourishment.[18]

Evocative nurture, then, builds on the view that worshipers desire and are ready for nurture and have the wherewithal to receive nurture and discern its meaning for their lives. That is, black worshipers come into the worshiping congregation seeking nourishment that affirms and responds to their capacity to receive it, struggle with it, and to discover, build on, and act on what is enormously important to their lives as Christians. Evocative nurture assumes that worshipers have the capacity to consider all that occurs in the worshiping congregation in light of what is already inside them. They are capable of positioning or making sense of the nurturing elements of worship in light of what Augustine calls "interior truth." For Augustine, "interior truth" is what already resides in a person that must be balanced with what the person hears from another.[19] I am using this term here to denote what we as black persons hold within us, as we worship, about the positive and troubling realities of life in general and our own lives in particular.

The interactive activities of the nurture-givers and nurture-receivers highlight the importance of paying attention to the approaches and the content that are being employed in the nurturing process as well as to what is being evoked through them. This attention is all the more necessary because the stories of black persons today trigger our quest for nurture that evokes new or renewed life meaning. In my earlier book, *Soul Stories: African American Christian Education,*[20] I stress that people do not come into any educational context as tabula rasa, or as a blank slate; and this is no less the case in the worshiping congregation. Black persons come into the worshiping congregation with the stories of our lives. We bring not simply beliefs or convictions to which the earlier mentioned worshiper referred but all of the "stuff" of everyday life. For black worshipers today, this "stuff" often reflects a dream not fully realized.

A Dream Not Fully Realized

It was assumed that the liberation agenda of the black freedom movement of the twentieth century would lead to the hoped-for future and to Martin Luther King Jr.'s publicly articulated dream of a beloved community in which oppression ceased and all God's people would dwell in a land of peace, justice, and safety. Communal action centered on black persons' historical faith in God's faithful nearness and activity on our behalf, and in God's empowerment of God's people to bring about relational wholeness and ongoing hope-oriented living for all. The assassination of Dr. King, the black freedom movement's leader, brought grief and discouragement to hope-filled people. The liberation agenda was not fully realized; and hopelessness began to appear in persons' despair at being unable to imagine a positive and realizable future that differed from the present. By the dawning of the twenty-first century, strides were made by many who moved into situations of accomplishment while, at the same time, black persons grieved needed and unseen progress.[21]

Clearly, we have witnessed opportunities for educational advancement, social position, and material gain for increasing numbers of black persons. Yet, this situation lies in stark contrast to the failure of life chances and abject poverty of many others. There is great concern, says Michael Dash and his associates, that "too many of our people are unemployed or underemployed. Far too many of our young men and women experience life in terms of its horrifying meaninglessness, love-lessness, and hopelessness."[22]

Health researchers and advocates also remind us that a disproportionate number of black persons grow up in poverty, struggling for adequate food and shelter in the world's wealthiest nation. Most of the two million Americans detained in our nation's jails and prisons are nonviolent substance-abusing black American offenders whose disease of addiction and need for spiritual wholeness go unaddressed by their incarceration in lieu of health care. Black people are not only disproportionately represented among the forty-seven million Americans without health insurance but also "experience poorer nutrition, more untreated mental illness, more environmental exposure to toxins, and a lack of quality health care for elderly brothers and sisters."[23] We grapple with the epidemic prevalence of AIDS in the black community and the stigma of AIDS, which still "hampers efforts to educate people and treat the sick."[24]

This current age is also characterized by the reality that those with beneficial life circumstances and those without continue to share in common absurd and demeaning experiences caused by our particular ethnic racial identity in a racially charged society. Black people across the various ages or stages are commonly on the receiving end of racial epithets, incidents of racial profiling, and unfair treatment and brutality. In addition, we confront those challenges associated with the human condition not the least of which are predictable crises accompanying each age or stage, family and communal relational concerns, and quandaries about the meaning and purpose of life.

These stories of black persons, which come with them into the worshiping congregation, also include a bent toward individualism that is seen in a concern for the care of selves before the care of others. In the midst of a hunger for the felt experience and nurture of community or the village in a challenging and fragmented world, a disturbing theme in the stories of those who are part of the worshiping congregation is an emphasis on "me and mine."[25]

In short, the hope-filled emphasis of the past era of liberation has given way to present stories marked by hopelessness, purposelessness, and lovelessness. There is a pervasive sense that far too many in the black community consider themselves to be powerless to arrive at a lasting positive existence within larger society and within the black community. There is a correlative sense in which, to use Cornel West's words, "the high moment of liberation theology has passed."[26] In the face of an elusive full and holistic liberation and the embrace of individualistic values that negate a sense of community, black people, especially the young, are raising the questions: "Why and in whom shall we have faith? How can we count on what appears to be an evanescent God who is not good all the time and who does bad things to good people? What hope is there for life?"

The troubles of our times, the stories black persons tell of those times, and the reasons for their entry into worship say much about the source of their questions and the search for a deepening faith and an alive hope that underlays the questions. Black persons are searching for a deepening faith and an alive hope that is more than an individualistic orientation to faith and hope. There is a search for a communally shared or "village" faith and hope that evokes in persons a zeal to make faith and hope concretely felt in and beyond the congregation through actions intended to make a better world. I have become aware of the depth of this search from the poignant queries of youth who are part of congregations: "Faith and hope? How are we suppose to live it when the adults around us don't show it in anything they say or do?" The nature of these questions of youth and the earlier mentioned questions of adults point to persons' deep yearning for a reorientation of black Christian faith and how to live that faith in hope-filled, whole-some-producing, and justice-seeking ways along the seeming unrelenting howling wilderness journey of life. The situation points to a critical need for nurturing faith and hope within the black worshiping congregation.

Faith and Hope as the Center of Evocative Nurture

Living in faith and hope constitutes a dynamic mode of being in the world that opposes the languid and life-defying mind-frame of hopeless-ness, purposelessness, and lovelessness that pervade the existence of many black persons today. It is also clear from sermons, songs, and prayers in black worship that faith and hope are orienting metaphors. As orienting metaphors, faith and hope are integral aspects of nurture carried out in the black worshiping congregation that are meant to answer worshipers' needs. Faith is understood as our belief or trust in our relationship with God and God's relationship with us through Jesus Christ and the Holy Spirit. Hope is our expectation and endeavors to live confidently and courageously in community after the model of Jesus in times of triumph and in the midst of hard trials and tribulations.

An evocative nurture that centers on these understandings of faith and hope is directed toward our embrace of a religious perspective that can provide sustenance for the continuation of life's sojourn. Indeed, the faith and hope, which the nurturing process is to arouse in us, is a new or renewed imagination of how to keep moving individually and collectively through each present moment "to see what the end will be."[27]

Central to the nurturing process is kindling and rekindling worshipers' recognition and embrace of the able God, relational Jesus, empowering Spirit, valued identity, and journey from sin to salvation that move persons toward a different future away from the one that present life in our community and larger society would predict. Yet, the overarching aim inherent in the nurturing process is the evocation of awareness that it is God *with* us in the person of Jesus and the Holy Spirit at all times, and who has not forsaken us and will not even in the difficult wrenching trials of life. This God is the only valid source of faith and hope. Indeed, there is a divine pedagogy at work in the nurturing process, particularly in our participation in the sacraments of baptism and Holy Communion, or eucharist, in which God is the evocator.

In the pedagogical work of nurture, God comes as the evocator who reaches out and invites our reaching back and calls for our vow that we will not, in fact, "turn back . . . but will go . . . shall go, to see what the end will be."[28] This is the call for faith and hope to become more than nouns expressed through the embrace of belief in God and the promise of God that comes to us in our imagining possibility in an unknown future. It is the call for faith and hope to become verbs. As verbs, faith and hope become actions that evolve from our consciousness that God is the recipient of our vow or declaration and that the weight of that vow is on us, the vow-maker, to honor it. The action takes the form of our living up to our vows through the vitality of our faith and hope that spill over into the everyday stories of our lives. Thus, the faith and hope that is evoked in the nurturing process of the black worshiping congregation must become, ultimately, the story of faith and hope that we live and share clearly and persuasively with others in actions and words.[29] Faith and hope in action is our living up to our vows even though, as our forebears knew and Lovell reminds us, it may involve "a great variety of sufferings, narrow escapes, failures, reversals, and hard trials which [we] must bear without losing faith and from which [we] must rebound."[30]

In light of what I have already said, I must add that faith and hope are not what is merely cultivated in the head. Faith and hope are matters of the head and the heart. The goal of nurture is to bring forth our knowing the content of the faith and hope we are to embrace. Nurture is to "fill us" with and invite our "digestion" by way of critical reflection on what constitutes the nature of God, Jesus Christ, the Holy Spirit, a valued identity, and the journey away from sin to salvation. Moreover, it is to stimulate our creation of insights on what these themes mean for our lives. Nurture draws on and stimulates our thinking selves, but the goal of nurture is more than simply knowing "proper information" about the themes that are so pivotal to faith and hope. Nurture is also to arouse our deep feelings in response to what is evoked within us. In the black worshiping congregation, nurture is to bring forth our passionate embrace of what faith and hope mean to us and a zest for acting on both. Indeed, this arousal of emotion may move us to contemplative homage to God or to the point of clapping, shouting, dancing, or exclaiming "Amen!" "Hallelujah!" or "Say it! That's the truth!"

I often hear that the black worshiping congregation is too emotive and does not promote in worshipers a deeper grasp of the Christian message through focused attention to matters of reason, belief, and knowledge. While we may identify cases in which this is true, we may be just as likely to name contexts of worship in which there is a lively and meaningful balance between cognitive and affective acts. I am also aware of the critique of black churches that underscores their loss of "the covenant relation between spiritual intimacy with God and human care of others."[31] However, I believe firmly that there is evidence of the black church's continuing efforts to make concrete what C. Eric Lincoln called the black church's role as "the uncontested mother of black culture."[32] This clearly lived nurture and communication of faith and hope in the world is attested to, in fact, in Andrew Billingsley's landmark volume, *Mighty Like a River: The Black Church and Social Reform*.[33]

Is there room for more to happen in the black church's nurture of faith and hope? Yes! The stories of unfulfilled dreams serve as a "wake-up call" for greater efforts to nurture new and renewed faith and hope. Although black worshiping congregations still carry out the historical role of "nursing mother" to persons in need of spiritual nourishment, the challenge remains one of looking closely at this role and assuring that its engagement is alive and vital. There are models to follow. What are they? What are the approaches to nurturing faith and hope taking place in black worshiping congregations? What is the content that is disclosed? The book is written to answer these questions.

WHO THIS BOOK IS FOR

This book is a resource for those of us who seek to strengthen the role of worshiping congregations in bringing faith and hope to life as well as for those who are already part of congregations who are looking to them for answers to life's difficult questions. The book invites pastors, professional and volunteer leaders in Christian education, and musicians and other church leaders to reflect on our own responses to the quest for an alive faith and hope for today's and tomorrow's sojourn. It also beckons us to consider what approaches are yet possible and what new content might be helpful to stimulate our knowing ourselves as faithful, hope-filled Christians who have a passion for living out this identity in everyday life.

Seminary professors and students in Christian education, worship, and homiletics will also find the contents of the book helpful in preparing leaders who are skillful in carrying out the nurturing task of the church. Preparing persons for the pivotal task of nurture in this nihilistic age is a formidable one and one for which seminaries must take responsibility. The book offers opportunity for seminarians to consider the self's views of faith and hope, how these views were formed, and the nexus of these views with the shape of the self's present or envisioned ministry in the worshiping congregation.

The chapters of the book may also be used as means of engaging laypersons in conversation on their journey of faith and hope. Through this engagement, laypersons, with a pastor or church leader as a reflection guide, are invited to revisit experiences in the worshiping congregation that most nurtured their formation of faith and hope, to identify helpful ways in which this nurture was carried out, and to discover, together, what yet may happen. Such an exploration may well lead to greater attention and even changes to what is happening in the worshiping congregation as well as to further times for exploring the nature and meanings of faith and hope outside the worshiping congregation.

THE DIRECTION OF THE BOOK: A DEMONSTRATION OF NURTURING FAITH AND HOPE

Numerous volumes of sermons of black preachers, songs of black worshipers, and prayers of black prayer warriors affirm that the black worshiping congregation demonstrates a variety of approaches to nurturing faithful and hope-filled Christians. What emerge in the three pivotal nurturing pathways are the beliefs and values on which faith and hope are built. Voluminous materials document that sermons, songs, and prayers in the black worshiping congregation disclose convictions about God, Jesus Christ, the Holy Spirit, a valued identity, and the movement from sin to salvation. As a nurturing theme, each conviction is presented through specific cultural approaches that best accentuate its content or its essence and that allow its evocative function to emerge. In addition, the content of each theme further reveals the richness of the cultural qualities of the convictions. Moreover, apart from the nurturing pathways of preaching, music making, and praying, the sacraments of baptism and Holy Communion—also called the Lord's Supper or Holy Eucharist—appear as crucial events in the life of the worshiping congregation that nurture faith and hope.

The book is organized in three sections.

• Nurture for Belief Formation

• Nurture through the Events of Baptism and Holy Communion

• Nurture through Pathways of Preaching, Music Making, and Praying

Part One includes six chapters. Each chapter explores a major theme in Christian life on which nurturing faith and hope in the black worshiping congregation centers. Attention is given to specific kinds of evocative approaches to nurturing faith and hope and key content that are disclosed through the approaches. Each chapter concludes with a commentary that calls for consideration of concerns that arise and demand attention in any ongoing focus on nurture. The commentary is followed by my invitation to the reader to reflect on what is contained in the chapter.

Of the six chapters in Part One, chapter 1 presents evocative approaches and content of nurture focused on God. The chapter approaches the task of nurturing faith and hope in God in the black worshiping congregation through emphasis on the metaphor-rich language occurring in sermons, songs, and prayers in this congregation. Of special importance is the power of the language to evoke an awareness of God that goes beyond anthropomorphic images. Instead, the language of evocative nurture has the effect of drawing worshipers' attention to God whose nature is boundless and about whom human expression cannot be bound.

How the black worshiping congregation nurtures faith and hope in Jesus is the focus of chapter 2. The chapter draws primarily on sermons, songs, and prayers to describe how the black worshiping congregation expresses and heightens worshipers' consciousness of Jesus' character, Jesus' relationship with them, and Jesus' ministry on behalf of them and others. The chapter also accentuates the narrative and vision-shaping language of evocative nurture that centers on Jesus and on the important effort in the worshiping congregation of pressing for faith and hope in action. In this regard, evocation takes the form of hard questions intended to elicit critical reflection on the nature of everyday actions that demonstrate an embrace of faith and hope in Jesus. Content focused on the relational character of Jesus forms the basis for nurture that evokes an intent for mimetic action on the part of worshipers.

In chapter 3, evocative approaches and content center on faith and hope in the Holy Spirit that extends the exploration of nurturing faith and hope in God and Jesus Christ appearing in chapters 1 and 2. The chapter calls attention to the role of evocation through sermons, songs, and prayers in the engagement of worshipers in reflective imagination and linking biblical texts to life stories that prompt awareness of the nature and activity of the Holy Spirit. In a manner similar to chapter 2, questions form an interrogative approach that serves as an "open doorway" to imaginative reflection not simply on the nature of the activity of the Holy Spirit, but on human activity empowered by the Spirit that aims to create a better world.

Chapter 4 explores approaches and content appearing in evocative nurture in the black worshiping congregation that is directed toward bringing forth black worshipers' faith and hope in a valued personal and communal identity. The chapter highlights the role especially of sermons and songs in creating a participatory and evocative nurturing habitation that invites worshipers into a redefinitional ritual. The redefinitional ritual is presented as a key approach to engendering new or renewed faith and hope in the valued self and community that is given by God. The ritual emerges as evocative activity designed to stimulate the worshipers' differentiation of denigrating language and treatment in the social sphere from affirmative language that redefines the self and the relationship of God to black people. The chapter places reframing, renaming, and redefining activities and countervailing content at the center of the evocative nurture.

Chapters 5 and 6 utilize especially sermons and songs to demonstrate the evocative approaches and content that press worshipers to see in concrete, experiential language meanings of "missing the mark" and reversing the direction to opening the way for faith and hope in God's transforming and sustaining activity. The chapters explore the nature of truth-telling language, including rhetorical devices and narrative content that are designed to heighten consciousness of the realities of sin and salvation and to enkindle worshipers' seeing, affirming, and being moved by the reversibility of "missing the mark." Attention is given to evocation that stimulates worshipers' faith in the reversibility of sin not simply through God's activity, but through their spiritual quest for wholeness. Hope for wholeness is seen as a consequence of the inward journey and persons' forming and sustaining a relationship with the person of Jesus through whom a "new creation" is possible.

Part Two includes two chapters. Building on stories, chapter 7 presents the sacrament of baptism as one of two pivotal events that nurtures faith and hope. Nurturing faith and hope takes place as baptism draws black worshipers into a dramatic and emotional experience of God's presence and activity through Jesus Christ and the Holy Spirit. The chapter highlights baptism as an integrative nurturing experience that fosters the worshipers' connection to all the themes of Christian life presented in the foregoing chapters. Moreover, special attention is given to baptism as a nurturing event that calls new or renewed attention to and affirmation of the valued identity on which chapter 4 focuses. The approaches of naming, announcing, and claiming identity taking place in the ritual of baptism are presented as crucial means of evoking an embodied awareness of the self's identity that is valued and affirmed by God.

Holy Communion is the second of the two central events in Part Two that chapter 8 describes as an integrative nurturing event. Using stories, the chapter shows how this event invites worshipers to make connections between faith and hope in God, Jesus Christ, the Holy Spirit, the valued self, sin, and salvation. The chapter also emphasizes the emotional power of this nurturing event on worshipers' formation of faith and hope. Attention is focused on the power of the event that results from the image of the ritual as the "Welcome Table," from the enactment of God's welcome made known in Jesus, and language describing the brokenness of Christ that awakens or reawakens an awareness of brokenness in the world. Additionally, the chapter highlights Holy Communion as an event that fosters worshipers' experience of re-membering or of being and becoming a community of solidarity and a caring people in the world.

Throughout the chapters of the book, sermons, songs, and prayers are identified as critical pathways of nurture. The three chapters of Part Three explore in more complete detail the nature of the inextricable role of these pathways in the process of nurturing faith and hope in the black worshiping congregation. Chapter 9 presents preaching as an evocative medium that nurtures faith and hope through prophetic, priestly, and apostolic functions of the preached word as well as through the pastor's character. The nurturing role of music is described in chapter 10 in terms of unique imaginative and expressive manners in which music both evokes and shapes thoughts, attitudes, and feelings about the primary themes of the Christian faith explored in Part One. Music is also presented as evocative nurture that prompts a kind of "spiritual free-play." This metaphor is used to describe music as thoughtful, artful, and emotional nurture through which the worshiping congregation voices, reflects on, and responds to the nature and meanings of life challenges, living with faith under fire, and sojourning with hope. Chapter 11 focuses on prayer as nurture bearer that arouses in us a sense of rightness in talking with God. Prayer is presented as "primary speech" and evocative communication that nurtures faith and hope by enkindling and validating beliefs about who God is and how God acts, our need for God, and ways of responding to God.

By way of summary, this book focuses on the evocative manner in which worship life of the black church nurtures the faith and hope of the worshiping congregation. The book is intended to explore in depth how faith and hope are formed in persons in an age of nihilism. Moreover, the exploration of nurture in the black worshiping congregation seeks to capture new awareness that worship is a central context for the educational ministry of the church.

Part One

Nurture for Belief Formation

"Core beliefs are our working opinions about whether God can be trusted. . . . They have been acquired through life experiences, worship, and cultural exposure, and they can be altered likewise."

—Nicholas C. Cooper-Lewter and Henry H. Mitchell,
Soul Theology

FAITH AND HOPE IN GOD

For surely I know the plans I have for you, says the LORD, *plans for your welfare and not for harm, to give you a future with hope.*

—Jeremiah 29:11

THE QUESTIONS "Who is God?" "How does God act in the nitty-gritty of our everyday lives?" and "How do we know God acts?" are prominent ones that black people raise along life's journey, propose answers, and bring into the worshiping congregation for further reflection. Some of us bring into worship our thoughts in the form of doubt about God's existence and for-us-ness, especially in or because of tough situations or experiences of hard trials and suffering. Others of us express differing views through our testimonies of unequivocal belief in a powerfully present God who does not leave or forsake us, who affirms and opens before us life's promise, and who is able to carry us through life's raging storms. We also give hints of our ideas about God in the words we choose to name God. Our conceptions of God emerge in whether we see and claim God as the One who calls us to a unique place to be and to act with faith and hope in today's world.

With questions about God and varied answers to the questions, we enter worship in anticipation of some responses to them as well as a new or renewed experience of God and God *with* us. As worshipers, we seek a worship experience that addresses our questions, affirms our faith and hope in God, and provides sustenance for the journey ahead.

In the words of one worshiper: "I recognize that we come to church to praise God. But, I want to come away knowing more surely and deeply the God we praise. Now, I'm not talking about the kind of knowing that's in your head. Well, I don't want to leave that out because that's important too. But, what I really mean is that I want to go deeper and deeper in my knowing God in my heart. It's important for me to know deep down that God's not done with me yet and is not going to leave me 'hanging out there.' I also want to have a strong enough faith that I won't let go of God."

Through our participation in rituals, symbols, and language, we look for those moments—a "happening"—in worship that evoke or enkindle the kind of heart and head knowing to which the worshiper refers. The unfolding of the order of worship, the symbol of the altar and the language of sermons, songs, and prayers are among the intrinsic aspects of the "happening" that give to us "food" for the mind and our imagination of God's nature. In this way, worship nurtures our conscious knowing God. Yet, in the midst of these expressive dimensions of worship, there is also room for the divine pedagogy through which God comes as the divine Evocator, reaches out to us, and beckons our reaching back. Ultimately, this human-Divine encounter triggers our deepest heart knowing, our awareness of being part of God's story, and our anticipation of a sojourn in which, as my mother would consistently say to me: "Nothing is going to happen that you and God can't handle."

How, really, though, does black Christian worship become the environment within which head and heart knowing comes forth? What constitutes the method and content that nurture our deepening faith and hope in God? Answers to these questions are at the center of our exploration in this chapter.

EVOCATIVE METHOD: NURTURING THROUGH A PARTICIPATORY HABITATION

A STORY

As the soloist and the choir began to sing the song "Surely God Is Able," the pastor invited us to come to the altar to thank God for blessings we received during the past week and to lay our cares before God who knows our every trouble and our every need. There was good reason for the altar call on that particular Sunday. Many of us in the congregation had been joyful participants at a wedding the day before. But, in the preceding week, a funeral had also been held for a teen who had committed suicide. The altar was soon filled with persons of all ages, some on bended knee, and some standing.

In the moments that followed, the prayer of the pastor went something like this: "We praise you, O God, for your presence in times of both joy and sorrow. We know you as the God who rejoices in our happiness and who weeps with us during our times of unbearable grief." The pastor continued by calling on God's affirming, renewing, and comforting presence, "knowing that you, God, are with us every step of the way in our journey of life no matter how brilliantly shining it is or how unbelievably hard and daunting it is." The pastor ended by saying: "Help us to stay assured of your love and to rest in the hope that you, God, will make a way out of no way." Throughout the prayer and the continued softly rendered message of the choir, worshipers wept quietly, some remained silently bowed, while others cried out, "Yes, Lord!" "God, we know you're here." "We know you hear us."

An Overview of the Evocative Method

The prayer time described in the story was a time of nurturing—of evoking our faith and hope in God. It was an invitation to us to enter into an experience of knowing God at a deep gut level that addressed but went beyond any head knowing. Yet, this occasion of praying is but one means in the black worshiping congregation that is intended to call forth what may be described as our knowing that we *know* that we *know God.*

Nurturing faith and hope in God in matters akin to that occurring in the story is what we seek and in which many report they find in the black worshiping congregation. There is an evocative method of nurture used in black worship especially through sermons, songs, and prayers that stirs and affirms our faith in a present and able God and hope in God's promises declared in scripture. The method serves as a stimulus to our depth-full knowing that meaningful and purposeful Christian life begins, continues, and ends with faith and hope in God. Moreover, what comes into play are evocative approaches that inspire us to hold to our belief in God's constant presence in the changing and oft-times difficult sojourn of life and to wait for the still small voice of God in times of God's seeming silence. The method seeks to make possible our actual encounter with God and our deepening belief in God's for-us-ness even in the desert moments of our lives when God seems to be absent.[1] We are to discover and rediscover ourselves as people of hope—a people whose hope is in God who acts in our lives just as God acted in the days of biblical prophets.[2]

The kind of evocative method that is directed toward our knowing God in mind and heart actually involves the presence of a participatory habitation within which to engage in reflexive activity. We are not bystanders, but rather full participants in all that happens to evoke our imagination and experience of God. Indeed, these methods that enlist our full participation are also designed to stimulate our thinking "beyond the box" about God and our coming to awe-inspiring awareness of who God is. More specifically, the methods to which we will now turn include:

- a method of reflection-in-action occurring in a participatory habitation;
- methods prompting analogical discovery;
- methods evoking a serviceable orthodoxy; and
- methods evoking thinking "beyond the box."

Reflection-in-Action in a Participatory Habitation

The black worshiping congregation has always been, and continues to be today, a key participatory habitation for Christian nurture that engages us in probing, naming, and forming images and beliefs of God.

The expression of convictions about God and questions like the one appearing in a gospel song that asks us whether we know the able-ness of God[3] invite us to probe who God is in our own lives.

Songs, along with prayers and sermons, are actually oral narrative means of forming a participatory habitation for evoking our awareness of the qualities of God. Our singing, praying, and "talking back" during the sermon engage us in reflection-in-action on the nature of God's activity in lives of persons before us and in our lives today. Reflection-in-action refers to our pondering God's nature and activity *during* our participation in story-telling and story-listening activities. The narrative methodology is awareness-evoking means through which we link and identify with biblical stories of God's activity in persons' lives, with stories of God in the sojourn of Christians including black forebears across the centuries, and with persons' responses to God. In reflection-in-action, we envision that God relates to us today in ways akin to the human-Divine relationship in the past. We also discover a language to name and converse with God. We conceive of and anticipate continuing conversations with God. We build our hope in God and visualize our role in making this hope come alive.

Reflection-in-action in the participatory habitation of black worship precludes our passivity in partaking of nurture. Nurturing our faith and hope in God evolves from the whole community's contemplation and expressions of who God is, how God acts, and what our responses to God may be. These endeavors also have the capacity to carry us to a place where the numinous or mysterious and inexplicable presence of God is keenly felt. In this place, there can emerge a sense of knowing that we *know God* to the extent that God's presence overtakes our awareness of being with others. Such an experience can result in our saying, as one worshiper said, "Yes, God is here with and for everybody. But, God was really present to me personally. I felt God's presence." It is this knowing that the individual person takes from the worship service and that creates faith and hope needed for daily life. A participatory habitation makes possible Christian nurture that results in this kind of knowing.

Prompting Analogical Discovery

I have already mentioned the use of scripture that initiates reflection-in-action. Scripture is, in fact, an important means of drawing us into an analogical method in nurturing process. As alluded to earlier, this method stirs our imagination of God's current-day presence and activity in the same manner as God was present and active in Bible times. The approach is not a new occurrence. Beginning in slavery, worship of black people evoked their faith and hope in God by identifying analogous relationships or likenesses between their own life journey and biblical exemplars' journeys in which God was present and acted.[4] Consequently, historically, black people began forming beliefs about God in the throes of their entering the Bible, considering their own lives within the center of the biblical narrative, and seeing a constantly alive God. The same is true today. Again, the scripture with which this chapter began is an example of the continuing presence of this process. Through its unfolding words, the scripture evokes faith and hope in God who is able today to do what God did in the days of Jeremiah.[5]

Sermons of black pastors also utilize the analogical method to stimulate our awareness of God's nature and to nurture our faith and hope in God. In many instances, the sermon material draws black worshipers into analogical discovery through the kind of story-linking approach I describe in the book *Soul Stories: African American Christian Education*.[6] In this approach, the black preacher is the nurturing agent who links a contemporary story with a biblical story or text for the insights from scripture about God's nature, God's activity, and human responses to God that are important to consider in the contemporary story. For example, in her sermon "If the Worst Should Come," Carolyn Ann Knight begins by "painting a storied picture" of people's living with little expectation that the worst would happen only to discover that life can take a disastrous turn with little or no preparation for it.[7]

Knight then links this contemporary dilemma with the biblical story of Habakkuk. Habakkuk had a plan for confronting the impending national calamity among a people who turned their backs on God. This plan reported by Knight was "[to] wait for the awesome day of calamity, trusting in the great God who performed awesome deeds in the past at Mount Sinai and the Red Sea. . .," and to seek God's mercy.[8] In the linking process, Knight draws the analogous relationship between "calamitous circumstances, tumultuous times, and perilous predicaments" in contemporary times and circumstances in the biblical story. The primary insight Knight draws from scripture and evokes in the listener is that "God will give sure footing in slippery times" today as in the past; and it is this faithful God who is worthy of our praise and response in the worst of times.[9]

Evoking a Serviceable Orthodoxy

The method of nurturing faith and hope also draws black worshipers into an awareness of a "serviceable orthodoxy" or "a usable concept of God."[10] It emphasizes the responsiveness of God to human beings as well as humans' responsiveness to God. The method begins by arousing black worshipers' recognition of a relational God whose actions on our behalf merit and require our cooperation and faithful response. Stated another way, evocative nurture accomplished in this way seeks to heighten our awareness that the journey of faith and hope is contingent, first, on the relationship that every individual enters into with God. Evocation involves drawing our attention to the kind of relationship with God, says Alton Pollard III, that we enter from within ourselves—"the secret altar, the tarrying place, the midnight watch, the solitary moment on bended knee."[11] However, the outcome of the awareness-heightening method is to move us beyond the inner self to outer action. We are to gain keen awareness of the necessity of and kinds of faith-filled and hope-filled responses to a faithful God through action in the everyday community. We are to come to know that God hears the cries of people; yet, God also calls us to join God in hearing and responding to those same cries.[12]

Karen Black-Griffith's sermon is a powerful illustration of the method of stimulating awareness of a "serviceable orthodoxy" or a response to God's call to us to act in community. In the sermon, Black-Griffith refers to God's presence, guidance, and inspiration in Nehemiah's efforts to lead his fellow citizens of Jerusalem to restore a dilapidated wall and bring back moral integrity and order.[13] God responded to

Nehemiah's strong concern for his people and a sincere sense of religious zeal and duty."[14] Black-Griffith, however, did not stop with her depiction of the mutual responsiveness of God and Nehemiah. She extended her evocative method by placing the hearer in touch with God's responsiveness to black people who seek, as Nehemiah did, to reverse the "bad news" that pervades stories like that of Pearly, whom Black-Griffith related had been forced into self-reliance from about the age of eleven as the result of her mother's crack addiction and abandonment of her. Black-Griffith continues by telling of Pearly's joining a gang and going through initiation rites that left her pregnant and infected with HIV. The story then turns to the community's response: "The community's heart was saddened. An overwhelming sense of guilt and concern swept through like a tidal wave. But the condition of the community had so deteriorated that even though there were churches, it seemed, on every corner, there was none with the will or the resources to come to the rescue. The community's few sincere leaders felt helpless against the tide of affairs and mourned for a way out.[15]

Black-Griffith's evocative method of nurture situates the worshipers in the life of Pearly and in Pearly's community. From this participative stance, worshipers hear the claim that "all is never lost" when people have a mind to cooperating with God's help. The evocative trigger is the engagement of the worshipers in imagining their own responsiveness through forthright action to bring about transformation in the community.[16]

The key point here is that the evocative method seeks to arouse the worshipers' understandings and ways of being mutually responsive with God. As stated earlier, through this method, worship nurtures faith and hope in God by drawing attention not simply to God's nature and activity but to our inner and outer response to God. To this extent, nurturing faith and hope in God is a process of nurturing a "serviceable orthodoxy" or a concept of God that we concretely act on in everyday life. Of course, the decision to act on this concept is ultimately up to us. I am reminded of a sermon given by my father many years ago in which he sought to evoke in the listeners their concrete response to God beyond the worship service. As the members greeted him following the service, one person simply said: "'Rev,' I heard what you said about God and our response to God. I know you're right. But, I just ain't gonna do it." Of course, the point not to be overlooked, though, is that this member did, in fact, "get the message."

Thinking "Beyond the Box"

At its best, nurturing faith and hope in God in the black worshiping congregation is about evoking in us a deepening head and heart awareness of the able God and our response to God. However, sometimes, the awareness we form hinders the response we give because of what Samuel Proctor calls our equating "our own cultural habits with the voice of God."[17] As Proctor asserts: "One of the most serious tasks we face is learning to distinguish the voice of God from our own preoccupations and loyalties."[18] The sermon of James Perkins places this concern in the context of our confining God within a specified cultural framework. What emerges from his sermon is the necessity of nurture that fosters our recognition that "God can't be made into the image and likeness of our cultural preferences . . . [because] God is God with full divine freedom."[19]

Jacqueline Grant also points to the importance of the kind of nurture in black worship that calls to mind with utmost clarity the ways we "place God in a box."[20] Based on her sermon, it can be said that the intent of the evocative method in nurturing faith and hope in God is not simply to engage us in examining our tendencies to control God, but to challenge us to release the limitations we impose on God. For example, Grant calls for the examination of four kinds of boxes in which Christians often place God. One box is the *church box* in which some Christians place God by virtue of their view that everything centers around "our" church or denomination. A second box is the *class box* into which prosperous people sometimes lock God by their tendency not to see God who blesses them so they may bless others. A third box is the *race box* into which some Christians place God by their insistence that God not simply favors them but exists solely in their image. The fourth box is the *male box* that people create by virtue of their belief in a male/father God, even though the Bible reveals a God that is much more than a male image portrays.[21]

Grant evokes an image of a "big God" by drawing on the words of the black American spiritual: "God is so high you can't get over, so low you can't get under, so wide you can't get around—you must come in at the door."[22] Grant's challenge to worshipers lies in the statements: "We must learn that we cannot contain God" and "when we take God out of our boxes, we are freed up to be all that God created us to be."[23]

The point of Proctor's book and Perkins' and Grant's sermons is that our preoccupations sometimes force us to confine and abridge our understanding of God. In such a situation, we limit what God can do in our lives and, indeed, may fail to see fully what we are called to do in response to God. Faith- and hope-directed nurture challenges the limited framework in which we place God; and it does not shrink back from agitating within us a Divine-human relationship in which God is God with full divine freedom. This more agitative view of evocative nurture bears semblance to the Augustinian emphasis on wise eloquence that is both beneficial and truthful as well as on forceful kinds of speaking when there is need for listeners to be moved rather than simply instructed.[24]

A Summary of Evocative Methodology

To summarize, the evocative nurturing method in the black worshiping congregation has multiple dimensions that focus on our formation of a head and heart awareness of God and the nature of the Divine-human relationship. Faith and hope in God depends on this kind of awareness. The faith toward which nurture moves us is our knowing deeply the qualities of the able and present God who has not and will not forsake us and from whom we will not depart. The hope that nurture arouses in us is our vision and embrace of a service orientation that is made concrete in our actions to make a better world. Yet, as I have indicated in the Introduction and will continue to reiterate in the chapters to come, it is God, the divine Evocator, who ultimately reaches out to us and beckons our reaching back; and, in that moment when God's reach and our response link—in that instant of awe-inspiring connection—both faith and hope come alive.

GOD-CENTERED CONTENT OF EVOCATIVE NURTURE

Singing, praying, and participating in the sermonic event in the black worshiping congregation connect us with and nurture a faith- and hope-oriented, culture-specific, and metaphor-rich God language. Indeed, our participation in these acts of worship contributes deeply to our formation of a God language and beliefs about God. Specifically, the content of the nurturing process serves as a stimulus to our awareness of a culturally formed oral God language. The content reveals cultural ways of addressing, talking with, and talking about God. It reflects persons' concrete experiences of God and frames the nature of experiences yet to occur.

The two centuries of African American prayers compiled by James Washington in the voluminous collection *Conversations with God,*[25] the smaller volume called *Prayer in the Black Tradition* by O. Richard Bowyer and his associates,[26] and numerous volumes of sermons and songs attest to the richness of the God language revealed in the black worshiping congregation. The nature of God's personhood, spiritual essence, and activity form an essential linguistic content in the nurturing process that we internalize and use to a degree that it becomes our own. Of even greater significance, though, is that this content of evocative nurture reveals the black cultural notion that God may be known in widely varying terms. Moreover, God may be named in ways other than hierarchical, imperialistic, and dualistic terms that stress the distance between God and the world.[27]

The following lexicon derives from God language appearing in collections of black prayers, sermons, and songs, many of which are based on biblical images. The list typifies the kind of content from which black worshipers build a cultural God language and beliefs about God.

All-wise God
Almighty God

Alpha and Omega

Archive of incarnate love

Avenger God

Captain who has never lost a battle

Counselor

Creator

Daniel's God

El-Shadai (the Almighty God)

Empowerer

Eternal Spirit

Everlasting or Eternal God

God

God, my only hope

God of all goodness, mercy, and love

God of heaven

God of love, power, and justice

God of missions

God of my salvation

God of nations, people, and all creation

God of our forefathers

God of peace

God of unbounded mercy

God, our all supply

God, our Father in heaven, our Mother on earth as in heaven

God, the Divine Other

God the father to the fatherless, mother to the motherless, and friend
    to the friendless

God, the flame

Governor

Gracious God

Gracious Presence

Great God
Great God of tenderness
Great head of the church
Great Physician
Greatest of the greatest
Heavenly Father
Highest, best, eternal rock of righteousness
Hope of our race
I am that I am
Immortal, Infinite, Exhaustless Fountain
Infinite Amiableness
Jehovah
Jehovah-Jireh (the Lord will provide)
Jehovah-Shammah (the God who is there)
King
Light
Lord God almighty, Lord God of old
Lord God of hosts
Lord, my Lord
Maker
Mighty God
Precious Lord
Omniscient Spirit
Our life, our hope, our guide
Our refuge in the time of need
Ruler whom servants trust
Shepherd Divine, Chief Shepherd
Source of light
Spirit of holiness
Sustainer
The One who knows all about us

Thou Dazzling Sun
Tireless Champion
Wonder Worker

What is important here is that these diverse metaphors come out of the very real experiences of the people who have used them. They represent the God revealed to black people in their everyday journeys; and they speak of a God in people's concrete experiences whose nature is boundless and about whom human expression cannot be bound. However, it is important to say as well that while the nurturing process may engage people in hearing and practicing a widely diverse God language, it is only when we actually experience God in the ways reflected in the language that the nomenclature truly has meaning for us. That is, we may be exposed to a metaphor-rich God language in the worshiping congregation and may develop a broader awareness of who God is and how God acts as the result of that exposure. However, the depth of meaning of the language we hear, practice, and find ourselves voicing quite naturally and spontaneously evolves from our experience of God as "a living, personal presence that is insinuated at all times and in all circumstances."[28]

An additional dimension that must not be overlooked with regard to the content pertains to the invitation afforded us to critique God language. It is interesting to note, for example, that the later the era in which the prayers occurred in the Washington volume, the greater the use of male anthropomorphic images. Specifically, more references to God as "He" appear in the prayers said toward the end of the twentieth century. Why this is so is not clear. Perhaps it has to do with the enculturating experiences of black people in wider culture. Regardless of the reason, the metaphor-rich language used across the years summons us to revisit our heritage and the nurturing power of this language. This language came out of the experiences of black people in the heat of the trials and tribulations of life, and a deep relationship with God that was fostered in black church worship and nourished in daily life. The language reflects the kind of knowing God that became a way of life. It is language, in fact, that takes God "out of the box."

The importance of our critique of God language lies in what it portends for our claiming our views and convictions of God based on our connecting the language we hear and practice in worship with our actual experiences of God.

COMMENTARY

It is perhaps the case that not nearly enough attention is given to what, exactly, Christian worship reveals about the nature of God and whether, in fact, the views of God that are revealed and nurtured actually make a difference in persons' knowing God. It is important, I think, for pastors and educational leaders to engage in conversations with our members beyond the worship experience and to ask the question and to learn from the answers to the question: "What notions about God and what experiences of God would you say result from your involvement in the worshiping congregation?" It is equally essential that we are cognizant of those in our congregations who are struggling with what Gardner Taylor calls the view of an elusive or absent God and of the congregation as a place in which to hide from God.[29] What Taylor seems to confirm is that it is not necessarily the words or language through which God's reality is revealed. Rather, nurture that seeks to evoke our encounter with a speaking God, awareness of God's nature and activity in and beyond worship, and ability to discern meaningful responses to God will require times in congregational worship and times beyond it for us to sit silent before God. This time of silence is not simply moments in prayer, but rather times of just waiting and being open to hear from God.[30]

Particularly in black worship today, the nurturing process must be able to stir in us the will to silence by inviting silence and communicating the necessity and nature of silent moments, especially in light of our jubilant-dominated worship and our frantic, boisterous everyday lives. To do so is to make of worship more than a habitus that simply nurtures people's formation of views about God and a God language. Rather, it recognizes that true nurture engages people in both stirring and contemplative ways of facilitating our knowing and responding to God.

AN INVITATION TO REFLECT

1. What images of God do you hold dear? How and where did you form them?

2. What views of and metaphors for God are communicated through sermons, songs, and prayers in your worshiping congregation?

3. What material in this chapter affirms, differs from, and/or challenges your experiences of nurturing faith and hope in God through worship?

4. Consider the use and importance of silence to you as a way of learning who God is and how God speaks. To what extent is silence an integral part of the worship experience in your congregation? What is said about the need for silence? Explore your attitudes and feelings about silence and opportunities for silence as a stimulus for your actual experience of and response to God.

FAITH AND HOPE IN JESUS CHRIST

We have this hope, a sure and steadfast anchor of the soul.

—Hebrews 6:19

A NOTED GOSPEL SONG WRITER, Fred Hammond, tells the story of being back at his grandmother's church during the "testimony service" when someone would invariably stand up and excitedly proclaim: "Jesus is all the world to me."[1] Pronouncements like the one recalled by Hammond are not unusual because of the continuing prominence of Jesus in the black worshiping congregation and black Christian life. The whole of worship in this congregation gives exceedingly great attention to the person of Jesus. Indeed, the importance of Jesus in black churches is so great that the term "Jesusology" is sometimes used as a descriptor of black Christianity.[2]

In the worshiping congregation, we expect an emphasis on the One whom black Christians have historically recognized and affirmed as the zenith of God's presence in our lives. There continues to be an unmistakable message of faith in God's presence in Jesus that began in black worship from the era of slavery forward. Central to this faith is the conviction that Jesus is God—the King of kings and Lord of lords[3]—and that God's revelation in Jesus shows God's for-us-ness in our sojourn as black people.[4] Jesus is revealed in the black worshiping congregation not simply as God's presence in the world but as the One who was for our forebears and is today hope-bearing Friend, Protector, Liberator, and Reconciler along the oft-times treacherous daily sojourn. Jesus-centered worship is, in fact, an evocative experience that raises our consciousness of who Jesus is. This experience affirms or reaffirms our faith and hope by awakening our memory of Jesus, the suffering One who knows all about our troubles and as Hope-Giver in difficult circumstances when "anything that could go wrong . . . [comes] our way."[5] This chapter presents the methods and content through which this experience is carried out.

By way of prefacing my presentation of these methods and content, I want to call attention, briefly, to the evocative style found in them. In much the same manner as noted in our consideration of God in chapter 1, sermons, songs, and prayers are primary methodological tools and content conveyors. These activities engage us in expressing our convictions about Jesus while, at the same time, engendering our reflection on and fresh thoughts about our belief in him. As with nurturing faith and hope in God, evocative nurture focused on Jesus continues to function in worship in ways that pose and answer queries about him that surface in the midst of the messiness we sometimes experience life to be. Sermons, songs, and prayers do not dodge the questions we raise or the answers we give, think about, or need to hear. In evocative nurture, we search for, receive, and ponder answers to the pressing questions: "Does Jesus care? How does he care?"

The evocative thrust of the method and content is to affirm or reaffirm our faith in the relational Jesus by stimulating our recall of him as the Friend and Protector "when all others have forsaken you."[6] The language is vivid and compelling in its disclosure of a relational Jesus. It is meant to move us not simply to think about, but to see, experience, and know, as we know God, the compassionate Deliverer who frees us to continue on in times of trouble and to choose right over wrong.[7] Evocative nurture is the prompter of our deepening awareness of Jesus who is the reconciling One, through such messages as "You can't hate your neighbor when your mind is staid on Jesus,"[8] the caring One "who speaks to us on the stormy sea and makes the billows cease to roll,"[9] and faithful One who will make a way somehow.[10]

Our knowing the relational Jesus is the goal that the method and content serve in evocative nurture. Both method and content bring us face-to-face with this Jesus in our everyday lives. However, the method and content give equal attention to the role we should undertake as Christians as the result of knowing him. The same serviceable orthodoxy described in chapter 1 applies here. Yet, in evocative nurture focused on Jesus, the answer to an essential question must precede service on behalf of a better world: "Christian, do you love my Jesus? . . . If you love Him, why not serve Him?"[11] Evocative nurture stimulates our knowing—our experience of—the presence and character of Jesus to the end that we are transformed, inspired, or encouraged anew to follow him and to make our followership known in our Christian character and a service-centered lifestyle. In the black worshiping congregation, the goal of nurture is faith and hope demonstrated by this character and lifestyle.

As we move forward in our consideration of methods of nurturing faith and hope in Jesus, particular attention will be given to ways in which songs, prayers, and sermons foster our relational knowing of Jesus. As part of this consideration, we will look at methods of:

- evoking appreciative consciousness of Jesus' relationality;

- evoking analogical discovery of Jesus' life and our own; and

- evoking mimesis.

METHODS OF NURTURE: FOSTERING RELATIONAL KNOWING OF JESUS

I made the point in chapter 1 that, in the black worshiping congregation, nurturing faith and hope in God happens through an evocative process that comes alive through a participative habitation and the use of scripture. Furthermore, I indicated that sermons, songs, and prayers are primary pathways through which these aspects of nurture occur. These attributes necessarily carry over into nurturing faith and hope in Jesus Christ, especially because of the interconnectedness of references to God and the person of Jesus. The black worshiping congregation is a key habitation and scripture provides the central thrust for our probing and deepening our relationship with him.

Again, as in the case with nurturing faith and hope in God, I need to comment on the difference between head and heart knowing. Through methods of nurture, we may come to know *about* all the previously named qualities of Jesus and of him who serves as an analogue to black suffering.[12] Heart knowing, however, is more than the information we gather. Heart knowing derives from our involvement in a divine pedagogy through which God in the person of Jesus speaks or acts in our lives in a way that opens up a new reality and a new sense of our being in relation to God, ourselves, and the world around us.

Whether happening in worship or recalled in the throes of worship, a firsthand experience of Jesus moves us beyond knowing *about* Jesus to *knowing him*. Indeed, this kind of knowing is a testifying-evoking experience of faith and hope as being in a life not forgotten or left alone by God and in a life going forward because of God's nearness in the person of Jesus. More than the information that prompts our head-knowing, the divine pedagogy brings to vivid consciousness Jesus' role in our lives that moves us to the interpretation of that role in testimonies like the one expressed in the song: "I thank you, Jesus, 'cause you brought me a mighty long way."[13] It is also the results of the divine pedagogy that brings a new posture of the heart from which springs our view of his life as worthy of mimesis or of emulating.

My point here is that, in our exploration of methods used in the process of nurturing faith and hope in Jesus in the black worshiping congregation, we must not forget that two interrelated kinds of knowing—head and heart—are desired.

Evoking Appreciative Consciousness of Jesus' Relationality

Arousing an appreciative consciousness of Jesus in the black worshiping congregation is an outcome of nurturing faith and hope in Jesus that results from our involvement in singing, praying, and responsiveness during the sermon.[14] Appreciative consciousness is identified by our formation of new insights or interpretations of who Jesus is and the significance of his presence and relationship with us in our daily lives. In a manner akin to what I shared in chapter 1, the activities of singing and praying and the congregation's engagement in the sermonic event through the preacher's "call" and our "response" are methodological tools for engaging us in reflection-in-action. Through these "tools," we undertake interpretative activity leading to our appreciative consciousness of Jesus Christ. As such, these tools are pathways for a highly personal hermeneutical endeavor in which we ourselves say, hear, and reflect on who Jesus is, how Jesus relates to us, and the meanings of this relationship for our lives. This activity creates the fulcrum for our coming to know *about* Jesus; and it opens the way for our experiencing and coming to *know Jesus* or to interpret that experience and knowing.

Black worshipers describe what their formation of appreciative consciousness is like in a variety of ways. However, these descriptions tend to be similar to the following one that a worshiper shared with me:

> I come to worship to praise God. I also come to be inspired by what happens there and to learn more about what will help me in my daily life. That's why I come, and I keep coming because that's what I get. The worship I experience in my congregation ushers me into the presence of Jesus and Jesus into my space. It doesn't matter whether the choir is singing or whether I'm singing with others in the congregation, whether the elder's praying or the preacher's preaching, I can see Jesus there. I am reminded of who Jesus is and what he stands for. Frankly, I come to know Jesus a little bit better. It's hard to explain, but there are times when the presence of Jesus is so real, I can hear him speaking to me. When I hear him, I get a little more inspiration to go on with my life as a Christian."

The worshipers' testimony highlights that there is something about the activities of worship that can evoke a vision or an ability to "see" and even "hear" Jesus. Most especially singing, praying, and preaching have an evocative manner that has the power to engage us in interpreting Jesus' humanity and his relationship with us. Let us look more closely at what is involved in the hermeneutical method that is inherent in these activities.

THE CENTRALITY OF LANGUAGE IN THE HERMENEUTICAL METHOD

Singing, praying, and preaching are language-driven activities; and the language communicated through them has interpretative power. The significance of these forms of interpretative language is that it is cultural language. To build on Randolph Crump Miller's terms, it is language that comes out of the traditions and narratives of black persons' experiences of Jesus Christ; and because of this historical grounding, the language can enrich us and promote in us a reality of Jesus' nature that can sustain and transform us, as we have noted in the story of the worshiper that I shared above.[15] Interpretation through the language of songs, prayers, and sermons is a method in nurture that creates opportunities for black worshipers to participate in "painting" and internalizing "word pictures" of Jesus' humanity and character.

"Word pictures" become catalysts for our seeing and experiencing the relational Jesus. For example, this kind of picture is "painted" in the musical testimony of Robert Fryson who first tells of feeling Jesus' presence and, then, sets forth a query about others' experiences of the same warm embrace of Jesus, which has obviously brought him soul-deep joy.[16] Witnesses of this kind function as announcements of the nearness of God's presence in the person of Jesus and evoke our own preparation for anticipating and experiencing this same presence. Moreover, our vision of the relational Jesus is furthered by such songs as "In the Garden" which describes the Jesus who walks and talks with us in personally affirming, welcoming, and joy-enhancing ways.[17] In short, musical examples point to the evocative language through which the hermeneutical endeavor of describing Jesus' nature, affirming his nature in our lives, and stimulating our anticipation of this nature occurs.

Prayers also paint "word pictures" that stimulate our formation of images and expectations of the presence and guidance of the relational

Jesus. In his prayers before the congregation, for example, my father-in-law would invariably insert the words: "We know, precious Jesus, that you are with us and will never forsake us. Prop us up on every leaning side and give us a vision of your will for our lives."[18] We also glean images of the relational Jesus from prayers such as M. Moran Weston's that give us a glimpse of the multiple roles of Jesus to which we as people of color can relate. In Weston's prayer, Jesus is portrayed as Carpenter, People's Leader, Chosen One, Prisoner, Defendant, Condemned Man, and Confident Man through whom good, love, and life can triumph in every situation in life.[19]

Similarly, the prayer of Jeremiah Wright Jr. triggers our visualization of the relational Jesus. In the prayer, Wright thanked God for watching over the worshipers the previous night and for food, clothing, family, and loved ones. Through the words that follow, though, Wright engages the congregation in "seeing" Jesus whose relational character is worthy of our thanks to God because Jesus does not leave us alone to move by ourselves.[20]

As in songs, the language of prayer prompts our awareness and formation of a vocabulary that widens beyond the multiplicity of depictions of Jesus appearing earlier in this chapter. This language also has the effect of helping us put into words in ways we may not have previously thought of Jesus' activity in our own stories. In addition, the language fosters in us anticipatory images or expectation of Jesus' relational character and activity in our lives. The language is faith-forming and faith-affirming through the insights that come and the new or renewed embrace of Immanuel or Jesus *with* us that results. The language is hope-forming and hope-affirming through the promise that resides in that embrace.

The interpretative method that draws black worshipers into personal visualization of the relational Jesus in both songs and prayers actually entails a cultural oral-narrative approach found in the delivery of sermons. Story-telling and story-listening are central to interpretative method. This method also exists in sermons. Sermons are story-sharing events that invite us to "see" not simply the relational Jesus but the situations in our lives that call for him. An example is found in the sermon of Gail Bowman, which builds on the three parables of being lost and found (Luke 15).[21]

As part of her narrative-oriented interpretation-evoking method, Bowman links the biblical stories with the human story by stating, "We don't need to be the one lost sheep, the one lost coin, or the prodigal daughter to know the wonder of the touch of the Savior's arms embracing us and carrying us."[22] Two follow-up statements are pivotal in the process. The first is that "God seeks us and in Jesus we can never be lost but must always be found."[23] In the second statement, Bowman meshes the identity of the wholly relational Jesus with God and places the activity of God in the lost places of our lives by saying that we get lost from ourselves but not from the Good Shepherd: "In crisis, in curiosity, in questioning, in good times or in bad; in frustration, in anger, in the kitchen with the pots and pans, in the backyard with the mower, in the relaxing room with the TV remote, in the front pew, in the parking lot, in doubt, in despair, in that thing you did that you wish you hadn't, . . . you can't shake God, and you cannot shock God!"[24]

Bowman concludes her cultural narrative approach of drawing worshipers into the story by "painting a word picture" of the reason for God's seeking us without ceasing or pause: "We are God's. We are God's. Children of Mother Africa, Children of the Promise, Children of the Kingdom, we are God's. And, oh! What joy!"[25]

THE IMPACT OF INTERPRETATIVE LANGUAGE

I want to conclude this part on evoking appreciative consciousness of the relational Jesus by returning, briefly, to my ongoing argument about the difference between knowing *about* Jesus and *knowing Jesus*. However, at this point, I invite us to look at this premise with regard to interpretative language as a method in nurturing faith and hope in Jesus Christ.

Building on the assertion of David White and Frank Rogers in their discussion on existentialist theology and religious education, we cannot prove God except by meeting God and in this meeting arrive at *knowing God*.[26] Similarly, we cannot prove the relationality of Jesus without meeting Jesus and in this meeting fulfill our quest to *know Jesus*. To this degree, the language of songs, prayers, and sermons describe a narrative world in which Jesus exists as the relational human presence of God in our lives. The language hints at this narrative world. It is this description—the hints—that can prompt our formation of our own narrative world of the relational Jesus. We glean what there is to know *about* Jesus.

It is important to add, however, that reflection is going on during our engagement with the narrative world; and this reflective activity sometimes involves more than contemplation on meanings of the narrative world for us. Perhaps more frequently than is shared, reflection becomes a conversation with Jesus as in the case of the worshiper who said that when she sings the song, "I Want Jesus to Walk with Me," she is not really making a statement. Instead, she indicated that she is making an appeal to Jesus whereupon Jesus answers and affirms his ongoing presence with her. In the throes of this conversation with Jesus, she and Jesus meet. The conversation becomes a profound experience of *knowing Jesus*. Indeed, what occurs is faith and hope in action.

Evoking Analogical Discovery

In the preceding section, I referred to the sermon by Bowman that links the biblical story to our everyday stories. This linking our scripture with black experience is a prevalent method of prompting the kind of analogical discovery that I described in chapter 1. In this approach, we see connections between the story of Jesus and our stories. The method draws us into the story and prompts analogical discovery through uses of reminders or engages us in recalling a Bible story. In addition, the approach situates us inside the Bible story in ways that we conceive of ourselves as actual participants in the story, thereby calling forth a personal consciousness of Jesus in our story and us in the story of Jesus. Henry Mitchell's sermon is an example of this approach.

In the sermon "The Christmas Plunge," Mitchell calls attention to Jesus' situation in life beginning at birth by saying: "Christmas *reminds us* that it was a total incarnation as Jesus took the form of a human being. . . . Let us now *remember* that Jesus also suffered all the details of pain and indignity of birth."[27] Mitchell's reminder and invitation to remember promote the formation of a hermeneutical lens for interpreting and acknowledging Jesus' birth narrative contained in scripture by drawing us into the story. The reminder *brings us into* the scene of the story. The invitation to remember *situates us in* the story of Jesus so that the hearer experiences the self in the story. This aspect of the evocative nurturing process is further illustrated in Mitchell's words that "the manger and the stable were the least of all the hazards of this awesome incarnation. The greatest danger . . . [was] not unclean hay and breathing his first breath near a foul-smelling stable. The danger . . . was essentially the same danger babies face in the hood today: oppression by a cruel, impersonal system."[28] Mitchell goes on to recall the Christmas lullaby spiritual sung by black forebears in slavery, "The world treat you mean, Lawd. Treat me mean too. Dat's how things is down here. Dey don't know who you is."[29]

In this instance of evocative nurture, the reminder and invitation to remember clearly link the situation of Jesus to the circumstances of black people. The reminder and invitation accomplish the tasks of evoking our identification with Jesus and of emboldening our faith and hope in the One who "knows all about our struggles" because of his coming into the world as a lowly despised peasant.

Richard Wills' sermon "From Mundane to Marvelous" also draws on the biblical narrative of Jesus' birth to set forth a reminder that typifies the evocative nurturing process. He says, "Luke *reminds* us that there were shepherds, grown men, not children, who were keeping watch over their flock by night."[30] Wills' reminder serves as an evocative trigger that promotes our interpretation of the event of Jesus' birth, which Christmas celebrates, as one not simply for children. With this evocative trigger, though, Wills also leads us to identify Jesus' birth event as God's supernatural disruption of the ordinary duties of working people; and Wills calls forth our identification with the event's occurrence among those who are often "overlooked, neglected, insignificant, out-of-sight, out-of mind folk after all."[31] Mary Ann Bellinger invites us to recall another scene of Jesus' unfolding life and ministry in her sermon "Upright but *Not* Uptight."[32] In the sermon, Bellinger situates us in scenes of Jesus' unorthodox caregiving as part of her disclosure of Jesus' encounter with "a certain woman . . . who had been bent almost in half for eighteen long years."[33] Bellinger invites the listener's recall by raising a question: "*Remember* him at the well when the woman of Samaria came to fill her waterpots in the heat of the day and he talked to her? . . . *Remember* him at the dinner party given by Simon the Pharisee?"[34]

Bellinger's particular invitation to remember is a noteworthy example of evocative nurture that occurs through posing questions. Moreover, her use of interrogatives serves as evocative triggers or means by which she calls forth our participation in the story of Jesus' unorthodox caregiving. The call to participation occurs through Bellinger's invitation to us to imagine the feelings of the severely hunched woman and the character of Jesus who bent down to where this woman was in order to heal her and transform her to an erect position.[35]

In similar fashion, one of the spirituals handed down from black forebears that is often sung in the black worshiping congregation during Lent evokes our recall of Jesus' passion and resurrection through raising questions: "Were you there when they crucified my Lord? . . . Were you there when they laid Him in the tomb? . . . Were you there when He rose from the dead?"[36] The questions serve as evocative triggers that lead us, in the process of singing and listening, to consider and even attest to the impact of our participation in the events heralded in the song: "Sometimes it causes me to tremble."[37] Nurture of faith and hope in Jesus takes place through this kind of participative activity that calls forth our recall of Jesus' character and activity.

Evoking Mimesis

In addition to arousing our appreciative consciousness of Jesus' relational nature and activity through methods focused on recalling his story in the Bible, nurture in the black worshiping congregation moves us beyond this recall of Jesus and seeks to evoke mimesis. The goal of nurture is to inspire our emulation of Jesus. This emulation takes the form of the "serviceable orthodoxy" described in chapter 1. Methods of carrying out this emphasis highlight the character traits and values of Jesus, which we are to mimic, as well as the importance of our living according to the character traits and values of Jesus. The outcome of the methods is our visualization of what our taking on the traits and values of Jesus means and looks like in our daily lives. The uses of methods to evoke mimesis are particularly prevalent in sermons. These pathways of nurture are significant because of the uninterrupted time to focus on the centrality of Jesus in Christian life and faith and because of the thoroughgoing nature or the ability of the preacher to invite us into a systematic and multilevel "reflection-in-action." Of the many sermons appearing in published volumes, several will be mentioned here as examples.[38]

Included in the sermons I have chosen for comment are ones that engage us in critical self-examination by posing hard questions about what it means for us to follow Jesus and by the straightforward and inductive manner in which they proceed. They direct our attention to what it means to pattern our lives after the mind of Christ, Jesus' spiritual eyesight, Jesus' form of leadership, and Jesus' values of self-emptying, humility, and obedience. And, in light of the goal of mimesis as a necessary personal and communal endeavor of Christians, the sermons incorporate personalized language such as "we," "us," "you," and "our" as well as statements of challenge and uses of prescriptive terms.

EVOKING SELF-EXAMINATION THROUGH POSING HARD QUESTIONS

The sermon of Deborah McGill-Jackson is an example of an evocative sermon that prompts black worshipers' "reflection in action" by raising pivotal questions. Her evocative method includes the use of a pivotal declarative statement that "Christians are called to participate in the liberation of others, for we have become heirs of the message of freedom and inheritors of the liberation agenda."[39] She then raises key questions to evoke our self-examination of our role in the liberation agenda: "Are not men and women held captive by their past? Are they not ashamed and guilt ridden? Is not society caught in its own web of greed and abuse? Are there not among us those blind to the truth declared in love and overshadowed by ignorance of spirit? Are there not among us those who would oppress? Are we not frequently participants in the oppression of others on the basis of religion, race, wealth, sex, and nationality?"[40]

Sermons like McGill-Jackson's press us to confront attitudes and behaviors that run counter to those of Jesus. The questions challenge us to come face-to-face with our limitations on the one hand, but our obligation as Christians, on the other hand, to apply outside the worship context what best re-presents the person of Jesus.

EVOKING BLACK WORSHIPERS' PATTERNING AFTER THE MIND OF CHRIST

Sermons of black preachers utilize the evocative nurturing approach by presenting the qualities of the secure mind of Christ and by challenging us to emulate these qualities. For example, in the sermon "The Mind of the Insecure," Nan Brown demonstrates this approach by presenting to us three qualities or values undergirding the secure mind of Christ. These qualities include the mind that directs human acts of kindness, considerateness, compassion, leniency, and mercy; the mind that is quick-sighted, perceptive, and enthusiastic to the benefit of others; and the mind that centers on God through Jesus Christ and, therefore, reflects the spirit of God.[41] Brown uses statements of challenge in her evocative strategy to prompt our awareness of the significance of the secure mind of Christ for Christian life and an openness to acquire it: "I challenge you . . . Let this mind be in you which is in Christ Jesus . . . (Philippians 2:5–8) . . . I challenge you further to emulate the example of [the mind of] Jesus Christ."[42]

EVOKING BLACK WORSHIPERS' PATTERNING AFTER JESUS' SPIRITUAL EYESIGHT.

Suzanne Johnson Cook's sermon is an example of the evocative method that uses story-sharing and personalized language to embolden our for-

mation of Jesus' spiritual eyesight for the sake of our seeing and cooperating with God's extraordinary hand in daily life. In the sermon,
Cook discloses the unfolding scenes in the story of Jesus' ability to see
clearly with faith the wherewithal to feed five thousand people with a
few loaves of bread and fish (John 6:6–14). Her personalized and black
context-specific language engages us in envisioning how our taking on
the character of Jesus allows us to see as Jesus sees. For example, she
tells us: "When we walk with Jesus . . . we gain the capacity to see
through spiritual eyes. . . . It's seeing the possible while others are blinded
by the impossible. It's learning to see more than just a group of 'bad'
kids, as the world would say. It's seeing kids who are in the rough
being transformed into honor students. . . . [O]ur spiritual vision will
let us see them as our doctors and lawyers who are contributors to the
community."[43]

EVOKING BLACK WORSHIPERS' PATTERNING AFTER
JESUS' FORM OF LEADERSHIP

Both John Bryant's and Walter Thomas's sermons typify evocative methods of nurture that use story-sharing, prescriptive terms, personalized
language, and challenge to arouse in the hearers an anticipation of
their development of Jesus' form of leadership.

Bryant tells the story of Jesus' leadership style that centers on his
perspective of victor rather than victim. Central to the story is the scene
in scripture in which the disciples were hiding behind closed doors
after the crucifixion. However, as the story continues, the resurrected
Jesus "breaks into" the closed door to confidently declare that the story
is not over and that there is no reason to feel hopeless, helpless, and
defeated. Bryant's insertion of the prescriptive terms "must" and "need"
press us to apply Jesus' confident leadership in church and community:
"The church of the Lord Jesus Christ must come boldly out of hiding
in the twenty-first century. Politicians must be held accountable, communities must be cleaned up, families need to be saved, children must
be taught discipline and respect, racism must be fought, hate must be
challenged, and Satan needs to be rebuked."[44] Bryant uses the person-

alized language of "us" and "we" in his concluding challenge: "The future awaits us, and so we open the doors. We do not retreat! There is only one command—'Forward march!'"[45]

Thomas's particular prescriptive approach to calling for mimetic action in our daily lives includes the forthright statement: "The leadership that is required for the new millennium will understand that the mission is not simply to reveal Christ but also to become like Christ."[46] He continues with prescriptive language that activates our envisaging the qualities of Jesus that they are to emulate: "The answer is clear, and the answer is here. We must grow to the measure of Jesus. It is his form that we are to take on: the form of a servant, the form of a teacher, the form of one who is compassionate, the form of one who is powerful, and the form of humility."[47]

Evoking black worshipers' patterning after Jesus' values of self-emptying, humility, and obedience

In the sermon "A Prescription for Humility," Marjorie Leeper Booker uses the evocative nurturing method to prompt our adoption of the specific posture of Jesus we are to emulate. As part of the approach, she tells us of Jesus' emphasis on unity in community by relating the story of Paul, who encouraged the church at Philippi "to follow the example of Christ in seeking togetherness for the sake of meaningful and peaceful life."[48] Thereafter, she discloses to us three specific unity-making values—self-emptying, humility, and obedience—that help form the character and activity of Jesus; then, she prompts a vision for applying the values in our lives. The use of personalized language and prescriptive terms stands out. The following analytical framework summarizes her evocative method:

Movement 1

- Evoking images of Jesus' value of self-emptying: Jesus "emptied himself of the attitude of 'my rights'. . . [Jesus] was never concerned with making a name for himself. He was concerned with doing the will of God."[49]

- Prompting consideration of Christian life patterns: "We must empty ourselves of all that may separate us from God. To empty ourselves may mean that prejudice and superior attitudes must take flight. . . that we must let go of our egos."[50]

Movement 2

- Evoking images of Jesus' value of humility: "Christ humbled himself taking the form of a servant."[51]

- Prompting consideration of Christian life patterns: In our society those who are considered to be great and in positions of authority "are served and reserve special privileges for themselves. . . . In Christian discipleship the great must do the serving."[52]

Movement 3

- Evoking images of Jesus' value of obedience: "Jesus did not sell out. He remained obedient [to God]. When the forces of his day rose against him, he remained faithful. He believed God and accepted [God's] plan obediently."[53]

- Prompting consideration of Christian life patterns: "We need a faith like that of Christ, a faith 'that will not tremble on the brink of any earthly woe.'"[54]

The sermons to which I have referred here reflect in a very real way the mimetic presupposition that the character and the nature of life of the relational Jesus are worthy of emulation. The sermon materials make plain that the method for evoking our commitment to that emulation centers on our seeing Jesus' character and relational way of being and doing in the world as our own. From these materials, we also glean that mimesis is an unquestionable imperative in nurturing faith and hope through sharing the sacred stories of Jesus. Moreover, building on the claim of Constance Tarasar, I would also argue that, when we look back at the New Testament story of Jesus Christ that is so central to professed Christian identity, we discover the spiritual roots of faith and hope.[55]

This discovery is a necessary part of nurture in the black worshiping congregation.

JESUS-CENTERED CONTENT OF EVOCATIVE NURTURE

It is impossible to divulge methods that bring forth our deepening consciousness of who Jesus is and what it means to be like him without somehow referring to specific content or themes that disclose Jesus' character and how he lived in community. Consequently, the preceding focus on methods includes a partial and limited characterization of the relational Jesus that has emerged from the stories of persons' experiences of him. The predominant images are those of Jesus as friend, protector, guide, liberator, healer, and sustainer. We find in the further description of these images additional ones that point to a vast storehouse of a metaphor-rich language that rivals the extensive God-language to which I referred in chapter 1.

Jesus as Friend, Protector, and Guide

The content of nurturing experiences in the black worshiping congregation reveals Jesus as friend, protector, and guide along the oftentimes perilous and wilderness journey of life. The images, which appear mostly in songs, reveal to continuing worshipers, new members, and coming generations a deep faith and hope in Jesus and an expectation of the presence of this relational Jesus in the unfolding journey. The importance of these particular convictions is confirmed by the seminal study of Louis Charles Harvey that shows that more than five hundred black gospel songs tell about Jesus' companionship and friendship.[56] Current examples of songs bearing the themes of friend, protector, and guide appear in a variety of cultural-specific hymnbooks including the *African American Heritage Hymnal*,[57] *Yes, Lord! Church of God in Christ Hymnal*,[58] and *Lift Every Voice and Sing II*.[59]

The content of the songs reveals Jesus as One who was born to be our friend,[60] who is friend to all,[61] and whose friendship is inexhaustible.[62] Jesus is further revealed as the friend who watches day and night, knows our every care,[63] and is with us even in death.[64] The songs declare that there is no friend or protector like Jesus,[65] and that He is One whom we may ask to lead us,[66] and to guide our feet while we run this race.[67] Regarded by some as friend unseen,[68] and as heavenly friend,[69] Jesus communes with us as friend with friend.[70] He remains our trustworthy and compassionate friend,[71] the lily of the valey, bright and morning star, greatest of ten-thousand, comforter, strength, life, joy, rock in a weary land, guardian, One who assuages discouragement, and who is everything that one can ever imagine.[72]

It is important to add, however, that the theme of Jesus' friendship, protection, and guidance appears in the content of prayers as well. The content of prayers refers to Jesus, for example, as the shining way, strong Son of God, our healing wisdom, and ever-present friend.[73] Moreover, prayers that tell of past activities of Jesus in the lives of black people are especially noteworthy forms of evocative content because they stimulate in us images and expectations of the same activities of Jesus in the future. The following is an example of this kind of content: "We want to thank you Lord Jesus, because you have brought us a mighty long ways; you were our bread when we were hungry, our water in a dry and thirsty land, our shelter in the time of storm."[74] Sermons and testimonies of black people's actual relationship with Jesus bear similar content. Through this content, we hear not simply the beliefs that people hold, but the live experiences of others with Jesus. Whether through songs, prayers, and sermons, the content allows us to disclose our beliefs about Jesus, to provide a basis for reflection on those beliefs, and to nurture black Christians' faith and hope in Jesus.

Jesus as Liberator, Healer, and Sustainer

The content of varied experiences in the black worshiping congregation identifies Jesus as liberator, healer, and sustainer of faith and hopeful living. The content especially of songs refers to Jesus' presence as liberator in his redemptive works that lift us out of Satan's bonds,[75] his grace that bought our liberty,[76] and the power in his blood that gives victory over sin.[77] He is also referred to as the deliverer who brings us out of the miry clay into the golden day and sets our feet on a rock to stay,[78] who will make a way somehow,[79] and who heals and transforms us with a touch of his hand.[80]

However, over the years, sermons have continued to give particular attention to Jesus as the deliverer of persons from despair and as the One who brings about the resurrection of hope.[81] The theme of liberating and initiating actions of Jesus in the lives of black people interacts with those appearing in the preceding section to form a dominant part of the content in evocative nurture processes taking place in the black worshiping congregation. For example, William Watley presents the active roles of Jesus in our everyday lives in terms of Jesus as liberator to the bound, way-maker to the needy, Prince of peace to the disturbed, and friend to the lonely in order that we might grow and move beyond the stuck places of our lives.[82] Content such as this reveals and stimulates the worshipers' imagination of what, how, and toward what ends Jesus liberates, heals, and initiates faithful and hopeful living.

Other interpretations of Jesus as the liberator, healer, and sustainer may be added to those presented by Watley. An added dimension to these interpretations of the character and activity of God is the notion that we are not passive recipients of the activity of Jesus in our lives. In this notion, we see Jesus as One who imbues us through his initiatory action with the wherewithal to act with integrity, faithfulness, and hope in life's sojourn. Examples of this content appear in published volumes of sermons of black preachers.[83] These interpretations may be summarized as follows:

- Jesus is liberator of humans from oppression and deliverer from frailties of body, mind, and soul to the end that we are instruments of God's mission of righteousness, justice, and peace. Jesus is the One who frees us by calling us into relationship with God through him. Jesus is the One who transforms us in that relationship by revealing his nature to us and by inspiring in us the quest to rely on him and to be like him.

- Jesus is liberator of the human will to overtake oppression. Jesus frees us to accept and act on God's liberation agenda of confronting social structures and institutions that bind us. Jesus frees us to explore the parameters of freedom. Jesus frees us to make the choices that result in a richer, fuller life and to participate in a new community with others who have found their freedom too. Jesus frees us to take risks that go along with living as people with faith and hope; and as liberator, Jesus initiates in us the power to continue to strive to overtake oppression in whatever form or place without giving up.

- Jesus is liberator of the human ability to see worth and dignity in all of God's children from the least to the greatest; and Jesus initiates in us the desire to attain the best quality of life for all.

- Jesus is liberator of the human vision to grow in the goodness of God; and Jesus initiates in us the quest for an ever-deepening knowledge of who he is and can be in our lives.

Again, of particular significance is the emphasis on the need for human response to the liberating Jesus, as Carolyn Ann Knight says, "not just so we can go to heaven when we die. Not just so we may see God face to face. Not just so we may get rich and prosper."[84] Thus, the experience of being freed, healed, or lifted up by God through Jesus Christ is to be followed by our lifting up others.[85] The content of Deborah McGill-Jackson's sermon frames this serviceable-orthodoxy theme in terms of our Christian responsibility, that of contributing to the liberation of others because we are heirs of the message of freedom.[86] Walter Thomas's sermon also carries a similar theme in his depiction of Jesus the healer whose compassion "caused others to see the light and run to embrace it" and as One who calls us to be a reconciling presence in the world in like measure in the form of servants, teachers, compassionate ones, powerful, and humble.[87]

COMMENTARY

Because of the Jesus-oriented nature of everyday black Christianity, it is important to state there is a larger evocative context that helps nurture black Christians' faith and hope in Jesus and that becomes intertwined with nurture in the black worshiping congregation. Much interplay exists between Jesus-oriented nurture in the everyday black community and nurture occurring in the black worshiping congregation. Indeed, there is Jesus-centered "curricular" content that extends beyond the context of the worshiping congregation and that both reflects and informs nurture in that congregation. To this extent, black people neither enter nor leave the black worshiping congregation as tabula rasa.

As black people, we are exposed to the Jesus-centered "curricular" content both in worship and in interactions with one another in the larger community. Within and outside the worshiping congregation, black elders and other extended family members take on the role of nurturer as others hear them testify about and talk with the "Jesus who knows all about our troubles and who will be with us 'til the end." What actually happens is that the nurturing context of the worshiping congregation expands to the extent that it might well be termed "worship without walls." In this expanded and interactive context, the nurturers are not simply the leaders and congregational participants in the church. The nurturers include the people in our family, extended family, and the storytellers on records, tapes, compac discs, videos, and television who engage us in their stories about Jesus and their encounters with Jesus. Increasingly, the nurturing face-to-face church-based worship interfaces with the techno-environments of TV and cyberspace.[88] Moreover, especially where music is concerned, it is often what is heard in the larger public sphere that inspires the choices of songs in the worshiping congregation.

Black people connect what our churches teach about Jesus with what we learn elsewhere. We bring into dialogue in every part of the interactive "worship without walls" the very real circumstances of our lives; moreover, we connect, consciously or unconsciously, our participation in this interactive environment with our everyday lives. In a real way, then, the context through which Jesus-centered nurture happens is a broad one; and the nurturing process in this broad context is multidimensional. Nurture is cumulative and latent.

A Cumulative Process

Our views of Jesus Christ expand as a consequence of our exposure to various historical and contemporary perspectives that are disclosed within and beyond the black worshiping congregation. Consciously or unconsciously, we are nurtured by a cumulative process. In this process, we form images of Jesus, beliefs about him, and understandings of what it means to follow him.

However, this cumulative nurturing process is not a matter of "banking" or amassing ideas about Jesus. Rather, the process entails our exposure to the "storehouse" of images of Jesus within and outside the worshiping congregation; and it includes our drawing images from the storehouse that help us tell about and interpret our lives. The cumulative nurturing process allows us to engage in what Ross Snyder calls the "ministry of meanings" through which we develop and call on images from multiple sources to "organize" and give direction to our journey of faith and hope.[89] Evidence of the process is often attested to by the scriptures and songs about Jesus we learn in various contexts over time. It is shown by the scriptures and songs about Jesus we choose as our favorites and tell with ease when, where, and how we learned them. It is revealed in our testimonies of the impact of the scriptures and songs on our lives. In this respect, it may be both helpful and illuminating to form conversation groups beyond the worshiping congregation to intentionally reflect on images and beliefs of Jesus gleaned in the worshiping congregation, on other sources of our images and beliefs, and the meanings of the images and beliefs to us.

A Latent Process

The nurturing process is also a latent one, both within and beyond the black worshiping congregation. The process is a latent one to the extent that we form attitudes and beliefs about Jesus as well as perceptions of life in relation to Jesus without intentional effort and concentration. For example, hearing and internalizing messages in the worshiping congregation and in everyday life via songs on tape, record, video, or television are not necessarily consequences of our setting out to form specific beliefs about Jesus. Yet, what we have heard both within and outside the worshiping congregation does help shape our views and our choices of channels through which we seek further nurturing experiences. For example, younger black Christians who attend black church worship tend to prefer more spirited forms of nurture than many older black Christians. People, young and old, also choose contexts of worship within and beyond the worshiping congregation in which to be nurtured by song, sermon, and the very presence of Jesus.

What is important here is that the extent of the participation of both younger and older black Christians in the nurturing process depends largely on the type of process in which narratives of Jesus come forth. Worship and an encounter with Jesus is an intimate experience, even in the communal context of the worshiping congregation. As one elderly woman said, "In church, darling, I'm with everybody, but really, lots of times, I'm singing with the angels in the presence of Jesus. Sometimes, they sing, Jesus speaks, and I listen. Other times, they listen and sometimes, me, the angels and Jesus sing together. It's me, the angels, and Jesus. Nobody else."

The reality of the intimacy of worship creates a challenge for black worship leaders today. A primary demand is to be both cognizant of and responsive to differing preferences in worship styles. There must be appreciation for the process of nurturing black Christians in faith and hope in Jesus that really does evoke both black worshipers' personal knowing *about* Jesus and our *knowing Jesus*. Strength of nurturing faith and hope also lies in the ability of nurture to embolden our zeal to be his emissaries on a journey to make a better world.

AN INVITATION TO REFLECT

1. What assumptions do you have about the role of worship in nurturing faith and hope in Jesus Christ?

2. In what ways does congregational worship in your church connect with what you learn about and experience of Jesus outside the church?

3. What images and views of Jesus come forth in songs, prayers, and sermons in your worshiping congregation? About what images and views of Jesus do you become aware outside the worshiping congregation and what are the sources of this awareness?

4. What meanings does Jesus as friend, protector, guide, liberator, healer, initiator, and sustainer of faithful and hopeful living have for you? Where and how are these beliefs about Jesus communicated to you?

3

FAITH AND HOPE IN
THE HOLY SPIRIT

May the God of hope fill you with all joy
and peace in believing, so that you may abound
in hope by the power of the Holy Spirit.

—Romans 15:13

Nurturing faith and hope in the black worshiping congregation responds to the question: What does it mean to be moved by the Holy Spirit to fully worship, live, love, serve, and continue the journey of life with certitude of our ability to do so? The question is a pertinent one in light of the despair, struggles, and quest for hope and meaning that dominate the stories of so many of our black sisters and brothers in today's world. The answers emerge as nurture occurring through what we do and say in the worshiping congregation; and in those answers lie the nourishment or the support for our formation of faith and hope in God's nearness and counsel, which we find in God's Spirit.

There is no single answer. One answer to the question lies in the inspiration that moves persons to enter into quiet contemplation, shout, dance, clap their hands, and speak in tongues during congregational worship. The Spirit "speaks" or affirms a word of hope, direction, or prophecy that moves persons to a variety of spontaneous responses that cannot be controlled. These responses of persons awaken us to the numinous or mysterious activity of God through which God connects with the very core of our being and which we may await. An answer is also found in our singing songs such as "Let It Breathe on Me,"[1] which reminds us that the presence and activity of the Spirit and our welcome of the Spirit are interconnected and that we may not necessarily or automatically be open to the Spirit's presence or activity. Still another answer comes from the "response" to the "call" of the preacher during the sermon: "Yes! Preach it! It's the truth!" for example. This reciprocity between preacher and worshipers calls us to "see" the nature of worship as communal celebration and as *spirited* interactive evocative experience.

However, there are answers to the question that are apt to give us new or renewed appreciation of how our forebears continued on in the midst of hard trials and tribulations and how we may yet sojourn with faith and hope. The answer is epitomized in the words of one of the oldest members of a church to which I belonged sometime ago: "Child, you've got to understand that the Spirit is alive and well. No matter what happens, you can 'make it through' because God's not going to leave you be. God's Spirit will guide you, protect you, comfort you, and put you on the right path. You're bound to do the right thing if you are in tune with the Spirit." Whether in the form of witnessing statements, songs, or prayers, testimonies in the worshiping congregation call our attention to the Comforter, the Holy Spirit, whom Christ promised as assurance that he would remain with his disciples. Moreover, we become cognizant of God who, as the divine empowering agent, makes possible our surmounting sufferings, narrow escapes, reversals, and hard trials without losing faith. Testimonies serve as consciousness-heightening occasions as well, indicating that God desires and becomes instrumental in our efforts to make a better world than the one we now inhabit.

As in the preceding chapters, I again caution us to differentiate our cognitive discernment of answers that derive from what we observe and hear in the worshiping congregation. While this discernment is important to our awareness of the nature and activity of the Holy Spirit, it is not the same as our personal experience of the Spirit. This experience comes from our own tending to the quality of our lives before God, to our yearnings for God's alive presence, and our reaching out and welcoming God who is a living, personal presence who has already reached out to us. At the same time, the very nature of nurture to which I am referring in this book has to do with spurring persons' tending and reaching out by what is said and done in the worshiping congregation. This means that what is said and done has both a guiding function in that we want what is said and done to "say something" that is helpful and an evocative function that brings forth insight within the person. Both the role of guidance and of nurture cannot be overestimated. This is particularly the case with the Holy Spirit because of the wonderment of more than a few persons about who the Holy Spirit is, how the Holy Spirit acts, and why they have not or whether they should have experienced what they see others experiencing.

With both the role of guidance and nurture in mind, this chapter invites our further reflection on ways in which the opening question to this chapter is answered in the black worshiping congregation. Primary attention will be given to the storied content of sermons, songs, and prayers through which we glean answers.

EVOCATIVE METHODS: NURTURING THROUGH STORY

Evocative nurturing methods in the black worshiping congregation are about bringing forth our attention to and experience of the Holy Spirit. The process unfolds on the premise that, as in the case of nurturing faith and hope in God and Jesus Christ, faith and hope in the Holy Spirit does not derive simply from the presentation of propositional statements or the recitation of creedal formulations, although we must not discount the importance of them. Rather, our faith or belief in God's Spirit and our hope for or vision and anticipation of the Spirit's activity in our lives forms and deepens in us in the throes of our hearing and telling stories. Indeed, experiences in the worshiping congregation that connect together our human stories with the Divine story are pivotal to the nurturing process precisely because, to build on the words of Anderson and Foley, they stimulate our discernment of "what God is doing in our lives and how we need to respond."[2]

Stories contained in sermons, songs, and prayers prompt consciousness-raising in us and create opportunities for disclosing who the Holy Spirit is and how the Holy Spirit relates with us and acts on our behalf in the worshiping congregation and in everyday life. Pedagogically, these uses of story invite us into a communal experience in which all participate and in which together we become actors in reflective imagination of the nature and activity of the Holy Spirit, and "see" this nature and activity through our "mind's eye."[3] Stories are not simply catalysts for reflective imagination, but have the power to evoke emotions that cannot be contained, that liberate our firsthand experience of the Holy Spirit, and that open before us occasions to see and affirm the Holy Spirit's movement in others.

Evoking Consciousness-Raising through Linking Bible to Life

Recalling biblical stories focused on the Holy Spirit and linking them to life today are pivotal means of raising black worshipers' consciousness of the ongoing nature and activity of the Holy Spirit. Through this recall, we glean more of the nature of God and Jesus Christ and God's purposes for our lives. We become aware of the activities of the Holy Spirit in the lives of early Christians. These stories evoke our imagination and anticipation of our own experiences of the Holy Spirit. Moreover, the intent of the stories is also to challenge our views of the Holy Spirit and our understandings of what it means to respond to the Holy Spirit.

This kind of evocative activity is particularly central to the oratory of the black preacher. As an evocative storytelling medium, the sermon of the black preacher becomes a stimulus for raising the worshipers' consciousness of the presence, activities, and purposes of God made known in the Holy Spirit as well as of responses to the Spirit. Exploration of three sermons will be used here to demonstrate the evocative storytelling process. The three sermons reflect differing methods utilized in the nurturing process. Yet, all are alike in the uses of storytelling and in the pivotal use of scripture.

SERMON I

As an illustration, I call attention to Teresa Fry Brown's sermon on the Holy Spirit, "Breathing Lessons."[4] My emphasis on her sermon in this chapter is to highlight her particular uses of the storytelling method and questioning as part of that method in the process of nurturing faith and hope in the Holy Spirit. In her approach, storytelling may be rightly described as a catalyst for what I call imaginative reflection. What does this approach entail?

Inspiring Imaginative Reflection: The Human Story as the Starting Point

Imaginative reflection is our ability to ponder the nature and meanings of God's story in light of our story and to envision as well as to decide how we will respond to and participate in God's story. Brown inspires imaginative reflection through her storytelling method, which begins with her arousal of worshipers' remembrance of personal events that fracture one's sense of wholeness and cause one to call faith in an able God and hope into question: "As Christians, we face times when our spiritual respiratory system is out of sync. . . . There is pressure all around, hopelessness residing, complaints raging. Our spirits are weakening; the death rattle of our connection to life is imminent; spiritual death is overshadowing our lives and our ministries."[5] The starting point in Brown's sermon is akin to the everyday story of persons on which the first movement in my story-linking model focuses in *Soul Stories: African American Christian Education.*[6] Beginning with the human story is also a pivotal element in inspiring worshipers' imaginative reflection in the worshiping congregation because this approach honors the story—the agenda—that people bring with them into the worship experience. This opening focus on the worshipers' selves pays homage to the human story and points to the notion that the process of nurture evolves from inside our lived stories. In Brown's sermon, the human story as the point of departure suggests that God's story "speaks" or has something to say to our stories of brokenness and, in its "speaking," can inspire our response, decision, belief, hope, and willing participation in a reconstructed story.

Stimulating Imaginative Reflection through Linkage with the Bible

Brown's storytelling method links the human story of brokenness to the biblical account of Ezekiel in the valley of the dry bones (Ezekiel 36 and 37).[7] To accomplish her approach to stimulating imaginative re-flection, she creates an interactive communal ethos by interspersing questions throughout the scenes of the Bible story. The questions have the effect of promoting a relationship between the storyteller, the ac-tors in the story, and the worshiper as story-listener. Indeed, the ques-tions are posed from the worshipers' stance as "participant observers" *within* the story. From the stance as "participant observers," the wor-shipers hear the storyteller speak aloud the possible query of Ezekiel as he walked around in the heat of the day: "Whose son does that leg bone belong to? Whose mother is that skull? What promise lay in that small fragment? Who mourned them? Who missed them?"[8]

The process continues with searching questions that are central to stimulating imaginative reflection. Searching questions encourage our delving into our own thinking and imagining or creating a "picture" of our responses. At the same time, these types of questions also promote our comprehension of the contents of scriptural material being pre-sented to us.[9] The following typify the searching questions posed by Brown: "Can you imagine the bones of 4,600 people? . . . Can you imagine Ezekiel walking through the bones?"[10]

A follow-up searching question calls forth imaginative reflection on the nature of the shift in the direction of the story from the situation of the stillness of lifeless bones to a life-giving circumstance: "Can you hear a little movement in the valley?"[11] However, before proceeding to another query, Brown inserts the statement: "We, too, need to hear from God." This statement functions as a catalyst for the worshipers' imaginative reflection on personal meanings of the story. The question "Can you see it coming together?"[12] which follows shortly thereafter, is bidirectional, calling the worshipers to reflect on both the unfolding biblical story and the self's story. This point of bidirectionality contin-ues with the invitation to the worshipers to see, hear, and feel the *ruah* or breath of God's Spirit that "warms us when we become cold in spirit, [and] energizes us when we would give up and stop praising God."[13]

Brown's queries are to move worshipers to the point of seeing and claiming the conclusion that "the Spirit prevailed," in the biblical nar-rative,[14] that "God is a God of resurrection and new life. No matter where we find ourselves, if we breathe in the breath of life, we will live. God can restore us."[15]

Further Comments on the Use of Questions for Imaginative Reflection

Pedagogically, the kinds of questions used by Brown confront in an expert manner the problem of distantiation in the worshiping congregation. Distantiation is reflected in the treatment of worshipers as passive recipients of information given to them in the nurturing process. Likewise, distantiation results in the wonderment of worshipers who are thrust in the passive role: "So what? What does the story have to do with me?" The questions posed by Brown lessen the temporal and experiential distance between the centuries-old happenings in the life of Ezekiel and the current-day experiences of the worshipers. The reduction in distance functions as a catalyst for the worshipers' formation of imaginative interpretations of the importance of the nature and activity of the Holy Spirit in the story of Ezekiel for our lives. Moreover, this means of stimulating imagination is enhanced by the ongoing engagement of worshipers in the acts of seeing, hearing, and feeling. The experience of imaginative interpretation rightfully becomes an encounter that involves far more than abstract thinking.

At the center of the interactive communal ethos, to which I referred earlier, is a form of invitational communication. This kind of communication draws worshipers inductively into considering and responding to truths about the Holy Spirit as opposed to the more deductive-oriented information-giving strategies. I would also add that the storytelling method, with the insertion of varieties of questions, serves as an "open doorway" to imaginative reflection and, when used in the worshiping congregation, gives credence to the foundational assumption that worshipers are imaginative beings and are "capable of imagination and in need of it," as Mary Elizabeth Mullino Moore reminds us.[16] In addition, pivotally, worshipers do not simply receive story-oriented nurture or help in our formation of faith and hope in the Holy Spirit but we "live" the stories inside ourselves through questions that call forth the involvement of the seeing, hearing, and feeling self.

SERMON 2

The second sermon, "The Hot Winds of Change," by Samuel B. McKinney, also exemplifies a process of nurture by linking biblical passages on the Holy Spirit to present-day life.[17] McKinney places special emphasis on the story of Pentecost. This story is the means by which he draws attention to the story of God's pouring out God's Spirit on all assembled at Pentecost, which fulfilled "the longings of the Old Testament" and affirmed "that God is not dead but very much alive and at work in history and the universe."[18]

McKinney's method differs from Brown's in that it begins with the biblical story and then links with the human story. Moreover, his method does not rely to any great degree on questioning as a means of engaging the worshipers in reflection. Nonetheless, his method draws worshipers into a consciousness-raising experience that presents an effective way of nurturing faith and hope in the Holy Spirit. His method of linking the historic faith and hope of the followers of Jesus in the Holy Spirit with the worshipers' story unfolds in three ways: consciousness raising through describing the biblical story of Pentecost, cultivating awareness of the central role of the story in the stream of history, and raising a key question to arouse reflection on implications of the Holy Spirit's activity in the past for the present story of the worshipers.

Describing the Pentecost Story

McKinney uses description as part of his storytelling process. Pivotal to his description is the characterization of Pentecost as the "launching pad" of the church, God's divine purpose in history, and "the Spirit of the Eternal fashioning, molding, and making of a new people. . . . In Pentecost we see the breath of God energizing his children and making the dead bones of hope and promise live again. . . . The church, established by the 'winds of God' was marked by a new quality of life, a society of love, joy, and hope."[19]

The function of nurture in McKinney's description is that of arousing and moving the worshipers' recognition of the trajectory of faith and hope set in motion in the historical event of Pentecost contained in the Bible. The description serves as an introduction of the powerful and transforming nature and activity of the Holy Spirit in the lives of the church and individual persons; and the characterization of the Spirit's nature and activity at that momentous historical event of Pentecost functions as a reference point for assisting the worshipers' comprehension of the potential for the same transforming and hope-building work of the Spirit today. Nurture, then, takes place through the descriptive act of the preacher, which is to evoke the worshipers' consciousness of the role of Pentecost in the stream of history—a stream, in fact, in which today's black Christians are part.

Cultivating Awareness of the Role of Pentecost in the Stream of History

The sermon presentation method of McKinney suggests that nurturing faith and hope in the Holy Spirit requires the cultivation of the worshipers' awareness of how God's activity unfolds over time and links and makes sense of seemingly disparate happenings. On this basis, McKinney places the worshipers in touch with hope for a new age by presenting a "picture" of the transforming activity of the Spirit of God at Pentecost as God's tending to the ancient breach in human relations occurring at the Tower of Babel. That is, McKinney fosters the worshipers' awareness that the Holy Spirit of God acted in the stream of history to reverse the separation of God's people from one another during the Babel event by reuniting them at Pentecost.[20]

Pedagogically, the linkage of the Pentecost and Babel stories has the effect of placing in motion the worshipers' awareness of what Donald Capps calls a *three-story* universe.[21] One story is of the New Testament Pentecost event. The second story is of the Old Testament Babel experience. The presentation of these two stories and the connection of the two lay the foundation for the third story, which is the worshipers' story and the question of what the first two stories have to say for the worshipers' story.

Raising the Question

McKinney's evocative storytelling process opens the way for worshipers to identify with what he calls the "New Humanity" or the one family of God brought about at Pentecost. He invites the worshipers' reflection on the question, "What is expected of a new people?"[22] The single question posed by McKinney functions to stimulate and guide thinking or to evoke the worshiper's reflections on the self's story. This self-story is the third story of the *three-story* universe, which becomes the focal point of the worshipers's reflection on the black self and the black community in the stream of history. Consideration is now to be given to how, specifically, the presence and activity of God's Spirit may make a difference in that story at this juncture in time.

The question is open-ended to the extent that worshipers may retell within the self the events of the self's life that are critical touchstones for the transforming activity of the Spirit. However, McKinney offers some possibilities for self-reflection and discovery including a person's concretely felt experiences of racism, poverty, hunger, disease, pollution, and war. McKinney's use of questioning and the insertion of troubling aspects of the everyday stories of people in community nurture faith by inviting the worshipers to visualize, make some judgments about, and contemplate some responses to the current nearness of God through God's Spirit in these stories. Questioning nurtures hope by stimulating worshipers' expectation and welcome of the transforming activity of God's Spirit in our stories and those of others. Yet, McKinney's evocative nurturing method does not stop with raising the question and inserting troubling aspects of today's story. His method of engaging worshipers in reflection on a *three-story* universe concludes with his arousal of the worshipers' awareness of the necessity of our openness to the Spirit's transforming work in us in order to make concrete today Pentecost's reversal of Babel.[23]

SERMON 3

A final example of the pivotal-use role of linking Bible to life and the employment of questioning appears in the sermon "Are We Merely Gazing?" by Walter M. Brown Jr.[24] In his evocative process, Brown begins by calling forth the worshipers' primary attention to the nature of Christians' responses to the Holy Spirit and the necessity of placing oneself in the presence of the Holy Spirit. In this way, Brown's evocative process calls forth a great deal of deliberation on the activity of the Holy Spirit and the impact of the Holy Spirit on the worshipers' becoming faith- and hope-filled moral agents in today's world.

Walter Brown's storytelling method is primarily descriptive in nature and, through this means, he turns to the story in the first chapter of Acts of Jesus' ascension to disclose the new connectedness with God into which the followers of Jesus were thrust after that event. In this opening part of his storytelling, Walter Brown relates that the followers' movement forward in their new relationship with God became possible only after two angels broke their awestruck gaze at the spectacular ascension event.[25]

In the second part of his evocative storytelling process, Walter Brown uses the gaze of Jesus' followers as a pivot for evoking the worshipers' consideration of a similar kind of gaze of black people today, though taking place under different circumstances. Brown shares and therefore invites the worshipers' wonderment about whether there are black people today who are gazing at the extraordinary accomplishments of our people and are failing to see beyond them.[26] The evocative process continues with Brown's definition of the phrase "to gaze," which means "to merely appreciate an event, the victory, or the achievement without any subsequent action on the part of the viewer."[27] The definition is followed by a series of questions, each ending with the mantra "are we just gazing?" to stimulate critical reflection both on the meaning of gazing and on situations calling us beyond the act of gazing: "While parts of our communities are yet devastated by neglect, are we just gazing? While more babies are born *out of* rather than *in* wedlock, are we just gazing? While children are often left to fend for themselves, are we just gazing? While drug lords seem to be replacing our Lord in the inner cities, are we simply gazing? When the tension in many of our communities is as thick as a dense fog, are we just gazing? When God is decreed out of our schools, and we turn to legislators and lawyers for opportunities to pray, are we—believers, prophets, the people of God— merely gazing?"[28]

Pedagogically, the repetitious nature of the queries sets forth not only a searching function but also a review function. That is, the repetition of searching questions fosters the worshipers' own critical thinking, self-judgment, and contemplation of what the answers to the questions mean for future action. However, the repetition also calls forth a review of the pivotal nature of the questions.[29]

In the final part of his evocative storytelling process, Walter Brown poses a follow-up question that the angel in the story in Acts might ask today: "Why are you standing when there is so much to be done?"[30] This follow-up question functions as a climactic point of decision making. Or, to build on Butler's explanation, this type of question functions as an informal dialectic that he likens to that appearing in the Dialogues of Plato. He states that this form of questioning pushes the antagonist, to whom the question is posed, to move from the original position to the opposite position at the end.[31] In Walter Brown's sermon, the question is a means of eliciting the worshipers' movement from the negative or "dead-end" position of simply "gazing" to the active positive place of placing faith and hope in the life-giving Spirit of God.

Walter Brown draws on 2 Kings 4:38–41 to paint a "word picture" of the movement toward faith-filled and hope-filled response. The "word picture" evokes reflection on how to avoid a dead-end situation that resembles truth but is not, in much the same way as the plant brought back by an unnamed preacher to Elisha's cooking pot appeared edible but was not. Brown calls attention to the necessity of the substance of truth, which he likened to Elisha's wise addition of meal to the pot, which added substance and prevented death.[32] But, Brown's primary concluding part of the evocative storytelling process raised a challenge for the worshipers' action. That challenge was to place ourselves in the presence of the life-giving Spirit of the Living God through prayer, which, as in the case of the followers in the Book of Acts, can pull our gaze out of the clouds and give us "courage to go and turn an upside-down world right-side up."[33]

A Word about Consciousness-Raising through Songs and Prayers

In the beginning of this chapter, I referred to the song "Let It Breathe on Me" as a reminder that the presence and activity of the Holy Spirit and our welcome of the Spirit are interconnected endeavors. As a methodological tool, the song engages us not simply in the act of singing something about the Holy Spirit, but of considering what it is we are singing about the Spirit and what it means. The song provides "food for thought" that an openness to and welcome of the Spirit is a necessary prerequisite to our experience of the Spirit. Other songs invite our consideration of the Holy Spirit's direction as indicated in the spiritual "I'm Gonna Sing When the Spirit Says A-Sing"[34] and the Spirit's counsel as noted in the song "I've Got a Feelin'," which highlights the situation of all-rightness that results from the speaking Spirit.[35]

Prayers have a similar function in stimulating our reflection on the nature and activity of the Spirit while we are engaged in prayer. This is to say that we do not pray blindly or thoughtlessly. The prayers of others are apt to trigger something in us about the Holy Spirit most especially in times of trouble. We want to know how we are going to "make it through" when nothing else has seemed to help. We want to know how God's Spirit can help us. A part of the pastoral prayer my husband often prays in congregational worship is an example of nurture that provides both "food for thought" and a pathway for our seeing and receiving the Holy Spirit's movement. In the prayer, he draws on the words of the apostle Paul in Romans 8:26: ". . . the Spirit helps us in our weakness; for we do not know how to pray as we ought, but that very Spirit intercedes with sighs too deep for words." The use of this short pericope presents a way of thinking about the Spirit, a way of anticipating the movement of the Spirit, and a way of actually experiencing the Spirit in the very moments of praying.

CONTENT OF NURTURE FOCUSED ON FAITH AND HOPE IN THE HOLY SPIRIT

Spirit-focused content in the black worshiping congregation exists as a means of disclosing the nature and activity of the Holy Spirit. The content is what and how the Holy Spirit "speaks," which we discern through the action of the participants in worship and through spoken and musical communication. At the outset of this chapter, I commented on congregational responses to the Spirit that arouse new or renewed consciousness of the nature and activity of the Holy Spirit. By virtue of what these responses arouse in us, these responses constitute an essential kind of nurturing content. That is, swaying, clapping, running, shouting, and other forms of bodily and emotional expression comprise what may be called action content that promote worshipers' affirmation and formation of new appreciations of the presence and activity of God's Spirit.

I also mentioned the oral means by which the black worshiping congregation "tells" who the Holy Spirit is and how the Spirit relates to us. What the congregation says while engaging in what Butler calls "the reciprocity of 'conversation,'"[36] especially between the preacher and the worshipers, constitutes probably the most common form of content. Building on the content of sermons, songs, and prayers included in this chapter and other materials, brief attention will be given to this oral content. Particular emphasis will be given to what is communicated about who the Holy Spirit is, how the Holy Spirit acts, and the impact of the Holy Spirit's activity on our everyday lives.

The content of sermons, songs, and prayers reveal, and therefore raise worshipers' consciousness of the Holy Spirit or the Holy Ghost as the presence and activity of the able God in our lives. The Holy Spirit is the same One God who breathed new life into dead bones in the Ezekiel story, the One God who "poured out" on all assembled at

Pentecost, and who affirms God's aliveness in the world and for all times. The Holy Spirit is also characterized as the Spirit of holiness, the Spirit of the Eternal, life support, energy source, the *ruah,* or the breath or wind of God, the empowering presence of God through Jesus Christ in the lives of Christians that is able to transform, energize, prod, rebuke, charm, enchant, lift, restore, fashion, mold, direct, and equip us.[37]

The Holy Spirit "speaks," not necessarily in audible words but in ways that are recognizable to us as noted in the earlier reference to "the inner witness of the Holy Spirit . . . [who] when I say, 'I can't,' the Spirit says, 'Yes, you can'" and by turning our cowardice into courage and fear into faith.[38] The experience of individual persons and congregations of the activity of the Holy Spirit makes possible a new people, quality of life, and society. On this basis, a change in who we perceive ourselves to be, a difference in our attitude and character, and the transformation of our life habitus are consequences of our relationship with God's Spirit.

Yet, the content also holds that, even as the Holy Spirit seeks us out, we must seek and be open to the Holy Spirit, especially in our prayer life. In addition, we must be obedient to the Holy Spirit to which the content refers, as noted in the words of the earlier mentioned song, "Let It Breathe on Me." Our relationship with the Holy Spirit is to have an impact on how we live our everyday lives. This relationship is to affirm or reaffirm our faith or belief in the presence and activity of God even in the tough times and places of our lives; and it is to illuminate our hope or vision of our own life-affirming responses in our own and others' lives.

COMMENTARY

As in the case of nurturing faith and hope in God and in Jesus Christ, nurturing faith and hope in the Holy Spirit in the black worshiping congregation is about more than presenting dry propositions. Rather, it is about inviting understandings of the Holy Spirit through worshipers' experiences of seeing, feeling, and moving, and of being illuminated by a clarifying engagement with scripture. The various process approaches and the contents of nurture function as culturally based evocative means of awakening black worshipers' awareness of the nature and activity of the Holy Spirit.

The importance of the presence of both action content and oral content in the conduct of nurture cannot be overemphasized. Much emphasis is typically placed on rhetorical skill or on the oral communicative means of arousing reflection, insight, and understandings of the Holy Spirit. However, it is well to remember Butler's astute statement that "words do not equal nurture, although they may be a common vehicle of it."[39] All that occurs in the worshiping congregation serves to heighten our consciousness of the Holy Spirit and how the Spirit acts, including what we observe of the feeling selves expressed in the actions of others and what we experience of our own feelings.

Just as nurturing faith and hope in the Holy Spirit is not a matter of presenting propositions, so also nurture is not simply a matter of the leading of the mind. Nurture is a matter of engaging our whole selves— of enkindling our minds, emotions, and behaviors to the end that we truly see, move, and have our being in life in response to God's Spirit. Ultimately, our response relies less on human nurturing efforts carried out in the worshiping congregation and more on what Charry calls "the divine pedagogy."[40] Through this pedagogy, God through the Holy Spirit wakes us up and turns us in the direction of God's hope for our lives, made known in Jesus Christ.

AN INVITATION TO REFLECT

1. Recall when you first became aware of the Holy Spirit. Where did that experience take place? What happened or what was said or done that brought the Holy Spirit to your awareness?

2. What is communicated in your worshiping congregation about the nature and activity of the Holy Spirit?

3. Who would you say the Holy Spirit is? How would you say the Holy Spirit acts? What difference would you say the Holy Spirit should make in the lives of Christians?

4. Take some time to ponder what the Holy Spirit means to you. Revisit any personal experiences of the Holy Spirit and what these experiences mean to you. Explore ways in which you may discover more about the Holy Spirit.

FAITH AND HOPE IN A VALUED SELF

For it was you who formed my inward parts;
you knit me together in my mother's womb.
I praise you, for I am fearfully and wonderfully made.
Wonderful are your works; that I know very well.
$\qquad\qquad$ —*Psalm 139:13–14*

FROM ITS INCEPTION, a primary emphasis in the black church has been getting to know God who is revealed in Jesus Christ and the Holy Spirit, and becoming ever more assured that black people are neither "cursed of God" nor condemned by God. To use the words of C. Eric Lincoln: "The church brought the comfort and the security of God's love and redemption into the hopelessness of abject dereliction. The black response—the prayer and the preaching, the singing, the moaning, the shouting (or as DuBois put it, "the frenzy")— kept human spirit alive and the presence of God an assured consolation."[1] This role of the black church and the worshiping congregation remains an essential one today; and how the worshiping congregation undertakes this role is the focus of this chapter. Two opening stories will serve as a bridge to the contemporary call for evocative nurture. We will then explore the kind of nurturing process and content in the black worshiping congregation that evokes faith and hope in a valued self.

TWO STORIES AND THE CALL FOR EVOCATIVE NURTURE

Larry's Story

"Growing up black is not easy!" This statement of Larry, a young black teen[2] followed a harrowing experience on his way home from school one day. The youth had finished a longer than usual track practice in preparation for an upcoming track meet. Fearful that he would be late for his role as a peer mentor in a program sponsored by the congregation he attended, he left the school yard running, still donned in his athletic attire. A couple of blocks later, a police squad car pulled alongside him. Two white police officers swiftly exited the vehicle, commanded the young teen to stop, frisked him, and pushed him to the ground.

Larry described what followed as a wild ordeal of being told of a robbery that had occurred several blocks away and that he matched the description of the robber. After asking where he came from and why he was running, the police rebuffed the teen's story of leaving track practice and of trying to get to church on time for an appointment. They refused to heed his request for them to simply return with him to the high school to verify his story. Although he was a better-than-average student who had never been in trouble with the law, Larry found himself handcuffed, addressed by the word "Nigger!" thrown into the back seat of the squad car, and transported to a police precinct. After seemingly endless hours of interrogation, Larry was allowed to call his mother. She called the youth pastor who, in turn, called the track coach. The three met at the police station and received the devastated young teen upon his release.

In response to the incident, the youth leader began working with Larry to help him regain a positive sense of self. The task was daunting and prolonged. The leader also opened the way for other youth to share their stories of racism and guided the youth group in preparing for a worship experience centered on meanings of a valued self that comes from God. The message for the service highlighted the biblical passage, "For it was you [God] who formed my inward parts; / you knit me together in my mother's womb. / I praise you, for I am fearfully and wonderfully made. / Wonderful are your works; / that I know very well" (Psalm 139:13–14). During the service, an elderly member rose to tell a personal story of overcoming a difficult incident of racism. The testimony ended with the member's plea to the young people: "Don't you let nobody turn you around!"

Wilson's Story

In his autobiography, Wilson Goode documents his own dehumanizing experience as a young man and how the worshiping congregation became a place of nurture that evoked in him a renewed sense of self. He tells of being repeatedly on the honor roll in a predominantly white high school; yet, he was convinced by his white guidance counselor to give up any plans for college because, according to the counselor: "You don't have the background to make it in college. You're from the South, and college life is more than just knowing how to read and write and do your work. You would never succeed in college, if you made it at all."[3] Wilson was crushed by the reality that his diligent study and accomplishment had apparently meant nothing. The words of the counselor also placed before him the very real possibility of the same dead-end future to which so many other black youngsters were relegated.

However, Wilson was not to remain discouraged for long. Shortly after he began working at a tobacco factory, the pastor's wife in a local Baptist church spoke with him about his future. When Wilson repeated what the school counselor told him, the pastor's wife quickly retorted in a tone of restrained anger: "Willie, I don't care what they tell you. You are college material!"[4] Because Wilson had begun to doubt himself, he reminded her of his tendency to stutter. The pastor's wife quickly responded: "Moses had a speech problem. He put stones in his mouth to speak properly. God used him. . . . You go to college, Willie."[5] She continued her plea: "Save your money and we'll help you here at the church. Don't let them tell you, *you* can't go to college. You *can* go to college!"[6]

Wilson applied to four colleges and received acceptance letters from all four. He chose one of the four. The Sunday before he departed for college, Wilson attended his church's Sunday worship service. During that service, the congregation presented to him a financial gift and a special send-off following the pastor's sermon, the words of a church deacon, and a shout from the congregation, "Amen!"[7]

The Call for Evocative Nurture

The two stories highlight an ongoing imperative call for nurture in black churches that focuses on faith and hope in a valued self and that is grounded in our faith in God who, through Jesus Christ and the Holy Spirit, remains with us in our struggles and guides us through them. A dominant part of this task is also to evoke in us an expectation of discovering and fulfilling God's purpose for our lives. Yet, the task of nurturing faith and hope must necessarily include the forthright challenge to overcome the negative definition of black people found in the societal arena and negative self-definitions resulting from violent, castigating, and hurtful treatment in our communities and homes. Moreover, the challenge also includes paying particular attention to the impact on black selfhood of negative and abusive language voiced in popular musical genres today and heard on CDs, tapes, radio, and Black Entertainment Televison (BET).

The task of the black church is to redefine black personhood as a gift of God and, therefore, as valuable. By taking on this task, the black worshiping congregation becomes a catalyst for evoking in persons a knowing within the very depths of the self answers to the questions: Who are we? Where do we fit in the world? Nurture in the black worshiping congregation is evocative activity that gives answers to the questions through the congregation's integral involvement in sermons, songs, prayers, and with uses of biblical stories/texts.

As we have discovered in the previous chapters, black worshipers are not passive participants in the evocative process. Our active involvement continues to be the case in the matter of nurturing faith and hope in a valued self. Thus, nurture in the black worshiping congregation is participatory evocative activity that is directed toward our knowing with surety our valued "is-ness," or valued black person that he *is* and that she *is*, in the presence of God, one another, and in an alienating denigrating society. This activity includes sermons, songs, and prayers that pave the way for this kind of knowing and sustenance. Moreover, the activity extends to the congregation's vocal assertions of "Yes, Lord!" "Amen!" or "Tell it!" in response to the identity-reshaping words of scripture and sermons. In addition, the evocative pathway to black worshipers' knowing the valued self opens through the messages of scriptures like the one with which this chapter began. Songs and prayers, too, evoke our deepened knowing of our valued selves by virtue of our belief that God knows and hears us and provides us wisdom to discern that God created a good earth and that out of one blood God created us all.[8]

In short, the black worshiping congregation is a participatory habitation in which individual and communal identity redefinition takes place. Black worship may also be described as a "redefinitional ritual" focused on evoking—or stimulating—our knowing that inequalities, stereotypical views, denigrating language and all forms of oppression and animosity are, in fact, antithetical to the Christian faith and what God wants for our lives.[9] This "ritual" of the black congregation is evocative activity that contributes not only to our knowing ourselves fully as people of God but also to our realizing the capacity and choice God gives us to direct righteous indignation and any bitterness that we feel into meaningful action.[10]

In the next parts of this chapter, more focused attention will be given to the evocative nature of the redefinition process at work in the black worshiping congregation. Moreover, consideration will be given to the kind of evocative content, particularly the language of redefinition.

EVOCATIVE METHOD: REDEFINING SELFHOOD

Black worshipers expect the worshiping congregation to be a context in which the self is affirmed. There is the expectation that the congregation will provide nurture that counters the painful and self-negating realities of daily life. We come into the worshiping congregation seeking an important sustaining and guiding force that overrides disaffirmation and that points the way toward faithful and hopeful living in everyday life. Methods of redefinition entail this kind of overriding activity and, as such, become a means through which we become aware of alternative options for sharing our lives.[11] As part of evocative nurture occurring in the black worshiping congregation, redefinition methods invite us into renaming and reframing activities that are intended to bring forth restoration and sustenance of a valued self. These activities are directed toward evoking in us ways of thinking about the self positively, of viewing the self through God's eyes, and of responding to God's affirmation through acting to build up others in community.

The activity of renaming refers to the presentation, hearing, and practice of language that defines the personhood of black people in positive ways or in ways other than the negative ones encountered in life's sojourn. It is activity that centers on God's love and affirmation of all of humankind, including black people, and that invites us into a reflexive self-consciousness in which we critically appraise our views of ourselves.[12] The activity of reframing is part of evocative nurture focused on the uses, hearing, and practice of language that awakens our vision of life lived as a valued human being in response to God's affirming love. This activity is transformation-directed in that it pushes us toward a new or renewed kind of participation in life based on our views of ourselves as God sees us.[13]

Through both the activities of renaming and reframing, the redefinition method engages the worshiping congregation in evocative language that becomes quite personalized, focusing on the "I," "you," and "we." The language engages us in cultural and religious historical reflection, calling on memory; and it connects us with the very real social ethos in which we live as well as how, as Christians, we are to carry out our lives in it. Evocative language used in the renaming and reframing activities, then, has personal, social, and temporal dimensions.[14]

Evoking a Positive Sense of Self through Renaming

Because of black people's experiences of being on the receiving end of racial epithets, ridicule, and belittling comments from nonblack societal members and sometimes from other black people, black congregations know the power of language. These congregations are aware that language emerges from and informs our thoughts. It shapes how we think of others and think of ourselves. Black congregations are also aware that, if language has the power to negatively name and maim people, then it also can be used to positively rename and strengthen people. Through the activity of worship, our congregations insist that negative naming will not be the final arbiter of black identity. Consequently, an important part of evocative nurture in the worshiping congregation is the engagement of worshipers in renaming acts through which the nature of human life in general and black identity in particular are placed in a more truthful perspective.

In the black worshiping congregation, we are free to override the experiences of misnaming and to go about renaming in an intentional way. Black people as children of God is the most commonly found image of the valued self in sermons, songs, and prayers. This image carries a powerful renaming function and invites us into experiences of reflexive self-consciousness. For example, in her sermon "Singing the Lord's Song," Yvonne Delk discloses a personal history story that invites reflexive self-consciousness through association: "My family and I made it through the roughest part of our existence because we had support, the nurturing love of a faith community who reminded us every Sunday morning of our identity: 'You are children of God.'"[15]

Through her testimony, Delk conveys an evocative image of a valued self that interfaces the message of the Christian faith with a depiction of lived experience.[16] She conveys the point that the reiteration of this truth is an exceedingly important role for congregations. More than this, though, the words that she heard in her formative years constitute both a powerful and necessary ethnic-cultural renaming strategy that emphasizes who we are as Christians and in whom this identity is rooted. On this basis, Delk reminds us: "Our task as Christians is to keep clearly before all persons who they are and under whose banner they are marching. *We are God's people.* We are authored, anointed, and given our authority . . . by God. Our spirituality is rooted in God."[17] For Delk, the importance of the renaming task lies in its keeping us from the danger of hopelessness.[18]

The sermon "In This Moment, at This Dawn" by Frederick G. Sampson II invites the listener into reflexive self-consciousness through addressing the listener personally in the present moment by using "I" and "You." As part of the renaming language in the sermon, Sampson invites us into a firsthand conversation with an outside devaluing critic: "I may have a flat nose, I may not look the way you think I should, but you ought to see my history. God made me who I am, I am whose I am. I'm a child of the king."[19] Sampson moves from "I" to "You" through the evocative approach of posing questions as well as through positing an answer. In this way, he invites our reflection on God's value of and desire for the human self: "Don't you know you're a divine investment? And, don't you know that investment is because of divine intention? What's the intention? It is a covenant relationship. . . . The unimpeachable evidence of the love of God and the power of Jesus and the Holy Ghost is YOU!"[20] Sampson draws further on Psalm 139 to make the point that we are God's creations and were, therefore, known by God before we were born.[21]

John Porter's sermon includes a statement not unlike Delk's and Sampson's. However, as part of the renaming process, he invites us to remember a cultural history story of our enslaved ancestors whose names were forced on them and who were invisible as human beings to those who misnamed them. In this sermon, Porter engages us in reflexive self-consciousness by connecting us with the journey of our forebears and the wisdom coming forth through the "redefinitional ritual" in their worshiping community. To this extent, Porter draws attention to the importance of remembering in our engagement reflexive self-consciousness. Specifically, Porter engages us in recalling the renaming legacy of our forebears in which God, "the name above all names," provides the basis for our language of redefinition.

Porter tells the poignant story from the slave era: "When they finished their chores, they would sneak off one by one and gather at the feet of the old preacher, . . . as he told them: "Brothers and sisters, y'all ain't no slaves. God ain't got no slavery up in heaven. Y'all ain't no nigguhs. God ain't got no nigguhs in heaven. Y'all ain't all them names they give us either. Children! Do you know who you are? You are the greatest thing God put here. You God's Children. God have you a name just like he gave you a song to sing. So sing yo song and walk with yo head high."[22]

The evocative pathway to black worshipers' knowing the valued self also opens through the message of songs such as "He Knows Just How Much We Can Bear," which declares that all of us are God's children and are loved by God.[23] Furthermore, songs are evocative nurturing channels that offer us opportunity to articulate our desire for renaming and for an assignment of a new name by God through the person of Jesus, as noted in the song of our forebears called "Changed Mah Name."[24] This kind of song not only brings to awareness our personal freedom and readiness to engage in the renaming process but also makes clear that the new self-understanding derives from Jesus, as friend, whose qualities as friend are described in chapter 2.

As indicated earlier, prayers, too, evoke our deepened knowing of our valued selves. The value of this "primary speech" to evoking a positive sense of self is described by James Melvin Washington in his collection, *Conversations with God*. He states that "prayer in the midst of the abortion of one's human, political, and social rights is an act of justice education insofar as it reminds the one who prays, and the one who overhears it, that the one praying is a child of God."[25]

Evoking a Valued Sense of Self through Re-framing

I have already referred to reframing as activity in the black worshiping congregation that centers on our imagining how to live our lives forthrightly as valued human beings in response to God's affirming love. This approach to awakening an affirming sense of selfhood invariably implores us to enter into a historical cultural-contextual review of the Divine-human relationship, God's purposes for our lives, and ways in which we may carry out these purposes. A sermon of Jeremiah A. Wright Jr. "What Makes You So Strong?" is one of the most eloquent sermons that demonstrates this process.[26]

Like so many sermons of black preachers, Wright's sermon relies on the evocative power of personalized cultural-contextual oriented questions to engage us in reflective activity. Consequently, the questions, "What makes you so strong, black man? What makes you so strong, black woman?" are interspersed throughout the sermon. Yet, it is not simply the questions that draw us into reflexive self-consciousness, but the insertion of multitudinous examples of black people's accomplishments over the years in spite of incredibly daunting odds. Through this method of evocative nurture, Wright rouses our imagination of our strength as black people by placing into juxtaposition both the question of what makes black strength possible and illustrations of the concrete exercise of it in real life. In the reframing process, the underlying assumption of strength automatically pushes us forward beyond any consideration of weakness and into an arena of opportunity or possibilities for self.

Yet, Wright does not stop at the point of questions and examples. He draws on the biblical story of Samson as means of evoking critical reflection and decision making on the source of one's strength. He tells Samson's story and, while telling it, poses the problem of reliance on inappropriate relationships that endanger one's strength and survival and the requirement of committing to move through problems *"nevertheless . . . in spite of . . . anyhow."*[27] Likewise, Wright weaves together Samson's and black people's stories to advance the solution to the problem, which is our devotion to God and recognition that God had a special work for Samson and has a definite will for our lives as black people. Wright's evocative method assists our visualization of the nature of God's will through declarative statements: "God has a work of redemption and healing to do through African Americans. God will do through you individually, not only corporately. . . . Watch out for what somebody can do *to* you and *for* you. Don't let that become more important than what our God wants to do *in* and *through* you. Samson allowed a relationship that he wanted to have but could not have get in the way of the relationship that he already had with God."[28]

Wright closes with a recapitulation of the question phrased in communal rather than individual terms: "What makes us so strong?" The question serves as a stimulus for our ongoing reflection on God as the Source of strength and the Spirit of God as the enabler of our strength.[29]

In a similar manner, the gospel songs "I Am Redeemed," "The Call," and "Stir Up" serve as evocative triggers for the reframing task by evoking in us a highly personalized "picture" of ourselves as God's own, transformed by God, and with strength to live life given by God. The first song, "I Am Redeemed," engages us in describing our spiritual identity and the nature of the whole of life when we have been transformed by Jesus. The resultant reframed life perspective is one that brings forth the affirmative response that redemption has, indeed, been achieved.[30]

Through uses of the words "I" and "You," the song "The Call"[31] draws singer and listener alike into the reminder that the self belongs to God and that God has given to us sufficient ability to live life for the sake of the call in spite of the doubts we express to God about that ability and the fear of failure."[32] The call to which the song refers draws on words from Paul's letter to the Philippians (3:13b–14): ". . . but this one thing I do: forgetting what lies behind and straining forward to what lies ahead, I press on toward the goal for the prize of the heavenly call of God in Christ Jesus." However, in the song, the biblical text is paraphrased.[33] The song, "Stir Up," assists the identity reframing task by referring to and identifying "us" as recipients of God's gifts of power, joy, peace, and happiness, and a sound mind in the face of fear. It is these gifts that must be stirred up.[34]

CONTENT ON THE VALUED SELF

Black people's experiences of threats to the positive definition of self prompt a special kind of nurture and a specific method in the black worshiping congregation that move us toward a redefinition of self in social and spiritual terms. However, a particular sort of content is required to illuminate this redefinition process. Specifically, we have explored evocative nurture that incorporates a redefining methodology in the black worshiping congregation that entails renaming and reframing activities and methods. Yet, it is also true that the evocative power of this method relies on content that stirs within us a knowing of our valued self.

In the foregoing sections, this kind of content has already emerged in the form of images of us as children of God and as having dispositions such as strength and character necessary to carry out God's purpose for our lives. This kind of content is consistent with the goal of nurturing faith and hope. As indicated earlier, there is a relationship between our faith in ourselves that is demonstrated by our affirmation of ourselves as valued creations of God and our faith in the One who created us. If we are to trust God's for-us-ness, then we must see ourselves as deserving of that for-us-ness. Moreover, our embrace of this worthiness of self is a prerequisite to our seeing ourselves as acceptable followers of Jesus as well as to our vision of living confidently and courageously in community after the model of Jesus even at the risk of unpopularity. The nature of this worthiness is a key theme in the content of nurture that leads to faith and hope.

In a real sense, the content on which the redefining process relies is what may be called countervailing content. This content is language containing essential meanings and affirmations of human life authored by God. It consists of images, metaphors, and statements that bring into view the human self as valued in contrast to the devaluation of the self by others. As such, countervailing content is constructive in nature and discloses who we are as opposed to who we are not. Countervailing content depicts the Christian self as embodying a distinctive character to be lived out in a vocational manner in community in accordance with God's purpose as opposed to the purposes found in the secular ethos of human communities. On this basis, countervailing content is enactive in nature.[35]

Who We Are and Are Not: Constructive Countervailing Content

By its very nature, a redefining process necessitates countervailing content that is constructive in character. A constructive quality refers to content that lifts up the biblically affirmed God-given value of all of humankind over against human beings' tendency to devalue other humans. The pivotal nature of the constructive quality of countervailing content to the redefining and reframing process lies in its usefulness in evoking the worshipers' reflexive self-consciousness, alternative interpretations of self-identity, and imagination of life based on a valued self. Content that has constructive qualities is be-lief-building content.

Examples of constructive countervailing content appear in earlier mentioned sermons of Yvonne Delk, Frederick G. Sampson II, and John Porter and in the song "Changed Mah Name." The content of these sermons and songs focuses clearly on personalized imagery from which we build a language of faith and hope in the valued self and we enter into personally affirming conversation with one another by admitting as true:

- I'm a child of the King,

- I am redeemed,

- You are children of God,

- You are a divine investment,

- You are great too,

- We are God's people.

In addition, it is helpful to mention here an overarching view of the valued self shared in the testimony and advice of an unnamed old black church member in a worship service. The particular imagery presented by the member is an important one to lift up today because it centers on the truth of our valued identity as black people at every age and stage and for all times:

It says in the Word that God created the whole human race accord-ing to His likeness. Don't you know we're part of that whole? I'm here to tell you that we—you and me, and our children, and our children's children are included. I know it! I believe it! And I want all you young folks within the sound of my voice to believe it too. In this world of ours, some people aren't kind because they don't know what I know. But, the God that the Bible talks about and the God I know is no liar. So, you just keep on keeping on. You hold your head up high and don't you be ashamed of who you are. And, don't you let nobody turn you around![36]

The countervailing content of the member's testimony joins the other examples of content in its stirring quality. In a real way, this quality makes of the content what may be called "faith consciousness" content. That is, it is content that focuses squarely on meanings of the gospel in the throes of our concrete lived experiences as black people. Indeed, this kind of content becomes all the more striking when real emphasis and assent are given to declarative content of who we are not, like that appearing in John Porter's sermon:

- Y'all ain't no slaves;
- Y'all ain't no nigguhs; and
- Y'all ain't all them names they give us.[37]

What We Are to Do: Enactive Countervailing Content

In addition to the constructive quality of countervailing content, evocative nurture in the black worshiping congregation centers on content that has an enactive quality. This quality refers to content that reveals God's purpose for human life, including God's purpose for black people. This content is also a necessary aspect of the reframing strategies in the redefinitional process because it emphasizes our place and activity in life as God's people. It discloses what we are to do to act on our beliefs about ourselves as people of God, even in the face of fear. For this reason, enactive content is also vocational content. Its emphasis is akin to Martin Luther King Jr.'s view that God desires people not simply to accept their human value and dignity but to claim their capacity to make a creative contribution in life's sojourn. King challenged people to activate knowledge of their worth through developing a sense of responsibility to discover God's purpose for human freedom and untiring determination to "break through the outer shackles of circumstance."[38]

Examples of enactive or vocational content appear in the earlier mentioned songs, "I Am Redeemed" and "The Call" by Nee-C Walls, Da'dra Crawford, Steve Crawford, and Mary Tiller, in the sermon by Jeremiah Wright Jr., and in the song "Stir Up" by Rudolph Stanfield. The content of these materials suggest at least four different movements that link the renaming and reframing activities, and focus attention squarely on vocation. The movements include:

- an acceptance of one's identity defined not simply by one's knowing oneself as God's child but as one transformed by God through Jesus Christ;

- an acceptance of oneself as belonging to God, called by God to fulfill God's purposes, and able to fulfill that calling;

- an acceptance of one's strength to move through the tough problems of life and to commit to carrying out God's work of redemption and healing in the world; and

- an acceptance of the self as a recipient of God's gifts and willingness to stir up the gifts, even in the face of fear, for the sake of Christian vocation.

In short, the movements verify King's assertion that acting out of one's known valued identity requires more than her or his acceptance of human value. The content centers on movement that proves one's knowing the valued self and having faith and hope in that self.

COMMENTARY

Mainstream or popular culture has a way of constantly making us aware that value is assigned deferentially to human life based on ethnicity, class, sex, age, or accomplishment. Daily life in popular culture reveals an ever-widening chasm between differing groups of people, increasing incidences of devaluing and abusive behavior in community and family life, and an alarming escalation of disparaging language and images in music and the media. The role of the black worshiping congregation in countering these realities is a critical one. This role continues to be one of evoking in black people through both process and content a vital consciousness or knowing of our own worth and the worth of all humans that contrasts with the prevailing defferential and divisive ones in popular culture. There is strong evidence that our worshiping congregations have been engaged in redefinition processes and countervailing content necessary to get the job done. But, we must ask, "Is enough being done?" and "Is there what Augustine calls "eloquent wisdom" in what is being done?"[39]

Clearly, there is much at stake, especially with our young, if we fail to bring into view meanings of a valued identity and engage them in critical reflection on who they are, who they are not, and what they are called to do as Christians in today's and tomorrow's world. What is necessary is our determination and vigilance in singing the songs, preaching the sermons, and praying the prayers that draw them and us all into the language that moves us to the degree that it is impossible to become sluggish in acting on our faith and hope in our valued selves. Moreover, Samuel Proctor reminds us that we are called to an awareness that, in fact, Christianity was borne out of the startling countervailing example and teaching of Jesus who "reached beyond his own people and shed abroad the love of God in the lives of all people."[40] Moreover, the early Christian church, which followed Jesus' life and teaching, continued to press on with an emphasis on the countervailing notion that God has no favorites. Evocative nurture in the black worshiping congregation must also remember this core of Christianity.

AN INVITATION TO REFLECT

1. What are the evidences in your community that point to the need for an emphasis on redefining human worth and on countervailing human values?

2. Take some time to write answers to these questions: Who are you? What best describes you as a person? Where do you fit into the world? Then reflect on where and how your identity was formed.

3. What experiences have you had in your worshiping congregations that are similar to the ones described in this chapter? What experiences have you had that differ from the ones described in this chapter? Explain.

4. What suggestions would you make for changes in the way your worshiping congregation addresses concerns about human worth? How may your worshiping congregation address specific needs of young people?

FAITH, HOPE, AND THE PLIGHT OF SIN

We know that we are God's children, and that
the whole world lies under the power of the evil one.
And we know that the Son of God has come and has
given us understanding so that we may know him who
is true.... — *1 John 5:19–20a*

NOTED PREACHER AND PASTOR, J. Alfred Smith Sr. once said in a sermon, "If the black church is to have a worthwhile future, it must redefine theological concepts, like sin, into concrete, experiential language."[1] Smith's words come as a stinging indictment of the failure of the black church to help people to see plainly the nature of sin in the realities surrounding us and the very lives we live. Smith's words make abundantly clear that the concept of sin is not comprised of inert ideas that are sealed off from everyday life. Rather, sin is a very real human condition or human experiences that must be named and confronted as part of the evocative methods and content of worship in the black church.

Smith's words also address the critique often made by black religionists and laypersons about an overemphasis on other-worldly content without due attention to the practice of faith and hope in present and ongoing embodied life in the earthly community. It is helpful that worship raises black worshipers' consciousness and affirms our knowing ourselves as sojourners who are "passing through" this "lonesome valley" en route to the place that is not made with human hands."[2] Yet, there must be no silence on *how* we "pass through." Or, to use Smith's words: "People are not only asking, 'Will there be life after death?' They want to know, 'Will there be life after birth, and what kind of life will our children have after birth?'"[3] Incisive methods of nurture and evocative content are needed in the worshiping congregation that both prompt our capacity to truthfully name sin and ignite in us a continuing quest for and embrace of a transforming relationship with God. Taking this task seriously fulfills the imperative goal of nurture, which is to foster in us an alive faith or belief in God's for-us-ness and desire for our wholeness and hope for our participation in God's story by living confidently and courageously after the model of Jesus.

Importantly, there is evidence that silence on *"how"* we "pass through" or what promotes and hinders life after birth does not prevail everywhere. There are black preachers who do speak boldly within the black worshiping congregation about realities of sin in daily life by naming and describing it and the related reality of evil. These nurturers of faith and hope also refer to the disruptive sources and consequences of sin and evil. Likewise, there are sermons of black preachers as well as songs that reflect potently an embrace of the vital task of evocative nurture that seeks to arouse a deep consciousness of ways of moving from sin to faith and hope. The presence of these examples is the subject of this chapter. In what follows, selected sermons and songs will frame our exploration of particular methods and content used in black worshiping congregations.

As a way of prefacing our exploration, I want to share my observation that the methods of nurture and content found in sermons and songs used in the black worshiping congregation clearly place before worshipers a particular view of sin. This view is that humans are prone to be sidetracked on life's journey and to move in a direction away from God. Along life's journey, humans "miss the mark" in relating not only to God but also with others and with all of creation. Becoming sidetracked is the nature of sin and evil; and this reality of human finite existence occasions the particular emphasis in evocative nurture that utilizes moral truth-telling to prompt worshipers' knowing meanings of "missing the mark" and of the direction toward change. The nature of the method is evocative and centers on moral truth-telling.

EVOCATIVE METHOD: MORAL TRUTH-TELLING

Sermons and songs are especially potent carriers of moral truth-telling about sin. Through sermons, the evocative nurturing process in the black worshiping congregation gets carried out through a deliberate and uninhibited rhetorical language that unabashedly tends to truth telling.[4] This language exposes meanings of "missing the mark" and "mending the mark." It functions as a stimulus to the worshipers' coming to know these meanings through forthrightly signaling us to look squarely at the nature of the journey away from God. Likewise, the language used in the evocative method authoritatively points out the direction back toward God. The communication makes for confrontational and persuasion-oriented approaches to the evocative nurture that are meant for worshipers to take notice and, as Augustine would say, "so as not to become sluggish in acting upon what they know."[5]

CONFRONTATIONAL RHETORIC

Confrontational rhetoric in sermons is truth telling that carries out a particular kind of evocative nurture intended to arouse in black worshipers a deep consciousness of meanings of sin and evil and responses to these realities of human existence. In a manner similar to the description of God, Jesus Christ, the Holy Spirit, and the valued self discussed in the previous chapters, worshipers are actively drawn into reflection and critical analysis through the use of questions; and we hear and convey through songs vivid personalized language that targets "I," "You," "We," or "Us." Through this methodological orientation, the language "paints pictures" of the nature and effects of sin and evil in everyday life. It is truth-telling language that rebukes the role of sinners and stirs the listener toward the end that we hear, internalize, and come to know the gravity of sin and the need of action for its reversal.

The language is straightforward. For example, J. Alfred Smith Sr. identifies narcotic pushers and pimps as children of the devil, and cites the sin of black youth who condemn the white man for exploiting black women in slavery but who sexually abuse and exploit our daughters, sisters, and wives.[6] This frankness in language about the nature of sinfulness is further noted in Smith's description of "youth who disrupt classrooms, refusing to learn and preventing others from learning, and youth who see the sacred as profane," as being among the lost."[7] At the same time, Smith's frankness extends to setting forth a community's responsibility: "Rather than condemn them, we must help them to find salvation."[8] Those who perpetrate crime in the ghetto are killers, children of the night, and workers of iniquity.

Use of the straightforward pattern in the evocative method of nurture is noted as well in the sermon by Deborah McGill-Jackson who implores the listener: "We in the black church cannot afford to reject the gospel that convicts us in our comfort. The church must loosen the shackles of tradition, the irons of prejudice, the bars of isolation and suburban escapism—lest church people and their ecclesiastical palaces deteriorate in their own captivity, which is due to the sin of alienation."[9]

"Picture painting" in sermons on sin also reflects a rhetorical method in which binary contrasts are present. In this approach, two ideas stand in opposition to each other.[10] L. Venchael Booth uses this particular rhetorical device in a sermon that describes the confusion of our age of perversity and sin: "We don't like debts, nor do we like to sacrifice. We don't like discipline, but we want good schools. We don't like jails, but we insist on committing crimes. . . . We want a great moving and powerful church, but we want to work and pray it down from heaven."[11] This use of binary contrasts along with the incorporation of personalized language functions in the evocative nurturing process to arouse the worshipers' consciousness and critical analysis of positive goals gone awry in our lives.

In other sermons, a rhetorical approach is used that poses contrasting questions and answers. This form of rhetoric appears in the words of Carolyn Ann Knight's sermon: "'What must I do to go to hell?' The answer [is] 'Nothing!'. . . We can just stay as we are and we'll make it! But when Nicodemus asked Jesus a similar question[:] . . . 'Good Master, what must I do to inherit eternal life?' Jesus told Nicodemus, 'You have to do *something* to make it into the kingdom of God. You must have some worthy ambitions and some noble goals. Nicodemus, you must be born again.'"[12] In still other instances, the confrontational nature of the rhetorical method in evocative nurture entails the black preacher's use of disassociation.[13] This method distinguishes the Christian lifestyle from an impious existence as means of enkindling the worshipers' heightened awareness of what is at stake in choosing to act one way rather than another. The confrontational nature of the approach is found particularly in the language of warning that is used. For example, Deborah McGill-Jackson warns: "Unless someone proclaims the truth that can pierce the darkness, the sightless will remain captive. Unless someone delivers the empowered radiance of righteousness that can overcome the corrosive and destructive forces of unrighteousness, the creation will remain captive. Many will choose to remain in bondage to the fallacy of human security and self-gratification at the expense of others."[14]

Songs, too, reflect a confrontational style through the employ of a language of warning. This language draws worshipers' attention to the moral struggle that the temptation of sin and evil generate. For example, an African American spiritual warns that "Satan's a liar and a conjurer too; if you don't watch out, he'll conjure you," while another states: "Everybody talkin' 'bout heaven ain't goin' there."

Confrontational rhetoric in the evocative approach to nurture in the black worshiping congregation also draws us into "painting" our own "self-portrait" of wrongs. Taking the form of a command, this aspect of the process centers on evoking not simply personal critical reflection on meanings of sin but an intent to go in another direction. It also draws us into a mode of reflection on the reality that sin and evil are not simply the failings of those guilty other folk, but are our own failings as well. Words of a congregational song that arouse this kind of reflection is "Yield not to temptation, for yielding is sin. . . . Fight valiantly onward, evil passions subdue."[15] The evocative method in this song moves forward both with the directive and with information or advice on how not to succumb to temptation, including shunning evil companions, refraining from the use of adverse language, showing reverence to God, expressing thoughtfulness and kindness, and seeking the help of Jesus, the Savior.

Another example of the approach of command appears in Leotis Belk's sermon. The sermon draws on Isaiah 1:16, which says to "remove the evil of your doings from before my eyes. . . ."[16] Belk further demonstrates the use of command in the confrontational approach to evocative nurture in the following commentary on the scripture: "What [God] meant was 'Stop doing it.' Toss those intents, motives, egotisms, corroded loves away from you. Cast away that lust, that envy, that pride into the 'sea of forgetfulness where it'll never rise again to condemn you at the Judgment bar.'"[17]

In short, the confrontational approach to evocative nurture in the black worshiping congregation takes the form of truth telling that focuses the worshipers' attention on the existence of sin in everyday life, its consequences, and a way of living Christian faith and hope that counters it. The language of the approach rebukes, stirs, convicts, confronts, warns, and commands as means of heightening our consciousness of the essential message that is being shared. It is language intended, ultimately, for us to radically shift our thoughts toward meanings of faith and hope and our embrace of these generating forces of Christian life as verbs. As I indicated in the Introduction, this embrace results from our response to the divine pedagogy by vowing or declaring that we will make visible the vitality of our faith and hope in our everyday lives.

Persuasive Rhetoric

Persuasive rhetorical communication in the evocative nurturing process also centers on black worshipers' grasping meanings of sin and responses to it through truth telling and change-directed language. However, rather than a language of command as in the case of the confrontational approach, the persuasive approach involves a language of entreaty. It is a plea to stir within worshipers the will to see and forsake the false sense of joy or security that a sojourn away from God portends. The persuasive approach also entails the use of associative language or speech that calls forth our imagination of the connection between the direction away from wrong and toward meanings of being

faithful, hope-filled Christians. This form of truth telling has transformation at the center of the nurture. Songs and sermons are means
of employing persuasive rhetoric in the black worshiping congregation. These activities in worship present a methodological framework
that prompts in worshipers the necessity of forsaking the journey away
from God and embracing the journey toward God through the uses
of a plea, a call, or a reminder to forsake the wayward journey through
God's transforming power. Specifically, our participation as worshipers in listening to and singing songs opens the way for our familiarity
with truth telling and change-directed call language and our recognition of its meaning for us. The song "Sinner, please don't let this
harvest pass; . . . O, let God redeem your soul at las'" is an example
of the kind of music in which the plea or call is prominent. The particular use of the call is a method of persuasive rhetoric that also uses
associative language as means of engaging us in making definite connections between what is being said and concrete situations in our
everyday lives. Associative language entails the use of imagery, illustration, or example[18] like that used by Deborah McGill-Jackson. This
black preacher's use of associative language in the call method forms
a framework for evoking in us a consciousness of the response that is
needed to address destructive forces and powers in the world we live
in. McGill-Jackson states: "We are called to set at liberty a world
bent on self-destruction rather than the destruction of peace. Such
power to bring liberation—to set at liberty the blind, the poor, the
captive, and the oppressed—is ours, by appropriating the mind-set to
receive it and the lifestyle to use it, not for the praise of men and
women, but for the glory of God."[19]

TRUTH-TELLING AND CHANGE-DIRECTED CONTENT

Rhetorical communication in faith- and hope-centered nurture includes
truth telling and change-directed content. Indeed, this content is insinuated throughout the foregoing section. Specifically, nurturing faith
and hope invariably includes content that discloses, conceptually, the
nature of sin and meanings of reversing sinfulness. This content not

only includes sin as a concept but also consists of the idea of sin as a behavioral act and attitudinal disposition. This section will highlight these two kinds of content that appear to be important in nurture that arouses depthful consciousness of meanings, consequences, and reversals of sinfulness.

Sin as Concept and Behavior

Although the use of concrete experiential language is apparent in sermons of black preachers and in songs, there is no shying away from the incorporation of concepts of sin in the content of these "materials" or pathways of nurture. The conceptual and the experiential are linked together in a way that says that one need not be considered without the other. Conceptual images of sin and responses to it are important because they are the building blocks to the worshipers' belief formation. These notions contribute to our developing a faith or belief that sin does not have to have the last word. Rather, a more vital faith alongside hope is possible in the form of our knowing the nearness and love of God shown in Jesus Christ and our responding to this knowing through a sojourn that honors it. Content that includes conceptual images is important to our formation of faith and hope.

Several conceptual images appear in the material presented earlier in this chapter. First, sin is presented as a moral issue that takes the form of temptation to which we may yield or shun.[20] Yet, our embrace of sin is a reality; and, in its concrete presence in our lives, sin is a form of death after birth.[21] Second, sin is a rejection of the gospel,[22] and in this way, it brings about our "missing the mark." Third, sin is perverse existence[23] and a sightless way of living that entraps us in darkness.[24] Fourth, sin is a way of being attitudinally and behaviorally in the world that is self-condemning and that has consequences including, for example, alienation in community life and God's judgment.[25] Finally, sin is self-destructive behavior and is antithetical to peace in the world; but liberation from it is possible for us to the extent that we want to be freed and seek to glorify God.[26]

COMMENTARY

In his essay on "The Formative Power of the Congregation," Craig Dykstra makes the point that "Congregations are profoundly caught up in powerful patterns of sin and alienation . . . [Yet], precisely in the midst of its sinfulness, rather than apart from it, the congregation has power to mediate the gospel in such a way that the 'speaking' of it can re-structure and transform human personal life."[27] In this chapter, I have presented methods and content of nurture in the black worshiping congregation that give credence to this assertion. However, I have also made the point that it is only when we hear God "speaking" through the divine pedagogy that we glean fully the impact of sin in our lives and the imperative direction away from it to which God calls us.

To build on Dykstra's claim, it is not enough to engage us in methods and content that place before us religious language and concepts designed to raise our consciousness and our moral judgment. The truth is, to use Dykstra's words, "because the patterns of mutual self-destruction operate at a pre-reflective level, mere speech has no effect."[28] There must be an openness and acknowledgment on our part to the activity of God in our lives through which God beckons a new or renewed relationship with us; and we must feel this movement so deeply that we sense no alternative but to claim this relationship. My point in the Introduction still holds that, in the pedagogical work of nurturing faith and hope, God does come as the evocator who reaches out and invites our reaching back and calls for our vow that we will not "let this harvest pass."

AN INVITATION TO REFLECT

1. In what ways would you agree or disagree with the premise of J. Alfred Smith that appears at the beginning of this chapter?

2. What is your perception of sin and evil?

3. What understandings of sin and evil are conveyed in sermon and song in your congregation? What are your thoughts about what is communicated about sin and evil?

6

FAITH, HOPE, AND THE PROMISE OF SALVATION

Listen! I am standing at the door, knocking;
if you hear my voice and open the door, I will
come in to you. . . .

—*Revelation 3:20*

STORY IS TOLD BY Otis Moss Jr. in a sermon about the experience of salvation of a black forebear: "I was on a downward road, no hat on my head, no shoes on my feet, no God on my side, no heaven in my view. Too mean to live and not fit to die. The handcuffs of hell on my hands, the shackles of damnation on my feet, but the Lord spoke peace to my dying soul, turned me around, cut loose my stammering tongue, [and] sent me on my way. . . . I have found meaning, purpose, love, and truth, and that makes me a 'New Creation.'"[1] The sermon in which this story appeared reflects an ongoing and intentional purpose in the black worshiping congregation to foster black worshipers' awareness of meanings of salvation and concrete images of what the experience of salvation is like.

Nurturing faith and hope in the black worshiping congregation invariably focuses on the subject of salvation as a counter to sin. Sermons of the preacher, along with songs and prayers of leaders and laity alike, are primary channels by which this focus is disclosed. The whole worshiping congregation becomes the nurturing agent whose task is to bring forth what Randolph Crump Miller calls "moments of enlightenment which are life-transforming."[2] Sermons, songs, and prayers immerse us in a vivid storied methodology and content that evoke our reflection on, understanding of, faith in, and responses to God's salvific activity. Through these means, we are to "see" the promise salvation holds for our lives. The story-rich method and content form an evocative structure for engaging us in reflecting on, affirming, and responding to the transforming activity of God through Jesus Christ. Moreover, this structure of the nurturing process makes possible our formation of new understandings of what it means to make our salvation concrete in daily life and creates a space for the divine pedagogy in which God "speaks," moves, and transforms us or renews our life in Christ.

The storied method and content disclose a truth-telling language that is similar to the kind found in the black worshiping community's approach to sin and evil, which chapter 5 explores. Specifically, a rhetorical narrative orientation is maintained. However, salvation-focused truth-telling language emphasizes a reversal of the journey of sin to a journey of promise through the activity of God through Jesus Christ; and this language discloses that embarking on the journey of promise results in our deepening faith in and companionship with God. In this way, the language carries out the goal of nurturing faith and hope, which is to evoke in us a belief or trust in God's presence *with* and *for* us and our vision of and readiness to live confidently after the model of Jesus.

Importantly, the method and content also reveal that salvation is, in fact, holistic. It is spiritual, social, and emotional. Salvation-focused language invites our reflection on the holistic nature of salvation. It is evocative language that makes possible our acknowledgment of salvation already experienced or our affirmation that "salvation is in-a my reach."[3] This chapter gives attention to the method and content of salvation-focused nurture, which incorporates both truth-telling language and a holistic view of salvation.

TRUTH-TELLING DIMENSIONS OF SALVATION-FOCUSED NURTURE

Sermons, songs, and prayers are the language tools through which the black worshiping congregation receives, explores, and responds to meanings of salvation and its promises. Specifically, language appears as a rhetorical truth-telling strategy. The strategy is a way of communicating truths through sermons, songs, and prayers in order to carry out a nurturing process focused on salvation and the faith and hope resulting from it. A rhetoric of interpretation is used that serves the purpose of promoting the worshipers' awareness of and reflection on God's desire for our salvation, interpretations of the salvation experience, and meanings of salvation in or for our own lives. A rhetoric of affirmation is a storied approach that evokes within us a personal attestation of the reality of salvation already experienced, or of our movement toward salvation, or of the potential for the salvation drama to become our story.

Interpretative Rhetoric

Interpretative rhetoric is a particular use of language in approaches to nurture in the black worshiping congregation that focus on salvation. The evocative intent of this rhetoric is to bring about our reflection on and awareness of what salvation is and means for our lives. At least four key rhetorical devices appear in black sermons, songs, and prayers that stimulate this interpretative activity. These devices include interrogative and explanatory devices, metaphorical rhetorical devices, anaphorical rhetorical devices, and dialectical rhetorical devices.

INTERROGATIVE AND EXPLANATORY DEVICES

Interpretative rhetoric includes interrogative and explanatory devices. These devices center on raising questions and giving explanations of truths of salvation in order to prompt our reflection on the nature of salvation and to heighten our awareness of the spiritual and ethical nature of the salvation drama. Three primary aspects of this approach are found especially in sermons. First, interrogative and explanatory devices used in sermons draw our attention to the need for salvation. Second, interrogative and explanatory devices in sermons invite us to consider the difference salvation might make in our lives. Third, interrogative and explanatory devices stimulate our formation of a picture of the experience of salvation (or transformation) as a spiritual and ethical awakening with Jesus Christ at the center. As the result of these devices, we are also to envision the unfolding post-salvation journey in which we take on the character of Jesus for the sake of making a better world. Indeed, the approach being utilized presses us to see the link between salvation and answers to the questions that many persons, particularly our young, are raising, which I included in the Introduction: "Why and in whom shall we have faith? What hope is there for life?"

Reference to the sermon of Deborah McGill-Jackson was made in the preceding chapter. We will draw on her sermon again in this chapter to provide an example of the use of interrogative and explanatory devices in interpretative rhetoric. In the sermon "To Set at Liberty," McGill-Jackson places salvation in the context of a world in need of liberation. In this way, she evokes in worshipers an awareness that salvation is not simply an individual or even a male and female matter, but a spiritual and ethical circumstance with a far broader society-wide scope. She frames the need and stimulates critical self-reflection through the questions: "Are not men and women held captive by their past? Are they not shamed and guilt ridden? Is not the society caught in its own web of greed and abuse? Are there not among us those blind to the truth declared in love and overshadowed by ignorance of spirit? Are there not among us those who would oppress? Are we not frequently participants in the oppression of others on the basis of religion, race, wealth, and nationality?"[4]

The questions draw the worshipers into an interpretative framework that describes both the existential situation in the world that counters a faithful and hopeful view of life and the need for a liberation-oriented salvation. But, McGill-Jackson also evokes the worshipers' consideration of the self's and the congregation's connection to this broader existential need by inserting the words, "they," "us," and "we." The insertion of this personalizing language also situates the need within the context of the congregation.

By personalizing the interrogating and explanatory approach, McGill-Jackson creates the conditions for our further thought about the significance of salvation for our lives.[5] On one level, the questions direct our self-reflection or self-examination toward simple "yes" or "no" answers. However, it is not simply this level on which salvation-focused evocative nurture occurs. The use of interrogative and explanatory devices to evocative nurture necessarily moves us to ponder or to explain within ourselves the reasons for the "yes" or "no" responses. This approach also makes possible our raising and answering within ourselves during the sermon further questions of our own about the kind of alternative story that salvation makes possible, including for example: What difference does salvation make for those who are poor in spirit and material substance, for those who are ashamed and guilt ridden, for those who are caught in a web of greed and abuse, for those who do not know the truth and are ignorant of the spirit, and for those who oppress others? What difference ought salvation make for me and why? In other words, for example, the questions posed by McGill-Jackson at the level of the sermon stimulate internal queries and possible explanations at the personal level of the worshiper.

Finally, the specific use of an explanatory device is a means of assisting us in answering the questions. For example, the use of this device in McGill-Jackson's sermon proposes answers to the previously mentioned questions by drawing us into an experience of visualizing the journey into and beyond salvation and why. This aspect of interpretative rhetoric fosters our awareness of what constitutes our experience of salvation (or transformation), the outcomes of salvation, and why the road toward making the outcomes a reality is important. Again, in the case of McGill-Jackson's sermon, the explanatory device invites our formation of a visual picture of Jesus Christ who shows us the way of salvation. This way is explained so that we "see" the movement of the Spirit of God within and upon us, and that our "seeing" moves us to acknowledge the work of the Spirit as well as to embrace the life toward which the Spirit calls us. McGill-Jackson describes the focus of this life as implementing a liberation agenda in the world after the model of Jesus. Her explanatory strategy prompts in us the formation of a view that our salvation and the salvation of the world through Christian ministry in the world are connected; moreover, the life of Jesus provides a model for how this ministry should be carried out.[6]

McGill-Jackson's sermon also demonstrates a manner in which the explanatory device brings awareness of the "why" or the importance of salvation through her description of it as opening the way for the "consummation of all human hope."[7] The implementation of this approach is seen further in her drawing attention to salvation as an experience that makes possible a new identity given by God as "we give ourselves to the power and work of the Spirit."[8] She further raises our consciousness of the challenge to the "already saved, those being saved, and the shall be saved" to "follow the footprints of Jesus" by living a lifestyle in a hurting world that contributes to the construction of peace rather than to the world's bent toward self-destruction.[9]

In short, interrogative and explanatory devices in interpretative rhetoric found in sermons raise our consciousness of the nature of salvation and invite us to explore meanings of salvation for our lives. This approach is part of the process of nurturing faith and hope through sermons in the congregation that focus on salvation. However, it is also true that interrogative and explanatory devices appear in songs that are sung in the black worshiping congregation, although to a lesser degree.

In songs, interrogative and explanatory devices heighten the worshiping congregation's familiarity with the nature and meanings of salvation by engaging us in posing questions and giving explanations about the activity of God and our own activity in the salvation drama. The songs stimulate what may be called "reflection in action" whereby we contemplate various dimensions and meanings of salvation through raising questions and posing answers in the process of hearing and singing songs. For example, the hymn "Nothing but the Blood of Jesus" engages us in raising the question about the agent of salvation that can cleanse us and make us whole. Likewise, in singing the question "What can wash away my sin?" we present the answer that frames the song's title.[10]

The hymn "There's Power in the Blood" also engrosses the congregation in a question about the desire of individual persons for salvation that comes from freedom from sin. The song then involves us in advancing the description that is framed in the title as the means by which such desire is satisfied.[11] In still another instance, the gospel hymn "How Can You Recognize a Child of God?" enlists our reflection on the evidence of salvation that answers the question. It then engages us in proclaiming that being washed in the Lamb's blood is the answer."[12] Finally, interrogative and explanatory devices in the spiritual "Didn't My Lord Deliver Daniel?" call forth our deliberation on social salvation for all who are in need of it. Reflection is prompted through posing the question appearing in the title. The question is followed by a series of answers that draw our attention to God's deliverance of Daniel, Jonah, and the Hebrew children, after which there is the reassertion of the rhetorical question: "So why not-a everyone?"[13]

Prayers do not tend to incorporate questions like the ones posed in sermons and songs. However, we find in them a rich explanatory language that, even while the prayer-giver enters into conversation with God on behalf of the congregation, the worshipers become privy to images of sin we are to leave behind and of the One who enables a new way forward. For example, the prayer of Obie Wright skillfully draws our attention to the conditions from which we are to be saved and the One through whom salvation is possible: "Save us [God] from becoming the evil we hate. Save us from denial of abuses which daily crucify Christ afresh. Drive away the chilling cold, the wintry frost, of numbing detachment from others' pain, and our own hurts, also."[14] The words of another prayer focus attention on salvation as a spiritual quest: "Make us conscious of the fact that we are all Thy children in that vineyard, striving to work out our souls' salvation."[15]

METAPHORICAL RHETORICAL DEVICES

Metaphorical language often becomes part of interpretative rhetoric in approaches to salvation-focused nurture. This language usually takes the form of biblically based or biblically inspired images. As a device in salvation-focused nurture of faith and hope, these images closely resemble interrogative and explanatory devices in the objective of kindling our awareness of meanings of salvation and its promises for Christian living in community. Metaphorical devices also seek to evoke within us a vivid "pictorial knowing" or a vivid "inscape" of the experience of salvation and its promises. For example, a prayer literally "paints a picture" of salvation as an experience like that of being delivered by God from the "whales" of our lives just as God delivered Jonah from the belly of the whale (Jonah 1:15–2:10).[16] In the same prayer, salvation is likened to being loosed from Satan's grip.[17]

In a sermon, Alton B. Pollard III uses the metaphor of the "journey to within" to "paint a picture" of the experience of God who speaks to us in the voice of our own heart, making possible our finding joy, release, acceptance, love, power, redemption, and ultimately ourselves.[18] The metaphor builds on the passage from the Gospel of Luke: "Neither shall they say, Lo here! or lo there! for, behold, the kingdom of God is within you" (Luke 17:21, KJV), and from the psalmist's words: "Deep calleth unto deep"(Psalm 42:7, KJV). In a related fashion, the view of salvation as "redemption by the mighty hand of God" is metaphorical language, appearing in a prayer, that paints a picture of God's concrete participation in our salvation.[19]

Anaphorical rhetorical devices

The use of anaphora, or a series of lines beginning with the same word or phrase, constitutes a third interpretative device that is a kind of truth-telling method focused on salvation in the nurture occurring within the black worshiping congregation.[20] Indeed, this rhetorical device is a form of evocative nurture that purposely accentuates qualities of the story of faith and hope. With specific reference to salvation, the device incorporates emphatic repetition that functions to sharpen our view of salvation as a matter of faith in the One from whom salvation comes and salvation as a fulfillment of hope.

An example of the foregoing function of anaphora is found in the sermon of Prathia Hall Wynn. In the sermon, Wynn draws the worshipers' attention to the promise of healing that attends the salvation drama and that occurs when we look at Jesus: *Look at him*—wounded for our transgressions, bruised for our iniquities. *Look at him*—coming down from Bozrah with garments red as one treading the wine press alone. *Look at him*—deliverance in his step, healing in his touch, life in his voice, hope in his hand, love in his heart, our living in his dying.

Look at him—healing crippled lives as well as crippled limbs, healing our hurts, forgiving our sins. *Look at him*![21] In this instance, the repetitive use of the phrase "Look at him" draws us into the salvation drama and fosters our attentiveness to the transforming activity of Jesus in that drama in our own lives.

DIALECTICAL RHETORICAL DEVICES

A fourth interpretative rhetorical device that is part of the methodology used in salvation-focused nurture is the dialectic (thesis, antithesis, synthesis) or contrasting images to draw worshipers into careful consideration of a firsthand account of a salvation story. The opening story in this chapter is an example:

Thesis: I was on a downward road, no hat on my head, no shoes on my feet, no God on my side, no heaven in my view . . .

Antithesis: but the Lord spoke peace to my dying soul, turned me around, cut loose my stammering tongue, sent me on my way . . .

Synthesis: I met a man named Jesus, and I had an exchange with him. I gave him my sorrows, he gave me his joy; I gave him my despair, he gave me his hope; I gave him my torn life, he gave me his purpose . . . I have found meaning, purpose, love, and truth, and that makes me a "New Creation."

Again, rhetorical approaches such as the dialectical one draw us into a particular existential situation and a concrete experience of salvation in which to form images of what may take place in our own salvation experience or to reflect on our past experience of salvation. The above example also evokes images of the dialogical nature of the salvation drama; and it provides a cognitive map of the salvation drama on which to reflect.

The use of contrasting images in prayers like the following one of Frank Madison Reid also prompt our visualization of the promise of salvation by identifying differences between sin and salvation, death and life, or what Ignatius calls "two ultimate alternatives":[22] O God, liberate us *from* the domination of individual and institutional violence. Liberate us *for* the ministry of deliverance to the captives within and without. Liberate us *from* a self-centered spiritual materialism and liberate us *to* serve the present age. Liberate us *from* building our kingdoms and liberate us *for* the Kingdom of God."[23] Even while we enter into the prayer, the view of salvation that comes forth has the effect of prompting our awareness and consideration of the difference between thwarted hope and fulfilled hope and between a self-centered faith and faith in the Other who is God.

Affirmative Rhetoric

Affirmative rhetoric is a particular truth-telling approach to nurturing the black worshiping congregation's faith in God's salvific activity and the promise salvation holds for individual and communal life. This kind of rhetoric intends to evoke in us an avowal of the reality of salvation; and it activates our recall either of our own experience of salvation or of its possibility for our lives. Indeed, affirmative rhetoric evokes our knowing or corroboration within ourselves that salvation is possible and it actually happens in persons' lives. At least two key affirmative rhetorical devices are used particularly in sermons and song. The first approach entails the use of a first-person characterization of the salvation drama. In sermons, the device emerges in the black preacher's role taking or placing her- or himself in the first-person position of a biblical character. In songs, affirmative rhetoric appears as a testimony or personal witness to the salvation drama.

In the sermon, the preacher "becomes" a biblical character and invites the worshiping congregation to "overhear" the words of the character. Through this rhetorical approach, the preacher draws us into the salvation drama in the Bible so that this story can become our story.

In her sermon "Human Reclamation," Ella Pearson Mitchell enters into role-taking activity as part of the affirmative rhetorical approach. In the sermon, she takes on the role of the woman who wiped Jesus' feet with her tears (Luke 7:36–50), and invites us into the narrative: "Listen, if you will to the testimony of a woman who was once trapped in the street. They called her a sinner, a streetwalker, a woman of the night, a prostitute. I want to remind you of what Jesus did for her."[24] In the role of the biblical character, Mitchell testifies to meeting Jesus, "a man who was different . . . (who) looked beyond my faults and saw my need."[25] In that role, she told of Jesus' reproof of Simon who questioned and criticized the woman's response to Jesus.[26]

Mitchell moves toward a pivot in the narrative by testifying, "[Jesus] put his hand on my head and told me point blank: 'My child, your faith has saved you this very day; go your way in peace.'"[27] The actual pivot of the role-play appeared in the words, "I was saved."[28] The follow-up to the pivot is Mitchell's claim of the availability of Jesus' welcome and God's saving grace to those whom we would regard as "untouchables."[29]

The affirmative rhetoric in a sermon by Samuel Proctor differs from that of Mitchell because of its invitation to worshipers to reflect on the biblical truth "that no matter how poorly Christians have shown it in practice, Jesus treated all persons as though they were all God's children. . . . Paul's sermon in Athens is this very point: God has no favorites. [God] sent Christ to save us all. This is what makes Christianity available to everybody."[30] Affirmative rhetoric in songs takes the form of testimonies that arouse in both the singer and hearer a consciousness of the realness of salvation. Three examples will be mentioned here. One example is indicated in the words of an African American traditional song that draws attention to God's activity through Jesus Christ in the salvation drama: "One day when I was lost, He died upon the cross, I know it was the blood for me."[31] Second, the gospel song "He Looked beyond My Fault" also employs affirmative rhetoric that draws our attention to the activity of God. Specifically, the song heightens our awareness of the amazing grace of God through the person of Jesus, who has looked beyond our faults, has seen our need, and has bought our liberty on Calvary.[32] Third, the words of a spiritual are couched in affirmative rhetoric that declares, "there is a balm in Gilead to make the wounded whole . . . [and] to heal the sin-sick soul."[33]

In contrast to the three aforementioned songs, the affirmative rhetoric in three additional songs are testimonies that enkindle our recognition of the initiatory activity of individual persons in the salvation drama. In one instance, this activity is noted in the words: "Oh, it is Jesus . . . in my soul. For I have touched the hem of His garment and His blood has made me whole."[34] In the other instance, the message is: "I told Satan, get thee behind, Victory today is mine."[35] A third example of affirmative rhetoric also comes in the form of a testimony that both engages us in the process of disclosing the nature of salvation, of becoming more aware of its nature, and of reflecting on our experience of it. In the song, Jesus Christ is the liberator who "is my light and my salvation," and because of his liberating activity, the propensity to be fearful is removed.[36]

SALVATION-FOCUSED TRUTH-TELLING CONTENT

The content of sermons, songs, and prayers is essential to the truth-telling rhetorical method used to nurturing faith and hope through an emphasis on salvation. Indeed, what appears in the foregoing section on process are key aspects of truth-telling content that invite us to reflect, question, testify, and affirm the reality and the possibility of salvation for our lives as persons and congregations. The content also reveals a holistic perspective. That is, the content centers on salvation as a spiritual quest, as movement away from sin, and as liberation from personal, social, and emotional forms of bondage, including our proclivities to enslave others through greed and abuse. Furthermore, the content illustrates the pivotal role of God's salvific activity through Jesus Christ and the Holy Spirit in the salvation drama. This theme captures the message set forth in the first three chapters that any discussion of Christian faith and hope or any attempt to nurture faith and hope must necessarily center on God, Jesus Christ, and the Holy Spirit. More importantly, salvation-focused content is also faith- and hope-centered content.

In addition to the role of God, Jesus Christ, and the Holy Spirit, our role in the salvation drama is a pivotal theme in the content. Associated with this theme is the idea drawn from McGill-Jackson's sermon that salvation is the consummation of all human hope."[37] In short, the content centers on the nature of the salvation drama, the divine activity in the drama, and the role of human activity in it.

In what follows, I invite us to explore two intersecting motifs in the content, including socioemotional and spiritual motifs. These motifs appear as intersecting aspects of content in ways that contribute to a view of the holistic nature of salvation.

Socioemotional Motif

The socioemotional motif in content is important to any elucidation of the salvation drama that takes place in the lives of black people. The importance of this motif lies in our experiences of injustice in this country. As indicated in previous chapters, we know all too well the kind of oppression, abuse, and material need resulting from racism in our society and to which Deborah McGill-Jackson points in her earlier-mentioned sermon. Black people enter worship with a quest to know what salvation has to say to their sojourn of faith and hope in light of the existential reality of sin in its social dimension, which is also known as injustice. The socioemotional motif in the content of McGill-Jackson's sermon responds to this quest. This motif exposes the truth that there are, indeed, situations in the world today that call for social and systemic salvation; but the motif also reveals that God is actively involved with God's people in bringing about this salvation.

At the same time, the socioemotional motif does not evade the reality that even those who experience injustice are not immune to oppressing others, as noted in the personalized questions of McGill-Jackson: "Are there not among us those who would oppress?" Are we not frequently participants in the oppression of others on the basis of religion, race, wealth, and nationality?"[38] The appearance of this perspective on sin within the content of salvation-centered nurture coincides with the position of Stephen Ray Jr. In a discussion about sin-talk, he states that "there is no community, no matter what its particular social or economic position, that is safe from the danger of reflecting on sin in a way that profoundly marginalizes others. . . . No one is immune . . . from talking about the sin of others in a way that minimizes the reality of one's own sin."[39] Consequently, the content on salvation in the nurture of the black worshiping congregation rightly addresses black people's social responsibility as indicated in Obie Wright's prayer to God for salvation from evil.[40] Moreover, within the content is the view of responsible living that liberates others and builds peace.

Truth-telling content that addresses the socioemotional dimensions of salvation also focuses on life challenges experienced by black people, including life crises, negative personal experiences, and relational woundedness at home, in the community, at work or school, and even in the church. Moreover, the content gives attention to black people's contribution to these challenges. The earlier mentioned prayer of Obie Wright points to the experiences of personal pain, hurt, and abusive relationships that are on the hearts of black people who come to worship and to which they may play a part in others' lives. This socioemotional motif in the content points to the reality that the challenges and wounding experiences of daily life are not beyond God's recognition and that God's salvation has to do with our recovery from these experiences and our contributing the same recovery in others. In this kind of content is the further message that the Holy Spirit saves us not simply by healing the sin-sick soul, but by making the wounded whole.[41]

Spiritual-Oriented Motif

The content of salvation-centered nurture includes a motif focused on spiritual salvation. This motif presents the idea of human soul-sickness as one's failing to see oneself as a reflection of the *imago Dei*, or image of God. This failure results in one's "cold detachment from other's pain and our own hurts"[42] or our refusing to enter into positive relationship with God, self, others, and all of creation. However, the motif shifts to a view of salvation as the reversibility of soul-sickness through God's activity in our lives, our spiritual quest for our soul's salvation, journey inward, and our meeting at the depths of our being the person of Jesus who can make us "a new creation."

A Composite View of Salvation

A composite view of salvation appears within the socioemotional and spiritual motifs of the content of salvation-focused nurture in the black worshiping congregation. This view contains a storehouse of images including the following:

- salvation as transforming experience,

- salvation as liberation,

- salvation as deliverance or being loosed from Satan's grip,

- salvation as the experience of washing away sin and making one whole,

- salvation as the activity of God through Jesus Christ and the work of the Spirit made available to all,

- salvation as the consummation of all human hope or the fulfillment of hope,

- salvation as the experience of oneself as a "new creation," who has found hope, meaning, purpose, love, and truth, and

- salvation as finding oneself.

The real importance of these images does not lie simply in what they suggest about the nature of salvation. Rather, these images become significant only when we see them in relation to the stories out of which they come. That is, content that is part of the conduct of nurture in the black worshiping congregation is typically narrative. As we have seen in the excerpts of sermons, songs, and prayers, stories matter; and they matter because we are more apt to see ourselves in them and glean meanings from them for ourselves. Moreover, as in the case with nurture that draws attention to the reality of sin and evil, there is far more to salvation than simply being aware of the images mentioned above. Salvation is really a matter of the heart on which God knocks and asks to enter and, then, leaves it up to us to respond. Ultimately, it is this awareness of the meaning of salvation that counts.

COMMENTARY

As I have indicated above and as prior chapters have indicated, nurturing faith and hope in the black worshiping congregation is a narrative participatory activity. In addition, as chapter 1 reveals, worship in the black church nurtures people into the story of God that is revealed in scripture. Nurture is the activity of arousing our vision of the story of God and how it is connected to our human story. Our tending to the salvation drama in worship is part of the storied nurturing process. The varied rhetorical approaches and the nature of the content engage us in a way that we are enabled to see ourselves squarely in the center of the story of God's activity of claiming us as God's own. The salvation drama is, after-all, God's redemptive efforts in our lives. Nurture in the black worshiping congregation seeks to draw us into that story of God's activity, to elicit our reflection on it, and to evoke our response to God's redemptive efforts.

Faith is our willing participation in the redemptive activity of God, knowing that God will not forsake us in our struggles to overcome our bent to err with our quest for good. Faith is relying on this for-us-ness of God known in Jesus Christ and enlivened by the Holy Spirit. Hope is our seeing ourselves in God's story and making our part in that story come alive. As I said in the Introduction, this hope is activated in a way that opposes the languid and life-defying mind-frame of hopelessness, purposelessness, and lovelessness of many in our communities. It is salvation that is created around us by the intentionality with which we strive to live as Christians even amidst "sufferings, narrow escapes, failures, reversals, and hard trials."[43]

AN INVITATION TO REFLECT

1. Describe the meanings of salvation that you have become aware of from your presence in the worshiping congregation.

2. What in this chapter particularly "stuck out" for you? Why?

3. What is your perception of salvation?

Part Two

Nurture through the Events of Baptism and Holy Communion

Black worship witnesses to the vitality of the mystery of God's actions in the commonplace. The celebration of baptism and the Lord's Supper dramatizes the vigilant presence of God. They link the mystery that transcends human experience with the concrete realities of everyday life in tangible ways.

—Ethel R. Johnson and Charles R. Foster
Christian Education Journey

NURTURING FAITH AND HOPE THROUGH BAPTISM

Look, here is water! What is to prevent me from being baptized?

—Acts 8:36

THE RITUAL OF BAPTISM IN THE black worshiping congregation has persisted as a highly significant public nurturing event. The rite draws black worshipers into a dramatic and emotional experience of the mystery of God's presence and activity through Jesus Christ and the Holy Spirit. A newly baptized person described this quality of the occasion long ago: "While we were getting our baptizing clothes, we shouted praises, as the people on the banks sang. Some of us jumped up. When my time come, I started to the pond, and just before the preacher turned to take my hand, I shouted, 'Lord, have mercy,' and clapped my hand over my head. Somebody said, 'Dat child sho' is gitting a new soul.'"[1]

Although baptisms in rivers and ponds are now rare, though not extinct, the deeply moving nature of the ritual remains. The ritual of baptism is an event that has a profound impact on the baptism initiate and worshipers alike. The ritual is a profound occasion of nurture in which the concrete experience of the baptism initiate and the participation of the congregation in it evoke their discernment of "the more" that constitutes Christian faith and hope. For example, "the more" was described to me by a worshiper in the following manner: "There is just something that happens at a baptism, whether of an infant or an adult, that makes me want to shout. Baptisms remind me that God is still alive and that we are important to God. Baptisms point to the promise there is for us in the difficult world in which we live when we have a relationship with God and the person of Jesus Christ. Really, in baptism, we become new beings and we are set in a new direction in life to do what we can as Christians to make a better world. That's good news!"[2]

As a nurturing event in the life of the black worshiping congregation, baptism discloses a language of experience and words that holds special importance for black people. The language arouses black worshipers' acute awareness of the valued identity of persons in the sight of God and of the meaning of the communal identity. In addition, the language gives rise to black worshipers making integrative sense of the central ideas or beliefs on which faith and hope center.

NURTURING IDENTITY

As a nurturing event, baptism in the black worshiping congregation calls us to renewed consciousness and examination of our identity as individual persons and as a community before God. During the baptismal drama, this emphasis of nurture occurs through what may be described as naming, announcing, and claiming "acts."

The Naming "Act"

In the naming "act," the pastor requests the initiate's name, calls out the initiate's name, and refers to this name throughout the baptismal rite. Black pastors sometimes elaborate on the cultural and religious importance of naming in a manner similar to what John Porter says about naming in his sermon "Nobody Knows Our Names." Porter reminds us, for example, that "Names reflect an identity, a place in time and space, a heritage. . . . It is the Spirit of God which motivates us to name ourselves and our world,"[3] in ways that counter society's definition.

Black pastors also draw attention to the symbolic power of naming because of black people's experiences of being disrespectfully named by white society from slavery onward. The intentional emphasis of naming in the baptismal ritual is to raise within black worshipers what Meland calls an "appreciative consciousness"[4] or a maximum degree of receptivity to who and Whose we are. As a nurturing event, then, baptism contributes to the redefinition process described in chapter 4. Baptism exists as a pivotal opportunity for our grappling anew with the question of identity and for affirming and reaffirming our worth as God's creation. Naming becomes a meaning-making aspect of nurture that is directed toward our grasping the point that God gave us a valued identity and a name just as God gave us a song to sing. In fact, the emphasis on naming as an aspect of nurture is to evoke our knowing that "No, we are not invisible. Somebody knows our name. God knows our name."[5]

The Announcing Act

Announcing the identity of newly baptized persons is part of nurture taking place through the baptismal rite. As part of the baptismal rite of infants and small children, the "act" of announcement occurs through the pastor's lifting high the baptized child on completion of the baptism and the reciting of baptismal vows by the parents and/or sponsors. At times, the pastor then carries the child throughout the congregation and introduces the child by her or his birth name followed by the name "God's child," and by the name "Our Child" or "the child of Christ's whole family and the extended family of the congregation." Older children, youth, and adults are most frequently asked to face the congregation after repeating the baptismal vows; and in these situations, similar references are made to their given names and to their identities as children of God and important members of Christ's extended family of which the congregation is part.

The "act" of announcing identity has the effect of engaging us in a "phenomenologizing" experience. Through this experience, all who are part of the baptismal ritual are to see or perceive what is happening regarding the definition of self not simply as a valued creation of God but as a valued member of Christ's family called the church. We are to hear what is described about that identity and to form images of the meaning of that identity for the lives that the baptized person and the whole congregation are to live out in community. The announcing "act" is nurture that invites us into probing the meanings of black identity in the context of the Christian family in which faith and hope are central.[6]

The Claiming Act

The "act" of claiming identity occurs as the pastor engages the congregation in recognizing our communal identity as God's people, as the extended family of newly baptized persons, and as Christian life models for and nurturers of these persons. The claiming "act" invites worshipers into an extension of the "phenomenologizing" experience occurring in the "act" of announcing identity. Through this experience, the worshiping congregation not only becomes aware of the communal identity and the important role that is to come alive in the lives of newly baptized persons but also enters into a preliminary role enactment. It is more than simply naming and announcing identity that comes into play here. Nurture through the claiming "act" is to evoke an embodied awareness of who we are and how we are to act as Christians in church and world.

An example of the form of nurture that raises embodied awareness is demonstrated by the invitation of the pastor to the worshipers to move physically toward the baptism initiates. Depending on the size of the congregation, this movement may be limited to the worshipers' extending their arms outward toward the initiate during either a baptismal confirmation prayer or a description of the nurturing role of the extended family of Christ as the body of Christ who, indeed, reaches out to, shows the way, and cares for the initiates. Alternatively, the worshipers might also be requested to place their hands on the shoulders of those directly in front of them so that there is an enactment of a human "web" that stretches toward and connects with the initiate. In still other situations, where immersion is not practiced, embodied awareness of the nurturing role of the extended family is prompted by the invitation to the worshipers to come forward to greet, affirm, and welcome the newly baptized person.

The point here is that the "act" of claiming identity is nurture directed toward the worshipers' embodied awareness of the experience of baptism as a crucial covenantal event in the life of both the baptized person and the congregation. It is the "act" of enkindling a deep "in the bones" awareness that what happens to the baptized member makes a difference to every other member to the extent that the congregation can never again be the same. Significantly, nurture raises this awareness not only through the congregation's physical enactment of the human "web" but also with spoken pledges to the initiate that, to use the words of one denomination's description: "Your joy, your pain, your gain, your loss, are ours, for you are one of us."[7] In this respect, the "act" of claiming identity becomes an experience of nurturing the nurturers. That is, the congregation is being nurtured into the role of nurturer through embodying or "living out" the onset of the nurturing role during the baptismal event.

NURTURING AN INTEGRATIVE SENSE OF FAITH AND HOPE

Although the emphasis on identity is of pivotal importance in the ritual of baptism in the black worshiping congregation, this focus does not happen apart from attention to the whole range of themes or beliefs explored in Part One. In actuality, the baptismal event is an occasion of nurture that arouses worshipers' appreciative consciousness of an integrative sense of the central ideas or beliefs on which faith and hope center. Consequently, baptism may be called an integrative nurturing event because it arouses our awareness of the interrelationships of various themes or beliefs as well as the impact of the themes on the lives of both the baptism initiates and the whole congregation. The baptismal rituals foster our seeing the themes in a unity and as pivotal to the baptized person's incorporation into the faith- and hope-oriented body of Christ or Christ's family called the church.

The foregoing section has highlighted that baptism is also a nurturing event that seeks to bring forth our image of and commitment to our role in the life of baptized persons through "walking with" and being Christlike examples for them. In the main, it may be said that the ritual

of baptism nurtures faith and hope by evoking our formation of a gestalt or a bringing together in a unifying way the beliefs and the actions
around which the body of Christ and Christian life are organized. The
gestalt orientation to nurture is integrative in nature. Mary Elizabeth
Mullino Moore describes this orientation as "reaching out to the many
facts and ideas and drawing them into unity."[8] Stated another way, the
central themes or beliefs that black worship discloses are brought into
close proximity to one another in order that the worshipers can place
them in some sort of unity. Specifically, baptism brings together beliefs
about God, Jesus Christ, the Holy Spirit, the identity of persons, and
the nature of sin and salvation.

However, it is not simply a cognitive activity of putting together
concepts. Baptism in the black worshiping congregation is a celebratory
and interactive event that is often infused with joyful singing, clapping,
handshakes, embraces, and shouting; and in holiness/Pentecostal
churches, the baptized may speak in tongues, called glossolalia. As a
result, the black baptism initiate's and the worshipers' experiences of
the baptismal drama have a highly affective component. This component becomes integrally connected to cognitive endeavors and, therefore, becomes part of gestalt-directed nurture. Nurture through the
baptismal rite arouses the worshipers' consciousness of the interconnectedness of language communicated through words and the language
of bodily and emotional expression.

The following reconstructed segment of a baptismal rite that I attended shows something of the nature of nurture that invites the black
worshiping congregation into the formation of a gestalt appreciation
of faith and hope:

A Story of Baptism

The pastor began by telling the story of Jesus' baptism by John as the
inauguration of a new thing in the life of Jesus and in the world. Speaking to the child and the adult being baptized as well as to the congregation, the pastor continued:

> To each of these two precious persons, Chris and John [not their real
> names] who are here before us to be baptized, God is doing a new

thing in you. But that is not all. To every one of us here, God is doing a new thing in us too. God is sealing in us all a new relationship with God, with Chris and John, and with one another.

Through baptism, the ones who are here before us to be baptized are also being made new in Jesus Christ, the One whom God sent to show us how to live in this troubled world of ours, even when we think we don't know how to carry on. That newness radiates to us all who are to be examples of Jesus in the world, and to show Chris and John how to keep on keeping on.

God is doing a new thing through the Holy Spirit, the breath of God that is breathing new life in Chris and John and in us all. God is giving them a new identity, the identity of Christ's children. God is giving them a new home which is Christ's whole family called the Church and this local family made up of each one of us in this congregation. God is doing a new thing! God's new thing is to make us all whole—Chris, John and everyone here. God's wholeness-making is God's turning us around away from sin and toward Jesus, the Son of God. God is making possible our salvation or our readiness and will to show God's goodness in a tough world after the pattern of Jesus. God is doing a new thing!

This narrative of the pastor followed with the words of administration of the rite with water: "I now baptize you, [Chris], [John], in the name of the most high God, the Son, and the Holy Spirit." After this administration of the rite, the congregation was led in words of reception of the initiates into Christ's family and words of commitment to be and act before the initiates as followers of Jesus Christ in everything that is said and done. At many points during the ritual, numerous responses of "Amen" and "Hallelujah" burst forth in the sanctuary. At other times and at the close of the ritual, worshipers responded with rousing hand-claps.

Uncovering the Gestalt

The foregoing story points to an unfolding process of prompting worshipers' formation of a gestalt view. In at least six ways, the story reveals an unfolding organic interplay of the process and contents of the baptismal ritual, the persons being baptized, and the worshipers who were active participants in the ritual. The manner in which this interplay unfolds offers a guide for setting forth a process of nurture through the ritual of baptism that evokes worshipers' formation of a gestalt of the important themes on which faith and hope center.

First, the activity of God is at the center of the gestalt-directed nurture. Nurture of a gestalt perspective begins and ends by evoking an awareness of God as the primary influence on the baptism initiate as well as the whole congregation of believers. At the center of nurture that prompts the formation of a gestalt during the baptismal rite is the task of what Ellen Charry describes as spurring the worshiper to attend to God or to enrich that attending.[9]

Second, as a nurturing event, the baptismal ritual appropriately prompts the initiate's and the whole congregation's remembrance of God's presence and activity in the past, namely, in Jesus' life. Using the story as an example, the language of the pastor draws the worshipers' attention to the relationship of God and Jesus through reference to Jesus as the One whose ministry was inaugurated by God at Jesus' baptism. Moreover, references to the ministry of Jesus set in motion at his baptism invite worshipers to connect the trajectory of the selves' lives after the pattern of Jesus.

Third, impetus for seeing the relationship between God, Jesus Christ, the Holy Spirit, and a new identity become possible through references to the life- and identity-transforming activity of the breath of God. The articulation of this relationship serves to heighten the worshipers' awareness of God who addresses us, of Jesus who appears as model, and of the Holy Spirit who enlivens.

Fourth, the insertion of references to sin and salvation function to enlarge the worshipers' formation of a gestalt by arousing a sense of responsibility for sin and for seeing another way forward with God after the pattern of Jesus. Through these references, the worshipers are called to activate the redefinition of the self in light of what God has already shown in Jesus.

Fifth, the evocation of faith becomes inherent in the language that arouses the worshipers' imagination of the power of the unity that is disclosed to make a difference in their lives. Moreover, this same gestalt communication is evocative language that serves to arouse the worshipers' anticipation of actually being part of and living out God's story in the world. In this way, it gives rise to hope.

Finally, the welcome of spontaneous feeling responses nurture the worshipers' understanding that we "learn" through observation and participation how to surrender control and to be "possessed" by the Spirit in the safe environment of the congregation. The expression of emotion is part of the gestalt communication in the baptismal rite that arouses the worshipers' awareness that there is, indeed, an affective dimension that intersects with the cognitive awareness of the nature and meaning of baptism. The expression of emotion in the process of nurture through the ritual of baptism fosters the worshipers' embrace of the very real, but often overlooked presence and importance of what Berntsen calls "the disposition of the heart."[10] This aspect of integrative directed nurture means that we come to own and celebrate our own affective disposition and see this disposition as integrally tied to cognitive endeavors, and as evidence that we have "perceived, remembered, believed, or known something"[11] about the content and meaning of the baptismal rite.

IMPORTANCE OF REPETITION OF EXPERIENCE

At this juncture, it is necessary to add a word about the importance of repeated experiences of the baptismal ritual. The story shared earlier gives us some insights about nurture that evokes an integrative sense of key themes and our emotional response to their meaning. However, our fullest grasp of a gestalt does not likely happen during a single experience of the baptismal rite. Repeated experiences of the ritual are necessary to stimulate the kind of familiarity worshipers need to form some insights into the interrelationships of God, Jesus Christ, the Holy Spirit, the identity of persons, sin, salvation, and the connection of emotion to the understanding of these themes.

Every occasion of participating in the baptismal rite presents us with "central cognitive processes" as well as equally important affective content or "disposition of the heart." Both trigger and reinforce our memories of the themes, their interrelatedness, and their meaning for our lives. Our repeated participation in the ritual of baptism serves as ongoing nurture that enkindles in us an awareness of what Herbert Anderson and Edward Foley call "the sacrament of certainty" by virtue of "the rich story web of the human and the divine, the personal and the communal that [baptism] symbolizes."[12]

It may also be said that, while participation of the black worshiping congregation in the ritual of baptism contributes to the formation of an integrative sense of what we believe and hope for, this engagement is further enhanced by opportunities beyond worship for reflection. Intentional occasions beyond the event itself are needed for us to share our personal stories of baptism and of being participants in others' baptism, and to reflect together critically on the meanings of these stories for the larger story of faith and hope of which we are part. Through these shared happenings, our formation of a gestalt and how we act on it are enhanced by the differing stories of others, by what we discover of our denominational perspectives on baptism, and by further exploration of meanings of baptism disclosed in the biblical texts.[13]

COMMENTARY

Nurture in the black worshiping congregation that focuses on baptism offers three key insights. First, nurture taking place in the baptismal drama in the congregation suggests that we develop insights through our actual participation in the rite. The ritual of baptism is an event that evokes our consideration and interpretations of multiple dimensions of the Divine-human relationship. Moreover, the presence of affect is an integral expressive part of the event of baptism that both promotes and reflects our grasp of the mystery of this relationship. To this extent, nurture through the baptismal rite draws attention to the reality that meaningful insights form on several levels and that what we experience and come to know about baptism and its meanings for our lives, at least on one level, is not easily put into words. Indeed, we may find, at times, that the only response we can give to what we discover is a display of deep emotion.

Second, Berntsen identifies the general assumption in Western thought "that emotions, patterns and feelings are one thing while thoughts, reasons and beliefs are another; distinctions are often made between these for polemical purposes."[14] He makes the claim that "emotions and thought are not different floors of a building but connecting rooms in the same suite."[15] The baptismal experience in the black worshiping congregation provides an illustrative basis for seeing the richness of nurture that counters the Western tendency to dichotomize feelings and thoughts and to attach greater importance to cognitive dimensions. The ritual of baptism exists as a powerful integrative experience that includes the themes around which faith and hope are generated as well as the affective and cognitive domains of nurture. This experience is to be celebrated.

The earlier mentioned story in this chapter disclosed the kind of gestalt-oriented nurture that can foster worshipers' formation of integrated meanings of baptism for our lives as Christians. In a real sense, the story reflects an approach to the ritual that differs from the rituals typically provided by denominations. This alternative treatment of the ritual has the effect of evoking culturally consistent interpretations of baptism or interpretations that address the critical problem of black identity in this society. The narrative orientation serves as an important means whereby the baptism initiates and the whole congregation develop meaningful "handles" for understanding and interpreting the event of baptism.

Third, oral narratives accompanying the administration of the rite, along with songs such as "Wade in the Water"[16] and "Have You Been Baptized? Certainly Lord,"[17] nurture the formation of meanings of baptism and the expression of feelings associated with it. Focus on these narrative means to meaning-making ends serves as translations of what some perceive as "dead rituals" to alive ones. At the same time, it must be added that there are those for whom the traditional rituals have great meaning. For this reason, care must be taken by pastors to discern the kind of baptismal ritual that is likely to promote the greatest meaning for the initiate and the congregation. In either case, important attention is needed to prepare initiates for the baptismal event and to provide occasions beyond the worshiping congregation for mutual reflection and deepening insights on baptism and its meaning for our lives.

AN INVITATION TO REFLECT

1. Recount either your personal experience of baptism or your earliest participation in another's baptism. Then reflect on what either experience triggered in you about the nature of baptism, the meanings of baptism, and your own feelings.

2. In what ways have your understandings of baptism either changed or remained the same since your own experience of baptism or your earliest participation in another's baptism? If your understanding has changed, what brought about the change; or, if your understanding has remained the same, what has helped to maintain your understanding?

3. With what part of this chapter's focus on baptism did you most identify? Why? With what part of this chapter's focus on baptism were you least familiar? What meanings do you derive from the aspects that were least familiar?

4. To what extent are you aware of or do you participate in opportunities to explore the nature and meanings of baptism beyond the worshiping congregation or beyond the context in which the event of baptism takes place? What suggestions would you make about the kinds of opportunities that might yet be needed in your congregation? How might these occasions be organized?

NURTURING FAITH AND HOPE THROUGH HOLY COMMUNION

The cup of blessing that we bless, is it not a sharing in the blood of Christ? The bread that we break, is it not a sharing in the body of Christ? Because there is one bread, we who are many are one body, for we all partake of the one bread.

— 1 Corinthians 10:16–17

IN ADDITION TO BAPTISM, the sacrament of Holy Communion, also called the Lord's Supper or eucharist, is a highly revered ritual in the life of the black worshiping congregation because of its nurturing effects.[1] Historically, the meaning of this liturgical event for black Christians lay in these persons' discovery of the welcome of God through Jesus Christ that countered the repulsion and maltreatment they experienced in society. The event became known as the Welcome Table where no one is turned away and where the meal becomes the bread and substance of life or the spiritual food for the journey ahead.[2]

The experience of the Welcome Table persists today. One worshiper described the Welcome Table as an occasion that kindles a deep awareness of God who, in the person of Jesus Christ, welcomes, loves, feeds us as Jesus fed his disciples so long ago, and renews us. The worshiper also made clear that, at the Welcome Table, we remember the wounded bleeding Jesus; and, through the meal, we discover ourselves as re-membered, individually and communally. Another older black church member described the significance of the experience in the following manner:

A NARRATIVE

Every time I take communion, I recognize the real friend that Jesus is to me. Jesus doesn't leave me out, turn me out, or forget me like the way things happen with people everyday. When I take communion, I *know* I'm welcomed by the One who died for me and who is able to keep me from falling. I'm not sure when, exactly, I came to know it, though. Growing up, I remember hearing and then reading the words that went along with the communion ritual. After awhile, I pretty much knew the ritual by heart. But, what has stayed with me are the words, "Come to the table of the Lord. You are welcome!" and the song, "I'm gonna sit at the welcome table." The words mean that I can take the bread and cup just as I am. It doesn't matter who I am, where I live, what I have or don't have. And, you know, God's table is not just spread for everybody right here and now. God's table is always spread. It's spread forever.

Also, the welcome table is the altar in my church, where we commune as a family and as friend-to-friend. The message that I learned as a child at the altar is that communing together makes us know ourselves as God's family. I learned, too, that we can leave our burdens and our sins there. The altar is the table where we leave all our troubles, the hard things in our lives, knowing that God's going to make all things right. And, it is the time to leave behind anything we hold against our neighbor. I take to heart the words in the communion service, "You are forgiven." I know that, in taking communion, I am receiving God's forgiveness and Jesus' love. And, I know I'm supposed to give the same to others. We're supposed to care for our neighbors. We used to sing another song, "Can't hate your neighbor when your mind is staid on Jesus; you got to love your neighbor when your mind is staid on Jesus." Well, taking communion means just that.[3]

The testimonies of worshipers underscore the highly intimate and integrative form of nurture occurring through Holy Communion. For black worshipers, Holy Communion is an intimate integrative experience of linking our particular everyday stories with God's story revealed in Jesus Christ. In a real sense, it is evocative nurture initiated by God and mediated by ritual acts that prompts our remembering the life of Jesus and his kinship with those whom society pushes to the margins. The intimate experience of Holy Communion is evocative nurture that stimulates our visualization of the nature of Christian community and our role in it. It engages us in re-membering. As in the case of baptism, God is the primary influence. God is the principal evocator who invites us into a divine pedagogy of discovering anew our human value and direction as Christians. The role of the communion ritual—the symbols and partaking communion—is that of inviting our participation in the divinely inspired nurture to the end that we feel ourselves renewed and that our faith in God's presence in our stories and our anticipation of God's love in the nitty-gritty of life is replenished.

In what follows, we will explore more fully the nature of remembering and re-membering in nurture taking place in Holy Communion as well as the role of hospitality or welcome and our encounter with the ritual symbols in the nurturing event of Holy Communion.

NURTURE AS ACTS OF REMEMBERING AND RE-MEMBERING

During the ritual of Holy Communion, the black worshiping congregation enters into a powerful form of nurture that immerses us in acts of remembering and re-membering. The two acts are related. However, each has a slightly different emphasis.

Remembering

At the center of the act of remembering is our formation of impressions, understandings, and meanings of Holy Communion by following the ritual visually and verbally, singing songs, hearing sermons, and partaking of the communion elements. These activities usher the officiating pastor, the communion stewards or deacons, and the whole congregation into an encounter with God while engaging us in remembering who God is, how God acts through Jesus Christ in our lives as black people, and what it means to respond to God.

In the black worshiping congregation, remembering as part of nurture during Holy Communion invites us to recall the biblical narrative of the Last Supper and Jesus' suffering following it as means of fostering the kind of analogical discovery that chapter 2 addressed. The biblical narrative becomes a means by which we draw analogous relationships or likenesses between our own life journey and the experience of Jesus. Nurture during Holy Communion entails our remembering the broken body and spilled blood of Jesus Christ as a sacrificial act on behalf of the brokenness and sin in the world in general and in the lives of black people in particular. This kind of recollection is triggered most profoundly by references in the ritual to the bread that Jesus broke and gave to his disciples in the upper room, saying "Take, eat; this is my body, which is given for you. Do this in remembrance of me." Our memory is further activated by mention of Jesus' taking the cup and offering it to his disciples saying, "This is my blood poured out for you and for many for the forgiveness of sins. Do this, as often as you drink it, in remembrance of me."[4]

These phrases in the communion ritual not only bring forth our awareness of the relational caring Jesus on which chapter 2 focuses but also prompt our recognition of Jesus' solidarity with and suffering on behalf of black people, past and present, and all suffering people. Holy Communion also becomes a nurturing occasion that kindles our vision, as the earlier mentioned story of the older worshiper revealed, of God whose table is always spread and who makes things right.

Music, too, opens the way for our recall that, although we are carrying out a ritual begun centuries ago with the Last Supper that Jesus hosted in the upper room, "Jesus Is Here Right Now," as the title says, offering us peace through the bread and wine.[5] The impact of this aspect of nurture is its confirmation that we have learned the central features, as Craig Dykstra puts it, "from others who have learned them before us, and they from others who in turn learned them from their forbears, all the way back to their beginnings."[6] Of course, the experience of Holy Communion entails more than the learning of central features. In this experience, we embrace the particular meaning of Holy Communion for our lives as black people. The essential task of nurture is to foster this meaning making.

Re-Membering

Nurture in the eucharistic ritual is activity that fosters our experience of re-membering or of our being and becoming a community of solidarity. Nurture in this ritual is also to prompt our seeing what this re-membering holds for us. The testimonies of worshipers disclosed at the beginning of this chapter reveal their views of the Welcome Table. Black people's embrace of these views is typically prompted by the historical ethnic-cultural interpretation of Holy Communion that is often shared in the black worshiping congregation. However, it is also clear from the testimonies that this perspective on Holy Communion comes from a personal awareness that God, through the person of Jesus Christ, welcomes not only individual persons but also the whole congregation—all of us—into a time of communing together. In addition, nurture is a divine initiative through which a consciousness of who we are in relation to others emerges.

Whether through human interpretation or divine pedagogy, nurture occurring through the Welcome Table has the effect of kindling black worshipers' recognition and experience of a communal "home." The Welcome Table personifies this "home" for people who experience a sense of "homelessness" in the everyday sojourn of life. As a nurturing event, the Welcome Table prompts our recognition of Jesus Christ as the host who includes homeless sojourners, offering them a shelter in the time of storm and spiritual food for the journey ahead. In her sermon "The Welcome Table," Ella Mitchell identifies this food as the "all-important Bread of Life."[7] The focus of nurture, however, prompts our responsibility for one another's well-being. As the older worshiper said, "We're supposed to care for our neighbors."

At the heart of re-membering as part of nurture is our becoming more deeply aware of God's family as an inclusive family. Nurture taking place during the experience of the Welcome Table centers on our recognizing who and Whose we all are during and beyond the table and what our responsibility is to those within and beyond our congregation in everyday life. In an important way, this form of nurture is redemptive experience through which we grasp not simply God's affirmation and reaffirmation of our human worth individually and communally, but what it means to act on it in life. In some respects, what happens at the Welcome Table is our unlearning negative views of individual and communal identities and uncharitable ways of relating and coming to a healing identity and mutually up-building story.

To this extent, nurture occurring during the Welcome Table takes the form of a eucharistic corrective and celebration that fosters what Mary Grey calls "redemptive knowing."[8] At the center of our coming to this kind of knowing is our formation of a communal ethic based on our knowing God's story shown in Jesus who welcomes us. Indeed, the end toward which this knowing points is what Stanley Hauerwas calls a hope-filled community of character that seeks to live rightly and faithfully the story of God.[9] Like baptism, Holy Communion stands as a crucial nurturing event that is meant to evoke our hearing and knowing God's story and our enactment of the story.

HOLY COMMUNION AS HOSPITALITY AND WHOLENESS-CENTERED NURTURE

A language of welcome and language focused on the blood of Jesus are distinctive aspects of nurture taking place during the sacrament of Holy Communion in the black worshiping congregation and to which I will give brief attention.

Language of Welcome

A language of welcome is used in the black worshiping congregation that assists worshipers in recognizing God's hospitality. The metaphor of the "Welcome Table" and the words "I'm gonna eat at the Welcome Table" promote our imagining the nature of God's present and future hospitality. The language evokes an image of the kind of intimacy mentioned earlier in this chapter. We feel comfortable in the presence of God in the person of Jesus, knowing that we are welcomed in a Divine-human conversation, and we can listen, speak, and be heard from the very core of our being. We are not strangers to God. We belong to and with God; and, this sense of belonging-ness inspires our vision of ourselves as eternally welcomed and nourished by God.[10]

In hospitality-centered nurture, there is power in words and there are words of power, to use Dolan Hubbard's terms.[11] The word *welcome* takes on a life of its own. The word *welcome* holds within it symbolic meaning that points beyond itself to another reality. Applied to the eucharist as a nurturing event, the word evokes the image, as the song says, of room enough for all,[12] which broadens faith and frees us to see greater promise for our lives.

The language of welcome during Holy Communion is a central part of nurture that draws us into enacting the hospitality of Jesus and, thus, forming a community in his image. Nurture is not simply telling the story of his hospitality. Nurture must be enacted. Thus, the Welcome Table becomes nurture that evokes our formation of a hospitable character and our preparation to live out this character in church and world. As a consequence of nurture, this character becomes a defining attribute of our identity as black Christians.

One issue does arise with respect to the use of the language of welcome and its enactment in the worshiping congregation that calls for intentional care. That is, there is the need for nurture to address the disjuncture between what the language conveys and what we do in the worshiping congregation. During the time some years ago when I directed a shelter for homeless persons, I found myself dismayed that the phrase "you are welcome," which was voiced during Holy Communion, was not always acted on in the reception of homeless persons within the congregation. Homeless persons appeared as strangers, and the fear or distaste of these "strangers" betrayed the very language of welcome the congregation had become accustomed to hearing. The tendency was to want to remove the "different" one as though to own and protect the language of welcome as that belonging to a chosen cloistered community.

The real measure of evocative nurture is its ability to wrench us away from our predisposition, as Hauerwas puts it, "to protect and enhance our most cherished pretensions."[13] Nurture is needed to incite our heart's knowing that inhospitality to the "stranger" is inhospitality to God and the One who is the center of the sacrament of Holy Communion. Nurture, then, becomes a task of helping us to see the requirement of being "hospitable to the ultimate stranger of our existence: God," and, thereby, opening the doors of hope for creating a hospitable habitation for all others who appear in our midst.[14]

Language Centered on Jesus' Blood

Language that centers on Jesus' blood is also a prominent part of nurture taking place during Holy Communion in the black worshiping congregation. This emphasis on the blood of Jesus provides impetus for black worshipers' renewed awareness of the scriptural account of Jesus' dying and death on the cross and the implications of this awareness for our lives. For example, the earlier mentioned testimony of the older worshiper identifies Jesus as "the One who died for me." On one level, then, the language calls forth an image of the personal sacrifice of Jesus on behalf of the wholeness of the self and, as the older adult said, to "keep me from falling," or to shield or safeguard the self from sin.

On another level, however, the language evokes an image of Jesus who knows all about the spilled blood of black people resulting from violence perpetrated by those outside and within our communities. For black worshipers, Jesus' blood stands as an irreplaceable source of strength in the overwhelming struggle for wholeness out of violence. In the situation of persons' experiences of violence, the nature of nurture becomes that of arousing our image and embrace of Jesus presented in chapter 2, whose blood liberates, heals, and sustains in the midst of tumultuous circumstances. This function of nurture is poignantly demonstrated in the story of a worshiper whose child was murdered. This worshiper identified profoundly with the words of the gospel song "The Blood Will Never Lose Its Power," which refers to the daily strength that comes from the blood shed by Jesus at Calvary."[15]

On a third level, nurture during Holy Communion that is carried out through reference to Jesus' blood engages worshipers in moral reflection. This reflection calls us to acknowledge our failures and sins and to accept forgiveness as a prerequisite to living faithful, hope-filled lives in church and world. An example of this function of nurture carried out during communion is reflected in the sermon of Margie Lewter-Simmons who refers to communion time as an occasion for giving "account of ourselves to God."[16] Her sermon further calls attention to Jesus' woundedness for our transgressions and injury for our iniquities, and, yet, he holds our accounts open "until we get them balanced and in good order."[17] Her stated purpose was to prompt self-examination during communion.[18]

The important point is that nurture is not complete without the dimension of moral reflection. At the same time, nurture must necessarily help worshipers to envision what it means, specifically, to live as Christians. More specifically, the function of nurture during Holy Communion is to invite worshipers into critical reflection on the quality of our relationships with others.[19] This is all the more important because, as Samuel Proctor reminds us, we are living "at a time when all values seem to be in flux, and when moral relativism shows up in family life, in political affairs, in international leadership, and in the world of work."[20] Building on Proctor's suggestions, the nurturing role of the pastor in the worshiping congregation guides worshipers' formation of an approach to life that applies the gospel to personal behavior, civic orientation, political choices, stewardship, health care and management, intercultural relations, and our view of the world.[21] In this way, nurture through the sacrament of Holy Communion brings forth in the worshipers the understanding that Jesus' blood, death, and resurrection was, on the one hand, a concrete historical occurrence; yet, on the other hand, nurture deepens our grasp of this reality of the story of Jesus as being contemporaneous with our stories today. The first century event is a present happening and has powerful meaning today.[22]

COMMENTARY

From slavery forward, black worshiping congregations have been nurtured in understandings of Holy Communion from within black people's experiences of devaluation and marginalization in larger society. The congregations are keenly aware, to use Browning and Reed's words, that the eucharist "speaks radically to the issues which divide us as a human family."[23] What the narrative of the eucharist offers us is an evocative habitation for self-reflection on and affirmation of who and Whose we are as well as a vision of how we are to act out our faith in the One whom we remember and who re-members us at the Welcome Table.

Holy Communion invites us into an experience of evocative and integrative nurture. It calls forth remembering that stirs in us a living faith or a sense of surety that God's presence with us can be counted on. It immerses us in remembering and re-membering that brings to life our hope that the broken pieces of our personal and communal lives can be put back together. It involves us in acts of remembering and re-membering that foster our vision of and commitment to carry out Christ's ministry in the world. Yet, we understand that God is the ultimate evocator in the nurturing process. Ultimately, nurture proceeds through God's divine initiative.

Clearly, an important continuing emphasis in the black worshiping congregation is on the Welcome Table and on nurture through it that activates our connecting our experience of this table to our expression of Christian character and hospitality in church and world. The power of the language of welcome and the language of the shed blood of Jesus Christ to heighten our awareness of the present significance of the ancient sacrament cannot be overlooked; and this language as a center of nurture has the ability to sustain us in a sojourn of faith and hope expressed through our being a community of Christian character.

As with baptism, a key challenge is to assure that there is what Anderson and Foley call a weaving of "the human story and the divine narratives into a single web."[24] I say this because I am aware that the historical cultural view of and insertion of its meaning in the eucharist is increasingly disappearing. I think that Anderson and Foley are quite right in their assertion that without integrating the story of God revealed in Jesus with our own present human stories, it is unlikely that our faith community will continue with vitality.[25] We risk, in fact, the engagement of persons in a dead ritual. Yet, where our cultural under-standings of Holy Communion persist, we are also challenged by the disjuncture between these understandings and our expression of the meaning of the ritual in real life. It is this challenge that nurture must not forsake. Moreover, as in the case of baptism, important attention is needed to prepare worshipers, especially new ones, for the event of Holy Communion and to providing occasions beyond the worshiping congregation for reflection and the broadening of insights into its mean-ing to us.

AN INVITATION TO REFLECT

1. Describe how the ritual of the eucharist or Holy Communion unfolds in your congregation. What is typically said and done? What songs are typically sung?

2. What key insights have you gained from your participation in the eucharist or Holy Communion in your church? What does this ritual mean to you and your life as a Christian?

3. In what ways does the discussion of the eucharist or Holy Com-munion in this chapter reflect and/or differ from your perceptions of it? In what ways does it reflect and/or differ from the celebra-tion of it in your congregation?

4. To what extent are you aware of or do you participate in opportu-nities to explore the nature and meanings of the eucharist beyond the worshiping congregation? What suggestions would you make about the kinds of opportunities that might yet be needed in your congregation? How might these occasions be organized?

Part Three

Nurture through Pathways of Preaching, Music Making, and Praying

No life is complete that does not make provisions for the place and significance of ceremonials. They are the moments of pause, of tarrying over meanings, of high celebration. . . . [W]e cannot escape the need for those experiences which summarize for us the inner meaning.

—Howard Thurman, *Deep is the Hunger*

9

PREACHING AS A PATHWAY
TO NURTURE

*For I am not ashamed of the gospel; it is the
power of God for salvation to everyone who has faith. . . .*

—Romans 1:16a

BLACK PREACHING IS ONE OF THREE essential pathways through which nurture of faith and hope are carried out in the black worshiping congregation. Preaching combines with music making and praying to nurture faith and hope by disclosing the religious beliefs and ideals on which Part One focuses.[1] Through hearing the preached word, we consider and form thoughts and feelings about what trust in our relationship with God and God's relationship with us means. Sermons are a key pathway for our discerning how it is possible for us to live courageously in the present and move forward with confidence. Preaching is a profoundly evocative nurture bearer. Like music making and praying, its place in the black worshiping congregation holds distinctive evocative functions and style.

As a nurturing pathway, the sermon is an evocative trigger that motivates black worshipers to live faith-full and hope-filled lives after the pattern of Jesus Christ. The black preacher is the evocator who herself or himself is guided and inspired by the divine Evocator. In the preaching role, as James Harris puts it: "The preacher is compelled to say something that addresses the needs of the people, directing the message to heart and head."[2] The intended communication on which nurture centers is at once relational, practical, specific, and intended to have evocative power. Indeed, the task of the preacher in accomplishing nurture through preaching, to use the words of Thomas Swears, is one of taking "the risks involved in evoking from others what is already in them and then in wonder and humility [watching] what God can do with it."[3] From this perspective, faith and hope-directed preaching is faith-filled preaching.

Preaching in the black worshiping congregation that nurtures faith and hope incorporates three primary functions: prophetic, priestly, and apostolic functions. The nurturing task of prophetic preaching is to literally "build a case," especially through story, that can evoke in worshipers a deepening faith in the nearness of the able God who was described in chapter 1. Furthermore, the task is to arouse in us a vision of the hope-filled plan of God for our lives made known in Jesus Christ and enlivened by the Holy Spirit on which chapters 2 and 3 focus. At the same time, prophetic evocation stimulates not simply our wideawake consciousness of what Gardner Taylor calls our proneness to "get carried away with our own freedom . . . and asserting our own pride and sovereignty."[4] Prophetic evocation also prompts our wakefulness of the One who calls us to justice, kindness, and humble relationship with God. Indeed, the prophetic word is to evoke our embrace of faith and hope as verbs—as actions in response to God, the ultimate evocator who beckons us to move into the unknown future with the will to be reflections of Jesus Christ in a hurting world.

The task of the priestly sermon in the black worshiping congregation is to arouse in us a surety of who and Whose we are. Moreover, it is to evoke in us what Olin Moyd describes as "the courage to struggle against dehumanizing forces and the power to transcend the human-caused trials and tribulations in countless otherwise hopeless situations."[5] Through these sermons, we are to be moved to imagine a worthy future and to move toward and into that future.

The apostolic function of sermons refers to the disclosure of the faithful heart and mind of the preacher, which is able to evoke in the heart and mind of the worshiper a response to the gospel.[6] The term *apostolic* refers to the function that centers on the establishment of the gospel in a believer, which includes the preacher. The manifestation of the gospel within the preacher calls for a response both from her or him and from others to whom this manifestation speaks through sermons and the character and life of the preacher.[7] More specifically, this aspect of preaching as evocative nurture regards the symmetry between the life of the preacher and the preaching of the preacher. At the center of this aspect is the pastor's character, which gets preached through the life of the preacher.[8]

In what follows, more will be said about the prophetic, priestly, and apostolic functions of the preacher's homiletical expression. Within this discussion, attention will be given to the distinctive dialogical style that transforms black preachers' homiletical expression into communal expressive action.

THE PROPHETIC FUNCTION OF FAITH AND HOPE-BEARING PREACHING

The black worshiping congregation expects the black preacher to carry out a prophetic function in the preached word. This function centers on the preachers' engaging black worshipers in seeing hope in the midst of chaos by disclosing in sermons a perspective based on faith in the divine imperative *"God wants you free!"*[9] This function in black preaching includes a view of nurture that involves "unsettling" worshipers in a way that pushes them beyond a position of complacency toward the necessary and intentional struggle for justice in everyday life.

Throughout the chapters in Part One, I continued to emphasize that it was not enough to evoke within worshipers an ever-deepening understanding of the beliefs on which the Christian lifestyle stand. The sermon was identified as pivotal in arousing the worshipers' awareness of the meaning of those beliefs for the daily sojourn. The sermon was presented as a central means of challenging worshipers to actually live out the beliefs in visibly concrete ways. Here, my focus is on describing the prophetic function of sermons that nurtures worshipers in a way that brings about heightened awareness and an existence that exemplifies an alive faith and hope in church and world. The phrase "a homiletic of protest" is a helpful descriptor of the prophetic function.

The protest sermon is an evocative instrument of nurture that aims to bring about black worshipers' critical internal assessment of the formation and use of an "internal propheticism," to use Dennis Wiley's term.[10] This kind of sermon charges black worshipers to be attentive to personally embraced apathetic attitudes and impotent behaviors that counter the gospel and that contribute to our failure to confront externally imposed oppression and internally adopted constraints to a valued identity and human wholeness. Underlying this aspect of the protest sermon is the view that dealing with oppression or dehumanizing treatment of human beings is as much an inner struggle as it is an outer battle. The prophetic sermon reflects the notion that dealing with any form of subjugation, denigration, or cruelty requires us to become uncomfortable and dissatisfied with any evidence of these "forms of inequities that we observe, participate in, and too often create."[11]

However, the prophetic sermon also seeks to clarify specific human behaviors or actions that are needed to address oppression in whatever form it appears. The sermon nurtures faith and hope by engendering images of freedom practices through uses of scripture and by provoking the worshiper to concrete action. Actually, through this protest emphasis in sermonic nurture, the skillful black preacher becomes a teacher prophet. In this role, the preacher seeks to bring forth within black worshipers a faith- and hope-centered prophetic spirituality through three specific nurturing movements including an authoritative disclosure, the critique of human behavior, and the challenge to act.

An Authoritative Disclosure

The black preachers' prophetic sermon pivots on the authority of scripture. In the preacher's hands, the Bible frames the nurturing function of the sermon that is to lead toward a faith- and hope-centered prophetic spirituality. The Bible is the basis for the black preacher's engagement of black worshipers in interpreting and critiquing the human situation; and the Bible provides the norm for the preacher's challenge for the worshipers' reflection on, correction of, or change of behavior. The black preacher nurtures faith and hope by stimulating the worshipers' entry into the biblical world; and through this means, the preacher intends for the worshipers to see the importance of the biblical text for their lives. Nurture through the prophetic sermon is about evoking the worshipers' self-reflection on the life-shaping impact of the text and the worshipers' experience of transformation or change by the text.

The prophetic function of the sermon emerges as the preacher engages the worshipers in their exploration of internal propheticism and their reflection on a faith- and hope-centered prophetic spirituality. Through this function, the black preacher evokes the worshipers' self-critical evaluation by framing biblical authoritative criteria. Patricia Gould-Champ's sermon "An Unfinished Agenda," incorporates this function. In the sermon, Reverend Gould-Champ draws attention to the Lucan account of Jesus' liberation agenda, which Jesus repeated from the book of Isaiah: "The Spirit of the Lord is upon me, / because he has anointed me to preach good news to the poor. / He has sent me to proclaim release to the captives / and recovering of sight to the blind, / to set at liberty those who are oppressed, / to proclaim the acceptable year of the Lord (Luke 4:16–21, RSV).[12] Gould-Champ also draws attention to Jesus' declaration that he did not come to bring peace but a sword (Matthew 10:34).[13]

The criteria set forth in this black preacher's sermon are found in her assertion of Jesus' unceasing faithful attention to the liberation agenda and the authority that this biblical account holds for black people's faithfulness and hope in confronting all kinds of human denigration and cruel treatment of human beings. The preacher also connects scripture to life through questions that are designed to engender critical self-assessment: "What should the church be about? What should the church be doing?"[14] The preacher later raises what she calls "a disturbing thought" by inviting the audience to look at the current state of things and to ponder the question of whether the agenda toward transformation has been finished.[15]

Implicit in the sermon is the notion that nurturing faith and hope has everything to do not only with black worshipers becoming clearly and newly aware of the faithfulness of Jesus that is proclaimed in scripture but also with these worshipers assessing their own faithfulness to the gospel of Jesus Christ. Moreover, there is the assumption that hope lies in the completion of the agenda for change that Jesus Christ has already inaugurated; and, an unfinished agenda runs counter to the biblical mandate and a hope-centered spirituality. What is important here is that scripture is the basis for the kind of nurture of faith and hope on which the prophetic function of sermons in the black worshiping congregation centers. Evocative nurture means not only arousing worshipers' awareness of the gospel message in the Bible but also raising and posing hard questions in ways that stimulate reflection on the self's attitudes and behaviors as well as on contemporary life in general in light of scripture. The sermon as nurture bearer is about voicing questions that go to the heart of what is possible, yet missing, in moving forward faithfully on the journey of life with hope versus despair.

The Critique of Human Behavior

The critique of human behavior in the sermons of black preachers exposes a prophetic function through straightforward descriptions of behaviors that counter the biblical norm or requirement for faith-full and hope-filled Christian life. The critique draws black worshipers into reflection on the disjuncture between the biblical norm and life in community.

Turning again to the sermon of Gould-Champ, we find a critique that calls for the church's adoption of Jesus' agenda. The preacher follows this plea with a narrative about human behaviors that hinder the church's ability to carry out Jesus' agenda. She states: "Many today are captives by choice. Alcohol, sex, greed, drugs, bigotry, and pride . . . Often we choose to be prisoners to our habits and our desires."[16] She goes on to say, "[F]reedom for some people in the world is dependent upon another's choice. . . . [S]ome are held captive to hunger and injustice . . . [M]any of us are still blinded by prejudice, bigotry, and pride and in need of recovery of our sight."[17]

The prophetic function of the black preacher's nurturing sermon is about evoking personal and congregational ownership of responsibility for faith-full and hope-filled Christian living. A key way of carrying out this function has been mentioned in earlier chapters. Namely, the preacher inserts personal pronouns such as "we," "our," and "us" that evoke the worshipers' identification with or seeing ourselves in the narrative material of sermons. This engagement of worshipers in identifying with and seeing the self in stories is central to the prophetic function of sermons and is a necessary means of arousing a sense of owned responsibility.

The intentional insertion of personal pronouns draws the worshipers into a self-critical mode and toward the formation of "internal propheticism." The importance of this kind of effort to form an "internal propheticism" lies precisely in its potential for persons' self-awareness and self-criticism. In fact, the formation of an "internal propheticism" requires self-awareness and self-criticism of attitudes, values, and commitments that, on the one hand, paralyze our abilities to address critical issues and that, on the other hand, empower our abilities. In this way, first-person language contributes to nurturing faith and hope through preaching.

The critical issues of the current age demand worshipers' critique of human behavior including our own. More specifically, nurturing faith and hope means bringing to the highest awareness our responsibility for confronting head-on the all-too-prevalent issues of racism, sexism, classism, HIV/AIDS, teen parenthood and other family crises, sexual immorality, homophobia, substance abuse and violence, incarceration, infant mortality, suicide, and end-of-life issues. The prophetic function of the skilled black preacher's nurturing sermon stands as a critical stimulus to our owning our responsibility as hope builders and our obligation to live the faith we embrace.

The Challenge to Act

The prophetic function of nurturing faith and hope through preaching in the black worshiping congregation is not complete without the worshipers' visualization and anticipation of concrete actions in everyday life that carry out the agenda of God made known in Jesus Christ.

Consequently, the black preacher's nurturing task is to awaken the worshipers' imagination of concrete actions that are consistent with the gospel and to evoke within the worshipers an impassioned will to faith-full action. The task is also one of activating black worshipers' grasp of the meaning of hope by moving us toward a realizable future.

Invariably, the task includes very clear prescriptive language or what may be called "prescriptive nurturing." Acts of resistance, acts of co-operative participation, acts in specific locations, and human capacities that empower action are typical prescriptive categories. For example, Gould-Champ employs elements of protest and obligation in her sermon by insisting that black Christians resist the status quo and participate in programs of reform in order to move toward freedom and away from personal choices, systems, and institutions that perpetuate life in bondage.[18]

Similarly, Samuel Proctor's sermon "Relevant Religion" sets forth kinds of cooperative action as examples of prescriptive nurturing. In the sermon, Proctor names the actions of licking stamps, ringing doorbells, and getting people elected to office who can curb excesses in our society.[19] In still another sermon, Delores Carpenter uses prescriptive language to help worshipers visualize God's call to action in the specific location of the city. In her words, "the city is one of the great intersections of rich and poor, powerful and powerless. . . . The city is where we can begin to bridge the great chasms of shelter, health care, security, and food. Here is where Jesus again wants to minister to his people and we are the instruments of his reconciling presence. But, we must first hear him calling us there. . . . Secondly, we must go *quickly*."[20]

The sermon of Magdalen Shelton highlights human capacities that empower actions in her use of prescriptive language. Shelton enters this particular use of prescription by posing the question that evokes visualization and anticipation of concrete action: "Lord, what must I loose that binds me?"[21] Shelton assists the evocative endeavor through the insertion of ideas for preparedness to act on which the worshipers could deliberate. She asserts that lives of hope become possible when you "take off complacency. . . . Loose yourself from negative compromise. . . . Loose yourself from mediocrity."[22]

I have already mentioned uses of personal pronouns to draw black worshipers into a self-critical mode. Evidence of this usage also appears in the aforementioned sermon of Shelton. However, black preachers also employ other linguistic tools in nurturing sermons in order to raise within the worshipers an awareness of the imperative nature of our acting beyond the context of the worshiping congregation. Some of these linguistic tools appear in chapter 5. However, I want to add here that hyperbole frequently appears as a way of arousing the worshipers' imagination and anticipation of concrete action in the world. For example, Gould-Champ concludes her sermon by saying: "I just want to remind you that *now* is the time. The captives can be set free—we've got to finish the agenda. *Now*, the blind can recover their sight—we've got to finish the agenda. *Now*, the oppressed can be set at liberty—we've got to finish the agenda."[23]

THE PRIESTLY FUNCTION OF FAITH AND HOPE-BEARING PREACHING

The black preacher carries out a priestly function in the preached word. The central focus of this function is building faith and hope within worshipers through intentional attention to the worshipers' identity-formation, views of life, and coping strategies amidst life's trauma. The priestly function centers on what Harris calls "uplift education."[24] The priestly function also has an emancipatory focus and is rightly called a homiletic of emancipatory uplift that is centered on faith in God's activity on behalf of persons' release *from* the things that bind them *to* a future of promise. The nurturing task of the black preacher is that of priest who evokes in the hearer an understanding "that his or her life situation does not have to remain as it is."[25] Through this task, the black preacher nurtures black worshipers by disclosing wisdom that is pertinent to claiming and maintaining the valued identity described in chapter 4 and that has already been given by God. Moreover, through the priestly word, the preacher helps the worshipers to envision a vocation and specific Christian life skills that are critical to living in families and in the world as Christians, even when our backs are often pressed to the wall by the challenges of life.

Wisdom-Sharing

Nurturing faith and hope through the priestly function of black preaching entails the black preacher's sharing pivotal information that helps black worshipers form positive views of self and life. For example, one of the historic sermons of Benjamin E. Mays utilizes biblical material to inspire faith to sojourn amidst the challenges of life. In part, Mays' answer is: "By every word that proceedeth out of the mouth of God or by everything that God provides above," but he does not stop with this statement. Mays shares an expansive pastoral theological perspective using pastoral images through which we can question, interpret, or reinterpret the realities and the direction of our lives. These images may be summarized as follows:

- Bread or material things are not enough; we must live by giving and receiving love and affection. Recognize that abundant food, air, sunshine, protection from the cold and heat are not substitutes for care, hugs, kisses, inviting smiles, and soothing words;

- We must live by forgiveness in families and communities and by God's forgiveness; Recognize that families and communities that hold together avidly seek God's forgiveness, the forgiveness of one another for trespasses great and small, and find ways of living in humane, respectful, loving ways;

- We must live gratefully by God's grace or by what we receive that we do not deserve. Recognize when we receive God's unmerited grace, such as the benefits of sun, moon, and rain, unearned honors, and gifts;

- We must live by faith in ourselves. No matter how difficult the road, recognize our usefulness and the contributions we can make in the lives of others; and

- We must live by our dreams. Recognize a worthy goal that exists beyond what we think we can attain, and continue to reach for it.[26]

The point here is that preaching that carries out the priestly function centers on evoking in worshipers self-examination, deepening self-understanding, affirmation of our valued identity that is given by God and lived out in community, and sustenance for the journey ahead. Indeed, it is through the priestly function of preaching that the kind of redefinition of identity described in chapter 4 takes place. Yet, this function also takes seriously that worshipers come into the worshiping congregation with the many facets of their lives. We come with stories great and small, promising and problematic about our identities, the places we live, our relationships, the direction of our lives, and the meanings we assign to our lives.[27] Preaching that carries out the priestly function tends to these themes of worshipers' stories and arouses in the community of faith its individual and communal understanding of the faith as being fully open to life and God's purpose for our being in the world. Carrying out this function may well result in testimonies like the one given by Harris: "This preaching helped me to believe that I could indeed finish high school and go on to college, although no one else in my family has done this before. This preaching was and is uplifting."[28]

Thomas Swears is also quite right in his statement that "there is too much pain and meaninglessness in the lives of the people sitting in Christian sanctuaries week after week to allow such a condition to go unanswered. The cost is simply too high."[29] Insofar as the priestly function of preaching is carried out, nurture that leads to faith, hope, transformation, and healing can arise.

THE APOSTOLIC FUNCTION OF FAITH- AND HOPE-BEARING PREACHING

In the beginning of this chapter, I made reference to the apostolic function of sermons. I indicated that at the center of this function is the character of the preacher. It refers to the establishment of the gospel in the life of the believer, including the preacher. I also mentioned in the introduction that one of the criticisms made by black youth today regards the lack of congruency between what Christians profess and how Christians live their lives. This criticism extends to preachers. This critique of our young is instructive of what must become a paramount matter to resolve if nurturing faith and hope through preaching is to be genuine. In fact, based on Swears' discussion of the person in the pulpit, nurture through preaching becomes a wholly believable endeavor only insofar as the preacher is a person of integrity, reflects authentic personhood, and expresses authority that is representative of the sacred.[30]

The integrity to which Swears refers is captured in the preacher's "transparent, consistent, intentional harmony of word and deed."[31] Authenticity is a quality that stands apart from sermonizing that is received, admired, and judged for its eloquence, theological brilliance, or the evocative artistry of the "hoop" alone. "Authentic preaching," says Swears, "requires of the preacher authentic living, which is best accomplished by the preacher's commitment to live intentionally in the presence of Christ."[32] Authenticity is the evidence that the preacher has a relationship with God through Jesus Christ that shows in the preached word and in the very life the preacher lives, and the truthful, caring relationships the preacher enters with others. Authenticity requires that the preacher is a listening presence with others in order to grasp who they are and the nature of their stories. Nurturing faith and hope through preaching requires an authentic and compassionate response to the existential conditions of people's lives. Authentic preaching also reflects the preacher's personal witness through appropriate disclosure of his or her story or disclosure that is relevant to the problems or experiences of the worshipers or that illuminates meanings of faith and hope with which they can identify.[33]

Authority in preaching is reflected in the preacher's recognition of the responsibility she or he has for others and for the communication of the gospel in such a way that it does, in fact, bring forth a new or renewed sense of faith and hope. This view stands in contrast to an assumption of power *over* the worshipers. Rather, authority is seen from the perspective of the preacher as caretaker of the gospel—a responsibility that comes from the preacher's own sense of accountability to God[34] and recognition, as Ellen Charry reminds us, that "God is the primary influence."[35] Indeed, if preaching is to spur the worshiper to attend to God or to enrich that attending for the sake of an enhanced faith and hope, then the preacher's attending to God and enriching her or his attending is of paramount importance. Through this attending, it becomes possible for God to address the preacher, for Jesus to appear as the model, and for the Holy Spirit to guide. In this way, authority is revealed in the preacher's comportment as God's representative or as "God-bearer," *a theotokos*.[36]

COMMENTARY

The importance of preaching in the black worshiping congregation cannot be overstated. Moreover, the distinctive "call and response" pattern appearing in the conduct of black preaching continues to be accorded great significance. Dash and Chapman describe this pattern in terms of "two kinds of simultaneous interrelationships going on, the interaction between the preacher and the Spirit and the interaction between the preacher and the hearer, the pulpit and the pew."[37] This interactive experience attests to the power of stories that evoke our connection with ideas, themes, and feelings of great relevance to our daily lives. The significance of storytelling and the dramatic manner in which they are told and received often leads to the exclamation of worshipers on their departure: "He/she surely did preach today!"

Yet, as indicated in the Introduction, the critique of our congregation's embrace of individualistic "me oriented" values and the correlative waning of a vital community service orientation calls for close and continued examination of whether prophetic preaching really is what it once was. Notwithstanding the proactive and positive demonstration of faith and hope in action appearing in the Billingsley resource, *Mighty Like a River*, Boykin Sanders states that there is, in fact, the need for "prophetic restructuring in Africa America."[38] The questions must be raised: Is this true? If it is true, how must we respond? Is there need to reaffirm the position of Dash and Chapman that the role of the preacher as witness is to move us to the point of "willingness to be available to God on behalf of others . . . [and] to transform worship in the sanctuary into work in the world that makes credible witness to God in our lives?" [39] My position here is that assuring the vitality of nurturing faith and hope in the worshiping congregation depends on critical dialogue undertaken by clergy and laity on these questions as well as on the character of the preacher on which I have given attention in this chapter.

AN INVITATION TO REFLECT

1. What is your awareness of the presence of prophetic, priestly, and apostolic functions of preaching in your congregation?

2. Describe your understandings of the prophetic, priestly, and apostolic functions of preaching and the need for them in your congregation.

3. What are the messages of faith and hope that are communicated through sermons in your congregation?

4. How would you answer the questions raised at the end of the commentary?

10

MUSIC MAKING AS A PATHWAY TO NURTURE

I will praise the LORD *as long as I live;*
I will sing praises to my God all my life long.

—*Psalm 146:2*

MUSIC IS AN INEXTRICABLE AND HIGHLY revered aspect of the everyday lives of black people and is central to the life of the black worshiping congregation.[1] Particularly in the worshiping congregation, music combines with preaching and praying as an essential nurturing pathway of faith and hope. In singing and listening to music, we experience tremendous evocative power that brings forth in us thoughts, attitudes, and feelings about the primary themes of the Christian faith explored in Part One. Music is thoughtful, artful, emotional nurture through which we voice, reflect on, and respond to what it communicates about the nature and meanings of the life challenges we encounter, ways of living with faith under fire, and sojourning with hope. Indeed, in the throes of singing and listening to songs in the worshiping congregation, we discover and rediscover what it means to believe or trust in our relationship with God and God's relationship with us through Jesus Christ and the Holy Spirit and to move into the unknown future with confidence. In this chapter, I invite us to explore these dimensions of music as nurture bearer.

As part of our exploration, however, I want to draw our attention, first, to the reality that, more than preaching or praying, the musical styles we encounter in the worshiping congregation have much to do with what music evokes in us. The genre of music selected for expression in the worshiping congregation often has the propensity to evoke strong emotion of either a positive or a negative, perhaps even rejecting, nature. Music has been known to create "culture wars" in congregations between groups of people, usually of differing ages or stages, whose musical tastes and preferences collide.

Many congregations struggle with how to bring peace in the midst of turmoil surrounding music. Some have discovered a way forward by embracing a "musical pentecost," or the use of multiple musical styles—from spirituals, hymns, anthems, and gospel music to Christian rap—within a given worship experience or by crafting separate worship services, each with a different musical and worship style. Still other congregations strive for mutual understanding across the generations and a common commitment to honor a "musical pentecost" through teaching and learning events beyond the worshiping congregation.

As part of the teaching and learning experiences beyond the worshiping congregation, persons from the differing ages or stages share a favorite Christian song, give a personal testimony of how the song became their preferred selection, and the meaning the song holds for them in their Christian sojourn. Others who choose the same song are asked to add their testimonies. What typically happens is the emergence of powerful shared autobiographies and the interface of these highly personal stories with the storied content of songs. In these settings, I have heard persons say to one another: "I understand where you're coming from. I see in your music something I never saw before. Thank you." I am aware of one situation, in fact, in which the older members taught the young how to "line a hymn" and the young taught the adults a Christian rap.

Times of sharing beyond church worship experiences result in an openness to one another and a readiness of persons to enter into the worshiping congregation in positive, affirming, and creative ways. From these experiences, the worshiping congregation holds the promise of becoming an environment in which music making can truly exist as a nurturing agent of faith and hope for the whole congregational family. With this in mind, we will proceed with our exploration of how music functions as a nurture bearer of faith and hope in the black worshiping congregation. Two specific functions will be explored including the imaginative function and the expressive function.

IMAGINATIVE AND EXPRESSIVE FUNCTIONS OF FAITH- AND HOPE-BEARING NURTURE THROUGH MUSIC

Music is artful nurturing activity that draws the whole congregation into an imaginative, freely expressed style of evoking views, attitudes, and feelings about the beliefs we hold or are forming. As we discovered in Part One, songs disclose ideas and meanings of pivotal themes of the Christian faith. In words and emotion beyond ordinary language, songs tell our communities' stories of faith and hope in God, Jesus Christ, the Holy Spirit, the valued self, and the movement from sin to salvation. Songs challenge us, too, to consider what these themes have to say for our everyday lives as Christians and to decide how we will sojourn as faithful and hope-filled followers of Jesus Christ.

We also discovered in Part Two that songs serve as a unique nurturing agent in the liturgical events of baptism and Holy Communion. Songs are an integral part of the celebratory and interactive event of baptism through which we make integrative sense of the Divine-human relationship and the ongoing responsibility we as Christians have for newly baptized persons, for one another, and for making a better world. As part of the celebration of the eucharist or Holy Communion, songs serve as evocative triggers for our imagining and experiencing the Welcome Table, where unconditional acceptance and open reception override experiences of unwelcome in daily life.

Imaginative Nurture

As we honor the broad spectrum of styles, music in the black worshiping congregation emerges as an imaginative nurture-bearing experience that reminds us about the nature and beliefs of a community of faith and hope about which we may have already grasped and claimed as important. Yet, imaginative nurture through music also places us in a position of unparalleled opportunity for imagining meanings of faith by *being* the community of faith and hope, by sharing the *experience* of its message through music.[2] One worshiper described the experience in the following way:

A Story

> It is easy to get completely and happily "caught up" in our church's music. Because of its vitality, music in our church draws us into an experience that is mind bending and heart rending. I can also say that it is life leading too. We sing what we know about life with God, and we come to know about life with God through the music. What happens is more than a head thing. Personally, my heart speaks through song and my heart receives the stories in song about God and us. I feel what is revealed in a song and what I'm singing. I can also go a step further because spirituals, hymns, gospels, you name it, help me to see a way out of no way. Music gives me a vision of hope for my life. I really think that music shows and builds black people's faith; and we make this fact known by the intensity of our singing and by the way we add onto our music as the Spirit leads.

Through the imaginative function of the songs we sing as congregational families or choirs, we externalize what others and we know or believe. Like the worshiper whose story appears above, hearing and singing is a faith revealer and faith builder. More than this, though, through the spirituals, time-honored hymns, and the lining of hymns of the church, we become aware of the memory of the older generation. We envisage the beliefs and the nature of hope that have continued to shape their lives; and the whole congregational family is placed in a position of imagining meanings of the songs for the self and the whole community. Through hearing and singing contemporary gospel songs, rock gospels, and Christian rap, we become aware of the concerns and vision of the younger generation; and together, the whole congregational family is placed in a position of imagining how memory and vision connect. Through hearing and singing gospel songs from the early and golden eras of gospel music and songs that straddle the musical genres, we become conscious of the religious views of the middle generation. These songs open to the whole congregational family a picture that brings together present reality, memory, and vision.[3]

In these ways, the imaginative function of songs nurtures an awareness of the criticality of the various generations' involvement together in the worshiping congregation. Indeed, this function makes of music a pathway for our imagining, redefining, and affirming our identity as black people and people of faith and hope in the manner described in chapter 4. Moreover, the externalization of what we and others know or believe draws us all into imagining, wondering, considering, and affirming the meaning of that knowing and believing in light of our own stories; and it summons children and others who may be new to the Christian faith into the same process. To this extent, the imaginative function of nurture-bearing experience carried out through music in the black worshiping congregation moves the worshiping congregation beyond simply rote or unmindful copied expression. It engages us in evocative experience that summons our thinking, reflecting, and feeling selves on the promise we have as children of God and creates a foundation for persons' ongoing participation in the worshiping congregation and, indeed, in the church's ministry.[4]

Expressive Nurture

Whether through congregational singing, choir selections, or instrumental music, musical expression in the black worshiping congregation does not ordinarily happen without bodily responses such as clapping, swaying, tapping the feet, drumming, or dancing. Music has a decidedly expressive function that happens spontaneously. However, liturgists and contemporary praise teams often openly nurture this kind of expressiveness by inviting worshipers to enter into it. Music becomes a nurture bearer of our black cultural ways of responding to the movement of the Holy Spirit. As one worshiper put it:

A Story

Most ordinarily, we don't just take the message of a song by simply listening, singing, sitting, or standing still. We're free to respond. We're free to "get happy!" Really, the Spirit won't let us sit still. Let me give you an example. For me, the words of the gospel song, "God is our rock, hope of salvation' a strong deliverer, in Him I'll always trust," puts me in touch with what happens. Something happens when we sing that song that I can't explain. It's like the Spirit takes over. Something happens all over the sanctuary. While we sing, people begin to sway from side to side. Hands rise into the air. It's like we move out of ourselves into another realm. People shout and say "Amen!" By what we do and say, we show that we know that God is the key to our goings on in our lives. Recalling the whole experience makes me want to shout even now.

It is appropriate to say that our bodily responses reflect the movement of the Holy Spirit that results in our "getting happy." However, it may also be said through music, we connect with the Spirit. This connection arouses in our bodies kinesthetic meanings of faith in God, our ability to give way to our expressive capacities, and what it means to hope or to continue into the unknown future with vitality and diligence as Christians. In another manner of speaking, expressive nurture through music engages black worshipers' "kinesthetic intelligence." That is, there is no need for explanation of what to do before we move. There is an indescribable intuitive knowing how and when to move.[5]

Yet, as we move, others who may be new to the worship experience, and especially the young, are very likely to enter into building a "movement vocabulary." They see what is possible. They become aware of the activity of the Holy Spirit. Their experience of seeing others move in response to music may also evoke awareness of the connection between movement and listening as well as the importance of stillness.[6] However, it is important to add here that black worshiping congregations are sometimes challenged to see the importance of stillness and quiet that allows for another level of hearing and responding to the Spirit. The challenge is to critically reflect on and assess the extent to which the intensity and profusion of action and sound overwhelms our ability to grasp the importance of stillness, especially active stillness that is anticipative listening and openness to the Spirit. Expressive nurture through music includes this dimension of the life of the worshiping congregation.

Two more comments may be made about expressive nurture through music. First, music expresses the depths of the innermost self—our very soul—and summons the whole self's expression. As such, choral and instrumental music in tandem with spontaneous and sometimes choreographed liturgical dance is nurture that awakens in present and successive generations a kind of black expressive spirituality. This spirituality is akin to what Urban T. Holmes III calls "thinking with the left hand." It is expressive activity that intentionally embraces more than rational thought.[7] Second, the imaginative and expressive functions of music in the black worshiping congregation combine to release within us an "inscape," or vision of faith and hope, that propels us beyond the communal context of worship into richer faith-filled and hope-filled everyday living.[8] In fact, it may be said that, as nurture bearer, music has the propensity to renew us, and even transform us by arousing our imagination, emotions, and attitudes that lie at the heart of Christian spirituality.[9]

NURTURE THROUGH MUSIC AS "SPIRITUAL FREE PLAY"

Nurture that occurs through music in the black worshiping congregation embraces, gives permission for, and fosters a spontaneous and improvisational style of expression. When the congregation or choir sings, or while an instrumentalist accompanies singing or plays at other times, the music in the worshiping congregation often becomes an experience of "spiritual free play." This metaphor describes music as thoughtful, artful, and emotional nurture through which the worshiping congregation voices, reflects on, and responds to the nature and meanings of life challenges, living with faith under fire, and sojourning with hope.

"Spiritual free play" takes place as a consequence of the heart's and the body's response to the movement of the Holy Spirit and the mind's connection with the message or content on which the music centers. In "spiritual free play," the whole self is released to delight in the personal experience of seeing and hearing God. Through this experience, we create and add new sounds, rhythms, and thoughts that respond to and add further meaning to a truth or belief disclosed in a song.

Immersion in the experience of "spiritual free play" becomes a catalyst for nurturing the worshipers' faith and hope as well as what John Berntsen calls an "emotion language."[10] In this sense, evoking our deepening awareness and appreciation of revered beliefs of the faith and our sense of promise beyond the present does not happen apart from feeling.[11] Stated another way, "spiritual free play" in the black worshiping congregation is our way of "thinking with the left hand" or discovering meanings that lie beyond what Urban Holmes calls the "logical operation imposed by society's categories of reality."[12] "Spiritual free play" creates a climate of imaginative experience and artistry that builds creative musical capacities from which life outside the congregation is embellished. It also enhances our understanding of faith and hope that guides life outside the congregation.

By further explanation, the improvisatory nature of "spiritual free play" engages the black worshiping congregation in at least five aspects of imaginative and expressive functions of nurture. First, improvisation is an act of responding and drawing attention to the mysterious work of God's Spirit that cannot be comprehended on the printed page. Through improvisation, black worshipers become open to the qualities of luminosity and a wholly affective religious experience that appends what we see, learn, and reproduce from a musical score.

Second, the improvisatory aspect of music making in the black worshiping congregation is a pathway for nurturing the meaning of surrendering to the "pull" within the self to sing, clap, shout, and pray when the Spirit says to do so. Improvisation also functions as a pathway of nurture that evokes our awareness of the "push" to lean into the future moment by moment by relinquishing a certain degree of control. In this way, improvisation is an act of coming to know something of the nature of transience and eternity. Improvisation places us in touch with the very real situation of our "knowing" what *might* happen, but of our not "knowing" what *will* happen. Improvisation evokes in us a kind of comfortability with what Nachmanovitch calls "the mystery of moments that are dependably surprising, ever fresh."[13] Improvisation evokes our sense of comfort with our own religious imagination.

Third, the significance of improvisatory musical experience to nurture in the black worshiping congregation lies both in its reflection of and stimulation of our awareness that life unfolds according to unexpected twists and turns. Improvisation in music both reflects and evokes within us, consciously or unconsciously, a cultural sensitivity to the reality of the unexpected events that occur in our lives. Moreover, the improvisational character of music affirms and reminds us, consciously or unconsciously, that unexpected life events call us to create, to improvise, and to proceed on the journey faithfully and imaginatively, as the spiritual says, "to see what the end will be."[14]

Fourth, by its very nature, improvisation is comprised of unique, nonrepeatable, and nonretrievable moments. The importance of this quality of music to nurture in the black worshiping congregation lies in what it can arouse in us about the uniqueness and preciousness of every moment in life. Improvisational musical expression calls our attention to the affective domain of educational ministry in which appreciation, reverence, and creative participation in every moment of life must be seen as a valid part of living with faith and hope.[15]

Finally, the evocative nurturing power of improvisatory musical experience makes possible, as well, our openness to God's speaking when God wants to speak to and through us. Improvisation opens the way for the divine pedagogy wherein, as indicated in the Introduction, God comes as the evocator. As evocator in improvisatory musical expression, God reaches out to us, invites our reaching back, and calls for our avowal that we will move forward in the journey of life. Moving forward means sojourning with resolute faith in the able God who is *with* us and with an expectancy of living confidently and courageously in community after the model of Jesus in times of triumph and in the midst of suffering, narrow escapes, failures, reversals, and hard trials.

COMMENTARY

Jeff Astley asserts that people probably develop religious attitudes, affections, and patterns of behavior as the result of learning that occurs through certain experiences, including experiences with other people.[16] Based on this assertion, our experiences of music in the black worshiping congregation are rightly viewed as imaginative pathways for nurturing or bringing forth in us the kinds of attitudes, affections, and patterns of behavior that promote and sustain faith and hope. In an important way, music in the black worshiping congregation stands as cultural "materials" that frame an imaginative expressive nurturing venture that fosters our ongoing awareness and embrace of Christian convictions that shape and flow from the stories of our lives.

We must not forget, however, that there is a *choice* that churches make about the kinds and contents of music to be shared in the worshiping congregation. Increasingly, choices are made regarding what is perceived as meshing with and promoting the particular musical genre, religio-cultural worldview and emotive style that will attract and retain the young in congregational worship. This focus on *choice*, however, also presents a challenge to church worship committees and liturgy organizers to consider critically the implications of what is chosen for the nurture of the whole intergenerational congregational family. *Choice* can and does provoke conflict in which differences of musical preferences, content, and emotive style exist; and this conflict is typically generational in nature. The issue of *choice* requires churches to ask the question: How may nurturing faith and hope through music be an inclusive experience?

A distinctive and powerful attribute of musical expression in the black worshiping congregation is what I have referred to in this chapter as "spiritual free play," which often includes improvisation and emotional and bodily affectivity. These qualities of music making in the worshiping congregation model an emotional intuitive, aesthetic nonverbal "right-brain and left-hand" mode of nurture that is often seen as antithetical and of lesser value than the more intellectual, analytical, verbal, and cognitive "left-brain and right-hand" mode of religious learning. However, this modeling in black congregational worship affirms an emerging position in religious educational circles that there should not be a wedge between emotion or experience and what we do to promote persons' grasp of belief or doctrine. To use Astley's words, "emotions have a logic: a grammar, form and determinacy which derive from, and must be understood in conjunction with, the accompanying thoughts, beliefs and objects of the emotion. The point is that the good health of Christian education is dependent on the operation of both lobes of the brain, so that Christian truth is learned both affectively and cognitively."[17] This point is no less true in the nurture of faith and hope.

AN INVITATION TO REFLECT

1. How would you describe the nature and role of music in your worshiping congregation?

2. Explore how the *choices* of music in your congregation's worship experiences are made. Why are the *choices* important? Over several occasions of worship, reflect on what in the music "speaks" to you and what in it does not "speak" to you and why.

3. In what ways does the description in this chapter of "spiritual free play" mirror or differ from what occurs in your congregation's worship experiences? Critically examine the nature and role of affect in nurture taking place through music in the worshiping congregation. What views do you hold?

4. How does music in your congregation respond to the need of every generation for ongoing nurture of faith and hope? What may yet happen for the role of music to be enlivened as a pathway of nurture across the life span?

11

PRAYING AS A PATHWAY TO NURTURE

Rejoice in hope, be patient in suffering, persevere in prayer.

—Romans 12:12

WORSHIP IN THE BLACK CONGREGATION proceeds with periods of immersion in soulful prayer. Nurturing faith and hope through prayer in the black worshiping congregation includes prayers from the "prayer warriors," who themselves disclose the deepest feelings of the soul in a fashion akin to our forebears. In worship, black people expect an invitation to talk to God on whom the ability to engage the sojourn of life depends. Whether offered by clergy or laity, we expect to hear the language of praise, gratitude, confession, lament, and petition that holds the cultural vocabulary of trust in the present and able God detailed in the opening chapter of this book and that reflects reliance on the promises of God. This language comes forth the moment the black preacher, liturgist, or layperson says what I have heard so many times: "With every head bowed and every eye shut, let us approach the Throne of Grace and talk to the God of our weary years and silent tears who has brought us this far by faith." Moreover, we enter into this language as an expression of both our individual selves and the whole community. In a very powerful way, then, prayer joins the preached word and musical expression as a primary means of nurturing faith and hope in the black worshiping congregation.

Prayer is "primary speech" or the natural expression of the whole self and the connected community to a faithful God and a God of promise to whom every desire and cry for help may be presented.[1] But, prayer is also evocative activity through which black worshipers become aware experientially of a model showing the importance and faith- and hope-building nature of conversations with this God. Through hearing and saying prayers, we become participants in and learners of cultural ways and meanings of "approaching the Throne of Grace and of coming before God, the full Fountain."[2] Through our prayers in the worshiping congregation, we tap into the spiritual legacy of our forebears who held to an impassioned faith and hope in God's for-us-ness amidst the ravages of hard trials and tribulations and awe-inspiring experiences of divine grace. Prayers in the worshiping congregation arouse in us a sense of all-rightness in crying out to God the heart's lament and even questions about God's seeming absence in times of tragedy; and, prayers become the medium through which we discover the activity of the Holy Spirit that can move us to shout, "Thank you, Jesus," in response to profound blessings of God.

Through praying, we practice the vocabulary of prayer and form our own soul's language with which we enter conversations with God. As such, the prayer life of the black worshiping congregation may be rightly called a bearer of nurture that presents to and engages worshipers in an oratory of faith and hope from which we build our own oratory.[3] As nurture bearer, prayer in the black worshiping congregation functions as both a pattern for relating with God and a cultivator of our individual and communal belief in and conversations with God.

This chapter is about evocative communicative functions and a language of prayer in the black worshiping congregation. We will explore prayer as an experience that nurtures faith and hope by arousing and validating beliefs about who God is and how God acts, our need for God, and ways of responding to God. Attention will also be given to the self-disclosive nature of the language of prayer that makes it a nurture-bearing experience. In addition, some comments will be made about meanings of developing an oratory of faith and hope as well as of nurturing expressive and dialogical prayer style.

CONVICTION VALIDATING FUNCTIONS OF NURTURE-BEARING PRAYER

The prayer life of the black worshiping congregation is nurture that raises in worshipers a view of prayer as a way of life with God undertaken by the children of God. Prayer in this congregation invites us into a life of faith and hope through engaging us in validating language or language that affirms core cultural beliefs about our relationship with God. Especially through the language of prayer, we affirm our beliefs and views about the nature of God and the Divine-human relationship. More specifically, nurture occurring through prayer in black worship is an experiential endeavor that affirms the faithful and hope-giving nature of God; and it validates through the language of prayer the faith- and hope-centered character of our relationship with God. Our very entry into the experience of prayer in and of itself communicates our need for it; yet, it is our actual participation in hearing and articulating the language of prayer that lets us know more surely the depth of this need.

Prayer as Validating Language of Who God Is and How God Acts

Wyatt Tee Walker states, "if preaching is indeed the heart of black worship, then praying has been the strength."[4] Prayer in black worship places the worshipers in the presence of God, the Source of all strength. We come to know that prayer connects us with a strength-giving God through praying words that affirm that truth, through testimonies of "black prayer warriors" of what prayer has done in their lives, and most importantly, through personally experiencing the impact or meaning of prayer in our own lives. Our making sense of this experience of nurturing faith and hope does not happen all at one time. It unfolds as the experience and the language become gradually our own and as the experience takes root and forms meaning in our everyday lives.

For example, a middle-aged black male shared with me his realization only after many years had passed that the knee-bent soulful cries to God by his pastor, other worshipers, and his parents were about tapping into God's strength. This person recollected that in his young mind, the knee-bending posture and fervent pleas to God at church, and at home for that matter, seemed silly. He remembered thinking: "If there was really a positive outcome to all that was being asked of God, then why was it necessary to ask the same thing time and time again?" He conceded, however, that, gradually, something important began to "sink in." He recalled hearing repeatedly during prayer time: "We as a people can't make it by ourselves. We've got to call on God who knows all about our troubles and who will not forsake us." The man gleaned from what was said before, during, and after prayers and from what he observed and began to experience himself during tough times that talking to God made possible an inexplicable kind of strength and resiliency in life. The man said that he came to believe not only that God is our strength and help in time of need but also that God's way and timing of answering prayers is mysterious. He also learned through others' testimonies of the powerful truth that "God might not come when you want God, but God comes 'on time.'"

In chapter 1, I explored God language as cultural content in the prayers of black people. In that chapter, my point was that prayers in the black Christian religious tradition inform black people of cultural perceptions of who God is and how God acts as a consequence of how God is named. It is important to restate here that prayer is a nurture-bearing pathway in black worship because it affirms views of not only who God is but also how God acts. For example, these views are couched in references such as God the wonder worker, gracious presence, our refuge in time of need, or great physician. These references validate the time-honored beliefs of some worshipers about God and arouse other worshipers' awareness of God's nature. By hearing these references, black worshipers become privy to, build, and reaffirm a vocabulary of prayer that tells of the One on whom we can call, who hears us, who will answer us in our desert places, and who is worthy of praise. Prayer exists as a nurture bearer through what it evokes in us and affirms about the nature and activity of God.

Prayer as Validating Language of the Divine-Human Relationship

Nurturing faith and hope centers on cultivating a dynamic human and divine relationship that enlivens our continuation on life's journey. The experience and language of prayer in the black worshiping congregation is an important means by which this goal of nurture occurs. Prayer evokes the worshipers' awareness of the interconnectedness of faith and hope in God, God's embrace of our relationship, and our need for entering into relationship with God.

Prayers in the worshiping congregation are disclosive faith-centered "lessons" revealing the able God and the trustworthiness of God's mercy and loving kindness.[5] Prayers reflect and nurture our understanding that God knows us and seeks us out for relationship and conversation.[6]

Nurturing faith and hope through prayer in the black worshiping congregation also happens as black worshipers engage in prayer language that calls attention to the need of human beings for God. Nurture through prayer evokes in us an awareness of the reciprocal relationship between God and us. Prayer is faith- and hope-filled activity through which we affirm our need for God by virtue of our entry into prayer. Prayer is activity that validates the Divine-human relationship by the opportunity it gives us to build a language to express our personal concerns and needs as well as the wider concerns and needs of churches, communities, social structures, and the world for God.

Thus, hearing and saying prayers in the worshiping congregation foster in us an awareness of our personal need for God as articulated in the prayer hymn "I Need Thee Every Hour"[7] and through the songs "Kum ba Yah" (Come by Here, Lord)"[8] and "Lead Me, Guide Me."[9] Yet, prayer also extends beyond the personal "I / Thou" language to the kind of corporate "We / Thou" phraseology that appears in the prayer hymn "We Remember You," which is often sung during the celebration of Holy Communion.[10]

It is not unusual for phrases such as the aforementioned ones to be heard in black worshiping congregations. To this extent, declarations and validations of need of this kind are, in fact, a way of arousing individual worshipers and the whole congregation's memory of the crucial connection between them and God that can spell the difference between hope and despair. Prayer in the black worshiping congregation is nurture-bearing activity that helps worshipers to recall, to get in touch with, and to articulate the language of our human need for God.

It is important to note that the human and divine relationship entered into and fostered by prayer does not happen through intentional and formal instructions on the prayer life. Indeed, praying is revealed to us as a Divine-human encounter that extends beyond instruction and that cannot be encapsulated in the word *nurture*. Rather, the prayer life of the worshiping congregation simply engages us, draws us into relationship with God the Source of all strength and the Author of faith and hope. This engagement summons the worshipers into a language world and realm of the Spirit that moves the prayer-giver to proclaim excitedly, as I have so often heard, "God, you are worthy of our gratitude and praise! Hallelujah!" followed by the words, "Let us bow before you, God, because your name is above all names and you are the One who is able to keep us from falling." Stated another way, praying immerses us in an experience with God in a manner recalled by James Washington, of slipping into "a different realm of existence," which is clearly not ritual but rather a mode of being, of talking and thinking with God.[11] In short, through the prayer life of the congregation, we form a distinctive "I" and "Thou" or "We" and "Thou" dialogical language that reveals and validates our faith and hope in God through Jesus Christ and the Holy Spirit. Indeed, prayer in the congregation is nurture that validates the view that, no matter the circumstance, or even the presence of doubt, God is personal enough, actively present enough, and believable enough to be a conversation partner.

Self-Disclosive Functions of Prayer

Nurturing faith and hope through prayer in black worship is activity that guides our answers to the question: "What are we allowed to say about our experiences and innermost thoughts and feelings in our conversations with God?" The black worshiping congregation answers these questions through the very real, spontaneous, and autobiographical nature of prayers by clergy, liturgists, and laity alike. The experiences of prayer engage black people in and, therefore, help us to express deeply heart-rending and extemporaneous thoughts and feelings that include laments, confessions, intercession, and commitments to God.

DISCLOSING THE LAMENT

Laments are the moans of the soul that arise from life's struggles and losses and that are brought to speech in prayer. Laments are our pleas for God's help. Prayers of lament in the black worshiping congregation are experiences through which we develop and affirm our human cries to God in times of trouble. Indeed, times of prayer in this congregation invite our cries when we are hurting as well as our copresence with and intercession on behalf of other hurting persons. Prayers of lament validate our awareness of a compassionate God who reaches out to us and welcomes our reaching back. Through these prayers, we become willing participants in the divine pedagogy in which the able God to whom I refer in chapter 1 is the divine Listener and the divine Evocator who seeks to arouse in us a profound sense of faith in God's presence and healing activity. The nurturing message of prayers of lament is that God can be trusted with our cries and that a perspective of hope cannot be wholly formed without the full disclosure of the depths of hurt and despair.

Participation in prayers of lament is activity that nurtures faith and hope through fostering the formation of a language of lament while, at the same time, evoking the creation of a posture of hope. Sometimes, the language takes the form of questions and a response to the questions, often built on biblical passages, like those in prayers I remember hearing across the years especially from elders. The prayers went something like: "God, sometimes, when troubles come, we want to raise the question to you, 'Why, God?' 'How long, O Lord?'" "Sometimes, we just can't seem to get beyond our deep groans of despair: 'Oh God, where are you? Just seems like we can't go on! Why have you forsaken me?'[12] But, God, we also know and believe the words of the psalmist that 'Weeping may linger for the night, but joy comes with the morning'" (Psalm 30:5b). Prayers like these validate and arouse in us not only the necessity of the lament but also the potency of words, including biblical guides, in helping us to deal with conflicting "images" of God as loving and kind on the one hand, and absent or chastising on the other.[13]

Through the lament, a storied language also emerges that reveals our need to "tell it like it is." That is, laments derive from the concrete stuff of our lives, which become part of the prayer life of the worshiping congregation. Thus, the prayer may be akin to Fred Lofton's lament of contemporary circumstances reflecting black people's mental enslavement and our forsaking God's purpose for us rather than God's forsaking us. Specifically, the lament is for our sons in jail, young daughters bearing children out of wedlock, dope running rampant in our communities, hoodlums besieging our neighborhoods, churches and houses being burglarized, brothers and sisters forgetting those left behind in ghettos, and the embrace of a destiny bent on self-destruction. Yet, the structure of the lament moves us from the complaint toward hope through pleas of mercy and help that come from God and from our being God's instruments of healing action in the world.[14]

Whether in the form of a complaint to God about God's presence (or absence) in life's sojourn or in the form of a lament about realities that reflect our own failure to fulfill God's purposes, prayers are evocative experiences that help us see ourselves and God more fully. Through these prayers, we become aware that we need not hide anything from God and that, in fact, prayers open the way for healing. In this way, prayers of lament nurture faith in God and ourselves and hope that carries us into the unknown future.[15]

DISCLOSING CONFESSIONS, APPEALS, COMMITMENTS, AND INTERCESSION

Prayer in the black worshiping congregation arouses in worshipers the importance and models of confessing sinfulness, appealing for forgiveness, and committing to Christian discipleship, which clergy, liturgists, and worshipers disclose. The worshipers' participation in the language of these forms of prayer become for us a way not only of learning what to say and how to say it but also of being enriched, nurtured, and even transformed in our relationship with God, others, and all things.

Mention has already been made in the earlier chapters on sin and salvation and especially in chapter 8 about prayers of confession and appeals for forgiveness in the ritual of the Welcome Table or Holy Communion. However, it is helpful to add here that prayers emphasizing sin, or what Howard Thurman calls "the imperfections of our lives,"[16] forgiveness, and commitment are integral aspects of our human biography that necessarily become part of faith- and hope-filled conversations with God in worship. In the worshiping congregation, these prayers heighten our awareness of our human difficulty to acknowledge our imperfections, our inability to manage them, and our tendency to be servants of our minds and will rather than God's, as Thurman's prayer points out.

Yet, the nurture that derives from prayer is not complete without the appeal for grace. Nurture depends on prayer that engages and guides us in forming and expressing language that leads beyond acknowledging imperfections to our appeal for guidance in confronting them as indicated in the gospel hymn "Give Me a Clean Heart."[17] Similarly, this appeal is found in the language of the gospel prayer song "Lead Me, Guide Me," to which I referred earlier.[18] In this latter instance, the theme of faith and hope appears in the assertion that all of one's trust is placed in God's leadership to direct the self toward the light and into servanthood.[19] Nurture is about engaging worshipers in prayers or structures for conversations with God that have ramifications for the Christian lifestyle beyond the worshiping congregation.[20]

Like so many other prayers of black people, prayers of confessions, appeal, and commitment also serve as models for drawing on scripture. The prayers present a biblically based language that is part of the black prayer tradition after which ongoing black prayer life is patterned. Such language is shown, for example, in prayers that are drawn from the reference in Isaiah 59:1-2 that ". . . the LORD's hand is not too short to save, / nor his ear too dull to hear"[21] and in Isaiah 6:8, "Here am I; send me!"[22]

In similar fashion, the gospel prayer song "Even Me" provides for black worshipers an approach to drawing on biblical material to frame a prayer of entreaty that the Savior would give showers of blessing to the thirsty soul (an allusion to Ezekiel 34:26) and would not pass the sinner by, but would, instead, bless even me.[23] Moreover, although not always present, the reference to scripture is found in prayers of intercession on behalf of the needs of those in the community as noted in the example based on Matthew 7:7 and Luke 11:9: "Lord, God-a-mighty, you done told us in your Word to seek and we shall find; knock and the door be open; ask, and it shall be given. . . and, Lord, tonight we is a-seekin. Way down here in this rain-washed world, kneelin here by this bed of affliction pain, your humble servant is a-knockin, and askin for your lovin mercy, and your tender love."[24]

DEVELOPING AN ORATORY OF FAITH AND HOPE

Praying in the black worshiping congregation is an "oratory of faith and hope." Building this oratory takes place through the intentional uses of metaphors of hope that affirm the valued identity of black people presented in chapter 4, and that center on God, the Source of our faith and hope. This oratory also builds on the assumption that faith and hope are to be acted on. A few more comments on prayer as an "oratory of faith and hope" need to be made at this juncture particularly on its nurturing role in affirming a valued identity, our embrace of God, the Source of our faith and hope, and ways of acting on the oratory.

Affirmations of Valued Identity and the Source of Faith and Hope

In chapter 4, I mentioned James Washington's statement that "prayers in the midst of the abortion of one's human, political, and social rights is an act of justice education insofar as it reminds the one who prays, and the one who overhears it, that the one praying is a child of God."[25] His statement aptly reflects the presence of prayers that not simply draw attention to our valued identity but that seek God's help in making us conscious of our existence as God's children.[26]

The black "oratory of faith and hope" is invariably nurture-bearing activity that not only affirms the one who utters it is a child of God but also identifies God as the Source of faith and hope by virtue of the strength God gives us; therefore God is worthy of the "Total Praise" that appears in the title of a gospel song."[27]

Assumptions of Faith and Hope to Be Acted On

Prayers in the black worshiping congregation assume that we are to respond concretely in life to that which we ask in prayer. Stated another way, our prayers function as messages to black worshipers to be faithful sojourners who freely live the Christian life without hope of reward or in spite of the human dilemma of not always experiencing and seeing clearly God's justice and love. Hope-filled prayer is, then, the act of guiding the believer to trust God's ultimate disclosure. Faith and hope-filled prayer "teaches" us to wait on the Lord who will renew our strength (Isaiah 40:31); and, it nurtures us in the exercise of "revolutionary patience."[28] With this kind of faith and patience, we recognize that an answer to a prayer may not come in the near or even far-flung future, but it is envisioned and spoken nonetheless in the heart and leaned toward by the verve of the spirit that is lifted and carried by the Spirit of the living God.

NURTURING EXPRESSIVE AND DIALOGICAL PRAYER STYLE

Prayer in the black worshiping congregation tends to be an expressive and dialogical endeavor. As alluded to earlier, prayers are often offered extemporaneously. Prayers said by the whole community are entered into rhythmically, intensely, and often through prayer songs or accompanied by music. The prayers of individual persons are punctuated by "Amens," "Yes, Lord," "Do, Lord," and "hallelujahs," as well as by audible sighs, and even obvious crying or shouting.

Without intending it to be so, times of prayer in the black worshiping congregation are "teachable moments" that nurture our understanding of what it means to be a thinking and feeling community in creative conversation with God. These moments convey the notion that it is not possible to nurture faith and hope through prayer without overt and expressive involvement simply because matters of faith and hope necessarily generate affect that cannot be suppressed. Consequently, what forms in the "teachable moments" of prayer is an appreciation, as Wyatt Tee Walker describes it, that praying is a patently rhythmic and poetic endeavor and that a certain kind of drama evolves when prayer combines with musical background. As stated earlier, in so many cases, black worshipers expect to hear the injunction for "every head to bow and every eye shut." Worshipers come to know that no moving around the sanctuary is tolerated and that the ushers' task is to guard the entrances zealously. They build an understanding that prayer time is talking-to-God time and that this conversation, like preaching and singing, will move toward a climactic finish.[29]

It must also be added here that praying through song provides an added nurturing dimension with "teachable moments" in which black worshipers form another expressive way of thinking, feeling, and talking with God. In prayer songs, we are allowed to repeat our ideas, rhyme our thoughts, and clap or engage in other bodily movements as so often happens in the musical appeal to God found in the song "Guide My Feet while I Run This Race."[30] Praying in song enlarges our prayer language. What evolves from the experiences of praying through singing is an awareness that, in song, we are enabled to express thoughts and feelings to God that we find inexpressible in spoken language.

In short, the overall experiences of prayer in the black worshiping congregation generate conscious awareness of a passionate style of praying; and these experiences have the effect of nurturing or evoking a desire for this style in new members and future generations. Moreover, repeated instances of overhearing, observing, and participating in expressive and spontaneous prayer are means of "practicing" and deepening this particular form of "primary speech" to the point that it becomes a mode of being rather than simply "a ritual."[31]

COMMENTARY

If we are to nurture persons' growth in faith and hope, then we must engage them in practices that actually make this happen. Prayer may certainly be regarded as a pivotal nurture-bearing practice in which we engage people in the worshiping congregation. However, it is also true that for prayer to *actually become* the mode of being of a person who is growing in faith and hope, it must increasingly become wholly part of that person. In other words, with regard to prayer, the growing individual person must continue to expand his or her understanding of prayer, and his or her participation in or even leading of it. Moreover, evidence of the deepening of our prayer life as part of our growth in faith and hope is noted both in our carrying out and sustaining our prayer life in varied ways in and beyond the worshiping congregation.[32]

With regard to prayer, to use Craig Dykstra's words, then, "it is one thing to recite a prayer . . . along with a congregation. It is another thing actually to *pray* that prayer."[33] Yet, people cannot do what they have not been taught to do. Of course, people learn how to pray by following the directions of the prayer giver, through imitating others, and through repeated recitations of prayers in the worshiping congregation. However, it is immensely important that there be times apart from the worshiping congregation when people become part of purposeful guidance and reflection on what we are really doing when we pray and how we grasp and deal with expectations or perceived outcomes of prayer.

Evidence of the importance of this appended approach to prayer was shown in an incident some years ago when a seasoned layperson was invited by the pastor to offer the invocation at an upcoming worship service as means of cultivating lay leadership in the service. The layperson replied, "Reverend, that's what we pay you to do." The pastor, as part of the weekly prayer and Bible study class, changed the approach to one of exploring meanings of the prayer life and kinds of prayer. Gradually, each member of the class took turns in offering prayer, and from this class, members became the prayer-givers during the morning worship. A remarkable thing also happened. The number of people attending the prayer and Bible study class grew. Moreover, periodically, a time of intercessory prayer was carried out in the worshiping congregation through what the pastor called the "de-centralization of the pulpit." That is, people in the pews were invited to turn to one another and form small clusters of two or three and share a prayer request or praise report followed by each one praying on behalf of the other(s) in the cluster. In this congregation, nurturing faith and hope through prayer became a mode of being of the community of faith.

Finally, the significance of prayer in our current age of depersonalization, busyness, and uncertainty about the future lies in the hunger of persons of all ages for practices that nurture faith and hope. People are hungry for what Jon Hendricks calls "generative futures"[34] in an age when many are raising the Nietzschean-like question, "Is God dead?"[35] The call of prayer is very real not simply for black people but across the spectrum of ethnic groups. Indeed, this may well be a time of new beginnings in prayer as a mode of being if we are to nurture people toward a vital life of faith and hope that can be lived fully in the present and into the anticipated coming tomorrows.

AN INVITATION TO REFLECT

1. What is the role of prayer in your congregation?

2. Who prays in your congregation?

3. How would you assess your own understanding of prayer and its impact on your life?

4. In what ways would you say there is need for greater attention to nurturing faith and hope through prayer in your congregation? In your life? What suggestions would you have for giving this attention?

NOTES

INTRODUCTION:
Black Worship as Nurturing Experience

1. Attention is given here to the role of Christian education in worship by Christian educators and others over the past two decades as found in: Charles R. Foster, Ethel R. Johnson, and Grant S. Shockley, *Christian Education Journey of Black Americans Past, Present, Future* (Nashville: Discipleship Resources, 1985), 22–33; Maria Harris, *Fashion Me a People: Curriculum in the Church* (Louisville: Westminister John Knox, 1989); Eugene C. Roehlkepartain, *The Teaching Church: Moving Christian Education to Center Stage* (Nashville: Abingdon, 1993), 12, 63; Jack Seymour, Margaret Ann Crain, and Joseph V. Crockett, *Educating Christians: The Intersection of Meaning, Learning, and Vocation* (Nashville: Abingdon, 1993), 101; John M. Hull, and others, "Critical Openness in Christian Nurture," in *A Reader on the Aims, Principles, and Philosophy of Christian Education*, ed. Jeff Astley and Leslie J. Francis, 251–75 (Harrisburg, Pa.: Gracewing Books through Morehouse Publishing, 1994); Charles R. Foster, *Educating Congregations* (Nashville: Abingdon, 1994); Jeff Astley, "The Role of Worship in Christian Learning," in *Theological Perspectives in Christian Formation: A Reader on Theology and Christian Education*, ed. Jeff Astley, Leslie F. Francis, and Colin Crowder, (Grand Rapids, Mich.: W. B. Eerdmans, 1996) 244–51; Craig Dykstra, "The Formative Power of the Congregation," in *Theological Perspectives on Christian Formation: A Reader on Theology and Christian Education*, ed. Jeff Astley, Leslie J. Francis, and Colin Crowder, (Grand Rapids, Mich.: W. B. Eerdmans, 1996) 252–65.

2. See Astley, "The Role of Worship in Christian Learning," in

Theological Perspectives on Christian Formation: A Reader on Theology and Christian Education, ed. Jeff Astley, Leslie J. Francis, and Colin Crowder (Grand Rapids, Mich.: W. B. Eerdmans, 1996), 244.

3. Roehlkepartain cites the Search Institute study as a motivating force in moving Christian education to center stage. See Roehlkepartain, *Teaching Church,* 12; Peter L. Benson and Carolyn H. Eklin, *Effective Christian Education: A National Study of Protestant Congregations—A Summary Report on Faith, Loyalty, and Congregational Life* (Minneapolis: Search Institute, 1990).

4. Roehlkepartain, *Teaching Church,* 63.

5. Ibid., 12.

6. Harris, *Fashion Me a People,* 63.

7. Seymour, Crain, and Crockett, *Educating Christians,* 101.

8. Astley, "Role of Worship in Christian Learning," 244.

9. Dykstra, "Formative Power of the Congregation," 264.

10. Ethel Johnson and Charles Foster, "Aims of Christian Education for United Methodists from the Perspective of the Black Religious Experience," in Foster, Johnson, and Shockley, *Christian Education Journey,* 24, 33.

11. Melva Wilson Costen, *African American Christian Wor-*ship (Nashville: Abingdon, 1993), 78.

12. Carlyle Fielding Stewart III, *African American Church Growth: Twelve Principles of Prophetic Ministry* (Nashville: Abingdon, 1994), 68–69, 102.

13. Stewart, *African American Church Growth,* 68.

14. Foster, *Educating Congregations,* 43.

15. Ibid., 40–41.

16. The words are part of the gospel hymn written by famous hymnist and preacher, Charles Tindley. The hymn is found in *Songs of Zion,* Supplemental Worship Resources 12 (Nashville, Abingdon, 1982), no. 10.

17. Iris Cully makes the point that, while nurture includes the educational goal of development, it "goes beyond the meaning of development, because it introduces a factor apart from the natural tendency of the organism itself to mature. It implies a person through whom this process can be implemented. The image of the nursing mother is there." See Iris V. Cully, "Christian Education: Instruction or Nurture," in *Who Are We? The Quest for a Religious Education,* ed. John H. Westerhoff (Birmingham, Ala.: Religious Education Press, 1978), 159.

18. A response given in an open dialogue session led by the author.

19. See James J. Murphy, *Rhetoric in the Middle Ages: A History of Rhetorical Theology from Saint Augustine to the Renaissance* (Berkeley: Univ. of California Press, 1974), 287–89.

20. Anne E. Streaty Wimberly, *Soul Stories: African American Christian Education* (Nashville: Abingdon, 1994).

21. Further background information on the trend from hope to hopelessness in the black community appears in Anne E. Streaty Wimberly, "A Black Christian Pedagogy of Hope: Religious Education in Black Perspective," in *Religious Education in the Third Millennium*, ed. James Michael Lee (Birmingham, Ala.: Religious Education Press, 2000), 155–58.

22. Michael I. N. Dash, Jonathan Jackson, and Stephen C. Rasor, *Hidden Wholeness: An African American Spirituality for Individuals and Communities* (Cleveland: United Church Press, 1997), 55.

23. Ronald L. Braithwaite and Sandra E. Taylor, eds., *Health Issues in the Black Community* (San Francisco: Jossey-Bass, 2001), xii.

24. Ibid., xii.

25. See Dale P. Andrews, *Practical Theology for Black Churches: Bridging Black Theology and African American Folk Religion* (Louisville: Westminster John Knox, 2002), 130.

26. West actually makes the claim that liberation theologies ushered forth in the works of liberation theologians such as James Cone, Mary Daly, and Gustavo Gutierrez carried impressive power and insight; and these theologies were expected not simply to change the world but to keep a precarious theology alive. West contends that the passing of the high moment of liberation theology is a hidden truth. See Cornel West, *The Cornel West Reader* (New York: Basic Civitas Books, 1999), 394.

27. See John Lovell Jr., *Black Song: The Forge and the Flame, The Story of How the Afro-American Spiritual Was Hammered Out* (New York: Macmillan, 1972), 323.

28. Ibid., 323.

29. Ethel Johnson and Charles Foster state that the aim of Christian education in the black church is to prepare persons "to share the good news of God's love' fairly, clearly, and persuasively." See Johnson and Foster, "Aims of Christian Education for United Methodists," 33.

30. Lovell, *Black Song: The Forge and the Flame*, 323.

31. Andrews, *Practical Theology for Black Churches*, 130.

32. See C. Eric Lincoln, "Introduction," in Andrew Billingsley, *Mighty Like a River: The Black Church and Social Reform* (New York: Oxford Univ. Press, 1999), xxiv.

33. Andrew Billingsley, *Mighty Like a River: The Black Church and Social Reform* (New York: Oxford Univ. Press, 1999).

CHAPTER 1:
Faith and Hope in God

1. The process bears some resemblance to the catechesis orientation or community of faith enculturation model that John Westerhoff III proposes as well as the congregational paradigm of Charles Foster in which persons form or are enculturated into religious beliefs and values See John H. Westerhoff III, *Will Our Children Have Faith?* (New York: Seabury, 1983); Charles R. Foster, "Faith Community as a Guiding Image for Christian Education," in *Contemporary Approaches to Christian Education*, ed. Jack L. Seymour and Donald E. Miller, 53–71 (Nashville: Abingdon, 1982); and Foster, *Educating Congregations*.

2. See Teresa L. Fry Brown, "Just Preach," millennium issue, *African American Pulpit* (Summer 1999): 59.

3. The gospel song "God Is Able," written by William Herbert Brewster, appears in *We'll Understand It Better By and By*, ed. Bernice Johnson Reagon (Washington, D.C.: Smithsonian Institute, 1991), 228–230.

4. See Thomas Hoyt Jr., "Interpreting Biblical Scholarship for the Black Church Tradition," in *Stony the Road We Trod: African American Biblical Interpretation*, ed. Cain Hope Felder (Minneapolis: Fortress, 1991), 30–31.

5. The scripture has particular meaning for black people who continue to experience themselves in exile and in search of "home."

6. Anne E. Streaty Wimberly, *Soul Stories: African American Christian Education* (Nashville: Abingdon, 1994).

7. Carolyn Ann Knight, "If the Worst Should Come," millennium issue, *African American Pulpit* 3, no. 2 (Spring 2000): 84–91.

8. Ibid., 84–86.

9. Ibid., 88–89.

10. See Major J. Jones, *The Color of God: The Concept of God in Afro-American Thought* (Macon, Ga.: Mercer Univ. Press, 1987), 48.

11. Alton B. Pollard III, "Journey to Within," *African American Pulpit* 2, no. 3 (Summer 1999): 41.

12. Manners in which this evocative method occurs are found in the sermons of Teresa Fry Brown, "Just Preach," millennium issue, *African American Pulpit* 3, no. 2 (Spring 2000): 60–64; and Diane Williams, "The Man Who Ran from God," millennium issue, *African American Pulpit* 3, no. 2 (Spring 2000): 105–110.

13. Karen Black-Griffith, "So We Rebuilt the Wall," in Ella Pearson Mitchell, *Those Preaching Women:*

African American Preachers Tackle Tough Questions (Valley Forge, Pa.: Judson, 1996), 11, 14.

14. Ibid., 9.

15. Ibid., 10–11.

16. Ibid., 14–15.

17. Samuel D. Proctor, *Preaching about Crises in the Community* (Philadelphia: Westminster, 1988), 69.

18. Ibid.

19. James C. Perkins, "The Burden of the Lord: The Need for a Prophetic Voice," *The African American Pulpit* 2, no. 4 (Fall 1999): 47–51, 50.

20. Jacqueline Grant, "On Containing God," *The African American Pulpit* 3, no. 3 (Summer 2000): 24–31, 24.

21. Ibid., 28–29.

22. Ibid., 25.

23. Ibid., 29–30.

24. See Augustine, "The Uses of Rhetoric," in *The Company of Preachers: Wisdom on Preaching, Augustine to the Present*, ed. Richard Lischer (Grand Rapids, Mich.: W. B. Eerdmans, 2002), 277–92.

25. James Melvin Washington, *Conversations with God: Two Centuries of Prayers by African Americans* (New York: HarperCollins, 1994).

26. O. Richard Bowyer, Betty L. Hart, and Charlotte A. Meade, *Prayer in the Black Tradition* (Nashville: Upper Room, 1986).

27. The Western hierarchical, imperialistic, and dualistic views of God are explored in Sallie McFague, *Models of God: Theology for an Ecological, Nuclear Age* (Philadelphia: Fortress, 1987), 19.

28. Washington, *Conversations with God*, xxxi.

29. Gardner Taylor's statement, which points to this need, appears in Kirk Byron Jones, "An Interview with Gardner Taylor, *The African American Pulpit* 2, no. 3 (Summer 1999): 87–92, 91.

30. See Ibid., 91.

CHAPTER 2:
Faith and Hope in Jesus Christ

1. See Fred Hammond, *Radical for Christ: Pages of Life, Chapter 1* (Nashville: Brentwood-Benson Music Publishers, 1998), 42.

2. The term "Jesusology" was put forth by Joseph Washington in his critique of African American church faith. His discussion on the term is found in Joseph R. Washington Jr., *Black Religion: The Negro and Christianity in the United States* (Boston: Beacon, 1964), 146–48.

3. The view of Jesus as God is conveyed in the old spiritual "He Is King of Kings," found in *Lift Every Voice and Sing II: An African American Hymnal* (New York: Church Hymnal Corporation, 1993), no. 96.

4. Brown-Douglass states that the understanding of Jesus as God in black Christianity communicates that God did not ordain and support slavery, that God sustains black people in their suffering, and that God frees them from their bondage. Indeed, says Brown-Douglass, "because black Christians have known Jesus, through scripture and in their own lives, they have known that God is for them and not against them." See Kelly Delaine Brown-Douglass, "Reflections on the Second Assembly of EATWOT [Ecumenical Association of Third World Theologians]," in *Black Theology: A Documentary History*, ed. James H. Cone and Gayraud S. Wilmore, vol. 2, *1980–1992* (Maryknoll, N.Y.: Orbis, 1998), 402.

5. These words appear in the gospel song "Good Times," written by B. Jones, J. Carruthers, E. Velz, E. Isley, C. Jasper, and M. Isley. The song appears in *WOW Gospel 2000: The Year's 30 Top Gospel Artists and Songs* (Franklin, Tenn.: Brentwood-Benson Music Publishers, 2000), 54–65.

6. See Montrel Darrett, "Oh, What a Friend," in *WOW Gospel 2000: The Year's Thirty Top Gospel Artists and Songs* (Franklin, Tenn.: Brentwood-Benson Music Publishers, 2000), 129–42.

7. See "I Must Tell Jesus" in *Lift Every Voice and Sing II*, no. 66.

8. The words come from an old Negro spiritual.

9. These words appear in the gospel song "Blessed Quietness," in *Songs of Zion*, no. 206.

10. The words appear in the gospel song "The Lord Will Make a Way Somehow," in *Yes, Lord! Church of God in Christ Hymnal* (Memphis, Tenn.: Church of God in Christ Publishing Board, 1982), no. 382.

11. The words are part of the traditional African-American spiritual "Jacob's Ladder." A version of the spiritual appears in *Songs of Zion*, no. 205.

12. See Hoyt, "Interpreting Biblical Scholarship," 29.

13. The entire gospel song "I Thank You, Jesus" appears in *African American Heritage Hymnal* (Chicago: GIA Publications, Inc., 2001), no. 532.

14. The use of the term "appreciative consciousness" is somewhat akin to Bernard Eugene Meland's description of the creative and dynamic nature by which people perceive and live truth. However, my use of the term suggests that people not only shape truth but also are shaped by the gospel of Jesus contained in scripture. Meland's use of "appreciative consciousness" as it applies to religious education is discussed in Randolph Crump Miller, "Empirical Theology and

Religious Education," in *Theologies of Religious Education*, ed. Randolph Crump Miller (Birmingham, Ala.: Religious Education Press, 1995), 150–51, 154–55.

15. See Miller, "Empirical Theology and Religious Education," 160.

16. The words are part of the song "Glorious Is the Name of Jesus" found in *Lift Every Voice and Sing II*, no. 63.

17. The words are part of the song "In the Garden," found in *Lift Every Voice and Sing II*, no. 69.

18. I recall these words of my father-in-law, Rev. Edgar Van Wimberly Sr. not simply in the congregations he served, but in family gatherings as well. He is now deceased.

19. See M. Moran Weston's prayer in Washington, ed., *Conversations with God*, 223.

20. See Jeremiah Wright Jr., "An Altar Prayer," in Washington, *Conversations with God*, 258.

21. See Gail E. Bowman, "The Elder Brother, the Coins, and Those Other Ninety-Nine Sheep," *The African American Pulpit* 4, no. 2 (Spring 2001): 44–48.

22. Ibid., 47.

23. Ibid., 48.

24. Ibid.

25. Ibid.

26. See David F. White and Frank Rogers, "Existentialist Theology and

Religious Education," in *Theologies of Religious Education*, ed. Randolph Crump Miller, 172–96 (Birmingham, Ala.: Religious Education Press, 1995), 181.

27. The italics are added in the quote to emphasize the use of a reminder and the invitation to remember in the sermon. The quote is found in Henry H. Mitchell, "The Christmas Plunge," *The African American Pulpit* 3, no. 1 (Winter 1999–2000): 38.

28. Mitchell, "The Christmas Plunge," 38.

29. Ibid.

30. The italics are added and, therefore, not found in the original quote. The quote appears in Richard Wills, "From Mundane to Marvelous," *The African American Pulpit* 3, no. 1 (Winter 1999–2000): 67.

31. Ibid., 68, 71.

32. Mary Ann Bellinger, "Upright but *Not* Uptight," in *Those Preachin' Women: Sermons by Black Women Preachers*, ed. Ella Pearson Mitchell (Valley Forge, Pa.: Judson, 1985).

33. Ibid., 70.

34. Emphasis added. Ibid., 71.

35. Ibid., 71–73.

36. A version of the spiritual appears in *Songs of Zion*, no. 126.

37. Ibid.

38. See especially Suzanne D. Johnson Cook, "Look for Your Miracle," *The African American*

Pulpit 2, no. 4 (Fall 1999): 19–24; Elliott Cuff, "A Great Gulf Fixed," *The African American Pulpit* 2, no. 3 (Summer 1999): 21–27; Nan M. Brown, "The Mind of the Insecure," in Ella Pearson Mitchell, *Those Preachin' Women: Sermons by Black Women Preachers* (Valley Forge, Pa.: Judson, 1985); Deborah McGill-Jackson, "To Set at Liberty," in Ella Pearson Mitchell, *Those Preachin' Women: Sermons by Black Women Preachers*, 35–42 (Valley Forge, Pa.: Judson, 1985); Leon C. Riddick, "This Is the Life," in *Outstanding Black Sermons*, ed. Walter B. Hoard, vol. 2 (Valley Forge, Pa.: Judson, 1989), 95–102; John R. Bryant, "Don't Give Up," millennium issue, *The African American Pulpit* 3, no. 2 (Spring 2000): 150–53; Walter S. Thomas, "Leadership for the New Millennium,"millennium issue, *The African American Pulpit* 3, no. 2 (Spring 2000): 171–78; Samuel D. Proctor, "The Recovery of Human Compassion," *Sermons from the Black Pulpit*, Samuel D. Proctor and William D. Watley (Valley Forge, Pa.: Judson, 1984), 9–23; Marjorie Leeper Booker, "A Prescription for Humility," in *Those Preachin' Women: Sermons by Black Women Preachers*, ed. Ella Pearson Mitchell (Valley Forge, Pa.: Judson, 1985), 85.

39. McGill-Jackson, "To Set at Liberty," 37.

40. Ibid., 37.

41. Nan M. Brown, "The Mind of the Insecure," 67.

42. Ibid., 66.

43. Cook, "Look for Your Miracle," 19–20.

44. Bryant, "Don't Give Up," 152.

45. Ibid., 153.

46. Thomas, "Leadership for the New Millennium," 178.

47. Ibid., 178.

48. Booker, "Prescription for Humility, 178.

49. Ibid., 86.

50. Ibid., 87.

51. Ibid., 88.

52. Ibid., 88–89.

53. Ibid., 89.

54. Ibid., 90.

55. Constance Tarasar, "Orthodox Theology and Religious Education," in *Theologies of Religious Education*, ed. Randolph Crump Miller (Birmingham: Religious Education Press, 1995), 115.

56. See Louis Charles Harvey, "Black Gospel Music and Black Theology," *Journal of Religious Thought* 43, no. 2 (Fall–Winter 1986–87), 27.

57. See *African American Heritage Hymnal*, nos. 201, 245, 299, 308, 363, 368, 372, 375, 378, 381, 382, 384, 408, 424, 430–31, 432, 524.

58. See *Yes, Lord! Church of God in Christ Hymnal*, no. 230.

59. *Lift Every Voice and Sing II,* no. 81.

60. See "O Holy Night," *African American Heritage Hymnal,* no. 245.

61. See "Blessed Be the Name," *African American Heritage Hymnal,* no. 299.

62. See "There's Room at the Cross for You," *African American Heritage Hymnal,* no. 245; "Christ Is All," *African American Heritage Hymnal,* no. 363.

63. See "Just a Little Talk with Jesus," *African American Heritage Hymnal,* no. 378; "What a Friend We Have in Jesus," *African American Heritage Hymnal,* no. 430, 431.

64. See "Where Could I Go?" *African American Heritage Hymnal,* no. 432; "Friendship with Jesus," *Yes, Lord!* no. 230.

65. See "No, Not One," *African American Heritage Hymnal,* no. 308.

66. See "Lead Me, Lord," *African American Heritage Hymnal,* no. 145; "Lead Me to Calvary," *African American Heritage Hymnal,* no. 253; "All the Way My Savior Leads Me," *African American Heritage Hymnal,* no. 469; "Lead Me, Guide Me," *African American Heritage Hymnal,* no. 474.

67. See "Guide My Feet," *African American Heritage Hymnal,* no. 131.

68. See "O Holy Savior," *African American Heritage Hymnal,* no. 408.

69. See "Jesus, We Want to Meet," *Lift Every Voice and Sing II,* no. 81.

70. See "I Am Thine," *African American Heritage Hymnal,* no. 387.

71. See "Tis So Sweet to Trust in Jesus," *African American Heritage Hymnal,* no. 368; "Satisfied with Jesus," *African American Heritage Hymnal,* no. 372; "I Must Tell Jesus," *African American Heritage Hymnal,* no. 375.

72. See "The Lily of the Valley," *African American Heritage Hymnal,* no. 381; "Jesus Is All the World to Me," *African American Heritage Hymnal,* no. 382; "Can't Nobody Do Me Like Jesus," *African American Heritage Hymnal,* no. 384; "Savior, Like a Shepherd Lead Us," *African American Heritage Hymnal,* no. 424; "Jesus Is a Rock in a Weary Land," *African American Heritage Hymnal,* no. 222; "There Is a Balm in Gilead," *African American Heritage Hymnal,* no. 524.

73. See *Conversations with God,* 269, 273, 278, 279.

74. The entire prayer appears in O. Richard Bowyer, Betty L. Hart, and Charlotte A. Meade, *Prayer in the Black Tradition* (Nashville: Upper Room, 1986), 39.

75. See "He's So Real," *African American Heritage Hymnal,* no.

237; "I Am Redeemed," *African American Heritage Hymnal,* no. 512.

76. See "He Looked beyond My Fault," *African American Heritage Hymnal,* no. 258.

77. See "There Is Power in the Blood," *African American Heritage Hymnal,* no. 258.

78. See "He Brought Me Out," *African American Heritage Hymnal,* no. 509.

79. See "The Lord Will Make a Way Somehow," *Yes, Lord!* no. 382.

80. See "He Touched Me," *African American Heritage Hymnal,* no. 273.

81. See Frederick G. Sampson II, "The Death of Hope," *The African American Pulpit* 5, no. 1 (Winter 2001–2002), 107.

82. William Watley, "Growth and the New Millennium," millennium issue, *The African American Pulpit* 3, no. 2 (Spring 2002): 185–86.

83. See especially Deborah McGill-Jackson, "To Set at Liberty," 35–42; Samuel D. Proctor, Finding Our Margin of Freedom," in *Sermons from the Black Pulpit,* 35–43; J. Esther Rowe, "Living in the Paradox," *The African American Pulpit* 2, no. 3 (Summer 1999): 56–63; Cynthia Belt, "Who Is Your Primary-Care Physician?" *The African American Pulpit* (Fall

1999): 9–13; Samuel D. Proctor, "A Nation under God," in *Outstanding Black Sermons,* ed. Walter B. Hoard, vol. 2 (Valley Forge, Pa.: Judson, 1979), 89–94; and Watley, "Growth in the New Millennium," 179–86.

84. See Carolyn Ann Knight, "You've Got the Power," *The African American Pulpit* 4, no. 2 (Spring 2001): 73.

85. Ibid.

86. See McGill-Jackson, "To Set at Liberty."

87. See Thomas, "Leadership for the New Millennium," 177–78.

88. An analysis and critique of the impact of cyberspace on congregational life is found in Anne Streaty Wimberly, "The Faith Community as Listener in the Era of Cyberspace," *The Journal of the Interdenominational Theological Center* 25, no. 2 (Fall 1977): 13–65.

89. The "ministry of meanings" is contained in a meaning-making paradigm that is presented in Ross Snyder, "Toward Foundations of a Discipline of Religious Education, *Religious Education* 62 (September–October 1967), 398.

CHAPTER 3:
Faith and Hope in the Holy Spirit

1. See "Let It Breathe on Me," *African American Heritage Hymnal,* no. 316.

2. Herbert Anderson and Edward Foley, *Mighty Stories, Dangerous Rituals: Weaving Together the Human and the Divine* (San Francisco: Jossey-Bass, 1998), 42–43.

3. Maguire highlights the role of story in affecting especially children's ability to listen, to think in words, and to exercise the mind's eye. However, the same role may be applied to adults. See Jack Maguire, *Creative Storytelling* (New York: McGraw-Hill, 1985), 13.

4. Teresa L. Fry Brown, "Breathing Lessons," *The African American Pulpit* 2, no. 3 (Summer 1999): 8–14.

5. Brown, "Breathing Lessons," 8.

6. See Wimberly, *Soul Stories*.

7. This linkage of the everyday story of humans with the Bible is akin to the second movement of my own story-linking model. See Wimberly, *Soul Stories*.

8. Brown, "Breathing Lesson," 10.

9. Types of questions for use in the nurturing process appear in J. Donald Butler, *Religious Education: The Foundations and Practice of Nurture* (New York: Harper and Row, 1962), 254.

10. Ibid.

11. Brown, "Breathing Lessons," 11.

12. Ibid.

13. Ibid., 13.

14. Ibid.

15. Ibid., 14.

16. Mary Elizabeth Mullino Moore, *Teaching from the Heart: Theology and Educational Method* (Harrisburg, Pa.: Trinity Press International, 1991, 1998), 141.

17. Samuel B. McKinney, "The Hot Winds of Change" in *Best Black Sermons*, ed. William M. Philpot (Valley Forge, Pa.: Judson, 1971), 40–49.

18. Ibid., 42.

19. Ibid., 42–43.

20. Ibid., 43.

21. I am reframing Capps reference to the three-story layers that are recognized in the therapeutic work of Eric Erickson. In that work, the layers include the story of the patient, Erickson's story to the patient of how things might be done differently, and Erickson's story or "teaching tale" of the outcome. See Donald Capps, *Living Stories: Pastoral Counseling in Congregational Context* (Minneapolis: Fortress, 1998), 84–86.

22. Ibid., 46.

23. Ibid., 46, 49.

24. Walter M. Brown Jr., "Are We Merely Gazing?" *The African American Pulpit* 2, no. 4 (Fall 1999): 14–18.

25. Ibid., 14–15.

26. Ibid., 15.

27. Ibid., 16.

28. Ibid.

29. See Butler, *Religious Education*, 254.

30. Brown, "Are We Merely Gazing?" 16.

31. Butler, *Religious Education*, 254–255.

32. Brown, "Are We Merely Gazing?" 17.

33. Ibid., 18.

34. See "I'm Gonna Sing," *Songs of Zion*, Supplemental Worship Resources 12 (Nashville: Abingdon, 1981), 81.

35. See "I've Got a Feelin'," *African American Heritage Hymnal*, no. 313.

36. Butler, *Religious Education*, 21.

37. See especially "Let It Breathe on Me," *African American Heritage Hymnal*, no. 316; "I've Got a Feelin'," *African American Heritage Hymnal*, no. 313; Gould-Champ, "An Unfinished Agenda," in *The Preaching Women: More Sermons by Black Women Preachers*, ed. Ella Pearson Mitchell (Valley Forge, Pa.: Judson, 1988); Teresa Fry Brown, "Breathing Lessons"; McKinney, "The Hot Winds of Change"; Walter Brown Jr., "Are We Merely Gazing"; Kenneth Walters Sr., "Would You Repeat That, Please?" *The African American Pulpit* 3, no. 3 (Summer 2000): 63–67; Richard Wiggs, "Try and Try Again," *The African American Pulpit* 3, no. 3 (Summer 2000): 75–80; Clara Mills-Morton, "The Blessings and Burdens of the Divinely Chosen," in *Those Preachin' Women: Sermons by Black Women Preachers*, ed. Ella Pearson Mitchell (Valley Forge, Pa.: Judson, 1985), 93–100.

38. Gould-Champ, "Unfinished Agenda," 78–79.

39. Butler, *Religious Education*, 21.

40. See Ellen T. Charry, *By the Renewing of Your Minds: The Pastoral Function of Christian Doctrine* (New York: Oxford Univ. Press, 1997), 213.

CHAPTER 4:
Faith and Hope in a Valued Self

1. C. Eric Lincoln, "Introduction," in *Mighty Like a River: The Black Church and Social Reform*, by Andrew Billingsley (New York: Oxford Univ. Press, 1999), p. xxiii.

2. The name and particular details of the story have been changed to assure the anonymity and the privacy of the person.

3. W. Wilson Goode, *In Goode Faith* (Valley Forge, Pa.: Judson 1992), 45.

4. Ibid., 47.

5. Ibid., 47–48.

6. Ibid.

7. Ibid., 49–50.

8. The prayer of William Donnel Watley makes this point more eloquently than it appears here. See Washington, *Conversations with God*, 263.

9. Building on the work of Barbara Myerhoff, Michael White describes a "definitional ceremony" as one that engages people, who are typically relegated to a marginal status in society, in reflecting on themselves and their lives in order to "become aware of options for intervening in the shaping of their lives." My use of the term, "redefinitional ritual" bears kinship to the "definitional ceremony," except that my particular term applies to what I have observed as taking place within the black Christian worshiping congregation. See Michael White, *Re-Authoring Lives: Interviews and Essays* (Adelaide, South Australia: Dulwich Centre Publications, 1995), 177–78.

10. See the prayer of William Donnel Watley appearing in Washington, *Conversations with God*, 263.

11. The process is one that invites black people into "reflexive self-consciousness that is akin to Michael White's uses of Barbara Myerhoff's work on definitional ceremonies in order that people may come to greater sense of their own worth." See White, *Re-Authoring Lives*, 177–78.

12. Ibid., 178.

13. White makes the connection between reflexive self-consciousness and one's "participation in the authoring of one's own life." Ibid.

14. David Buttrick makes the point that there are temporal, spatial, social, and personal languages comprising rhetorical intentions and that relate to particular modes of consciousness. From his way of thinking, the languages are separate distinctive ones because of the nature of human experience. More specifically, he states that "human experience is appropriated temporally (diachronic thinking), spatially (synchronic thinking), socially (corporate consciousness), and personally (self-awareness)," and "each of these orientations will produce a different language." My observation is that these orientations are actually different dimensions of the language black people use to redefine selfhood in the black worshiping congregation. See David Buttrick, "Designing Moves," in *The Company of Preachers: Wisdom on Preaching, Augustine to the Present*, ed. Richard Lischer (Grand Rapids: W. B. Eerdmans, 2002), 343.

15. Yvonnne V. Delk, "Singing the Lord's Song," in *Those Preachin' Women: Sermons by Black Women Preachers*, ed. Ella Pearson Mitchell (Valley Forge, Pa.: Judson, 1985), 57.

16. The use of association is described by David Buttrick as a form of Christian rhetoric used in preaching to demonstrate that our

Christian convictions are true to life. The rhetoric of association is a way of connecting Christian understandings with lived experience through a language of imagery, illustration, example, and testimony, for example. See Buttrick, "Designing Moves," 342.

17. Ibid., 56.

18. Ibid.

19. Frederick G. Sampson, II, "In This Moment, at This Dawn," *The African American Pulpit* 4, no. 3 (Summer 2001): 74.

20. Ibid., 73.

21. Ibid.

22. John R. Porter, "Nobody Knows Our Names," in *Outstanding Black Sermons*, vol. 2 (Valley Forge, Pa.: Judson, 1979), 85–87.

23. The actual song, "He Knows Just How Much We Can Bear," appears in *Songs of Zion*, 202.

24. A version of the song, "Changed Mah Name," appears in *Songs of Zion*, no. 118.

25. Washington, *Conversations with God*, 263.

26. The sermon appears in Cleophus J. LaRue, *The Heart of Black Preaching* (Louisville: Westminster John Knox Press, 2000), 184–91; Jeremiah A. Wright Jr., "What Makes You So Strong?" *Sermons of Joy and Strength from Jeremiah A. Wright, Jr.* (Valley Forge, Pa.: Judson, 1993), 147–61.

27. See LaRue, *Heart of Black Preaching*, 188.

28. Ibid.

29. See Ibid., 190–91.

30. See "I Am Redeemed," *African American Heritage Hymnal*, no. 512.

31. See Nee-C Walls and others, "The Call," *Wow Gospel 1998: The Year's Top Gospel Artists and Songs* (Franklin, Tenn.: Brentwood-Benson Music Publishing Company, 1998), 63–69.

32. Ibid., 66.

33. Ibid., 68.

34. See Rudolph Stanfield, "Stir Up," *Wow Gospel 1998: The Year's 30 Top Gospel Artists and Songs* (Franklin, Tenn.: Brentwood-Benson Music Publishing Company, 1998), 129–40.

35. This kind of enactive content appearing in the black worshiping congregation bears some kinship to David Buttrick's description of Christian preaching that focuses on disassociation. Disassociation distinguishes Christian understandings from common social attitudes and contrasts Christian lifestyles from the conventional ethos of human communities. See Buttrick, "Designing Moves," 342.

36. The testimony is one that I heard in a black worshiping congregation.

37. Porter, "Nobody Knows Our Names."

38. Martin Luther King Jr., "Three Dimensions of a Complex Life," in *Best Black Sermons*, ed. William M. Philpot (Valley Forge, Pa.: Judson, 1972), 10–11.

39. Augustine makes the point that unwisdom is marked by a flood of eloquence or fluent speech that is less than profitable and truthful. But, there is the need for wise eloquence that is both beneficial and truthful. See Augustine, "Uses of Rhetoric," 281–282.

40. Samuel D. Proctor, "Everybody Is God's Somebody," in Samuel D. Proctor and William D. Watley, *Sermons from the Black Pulpit* (Valley Forge, Pa.: Judson), 26.

CHAPTER 5:
Faith, Hope, and the Plight of Sin

1. J. Alfred Smith Sr., "The Future of the Black Church," in *Outstanding Black Sermons*, ed. J. Alfred Smith Sr. (Valley Forge, Pa.: Judson, 1976), 75.

2. This orientation is learned most notably from the prayers of black worshipers. See Washington, *Conversations with God*, 251.

3. Smith, "Future of the Black Church," 75.

4. William Jones Jr. states that, historically, black preaching has been uninhibited with respect to truth telling. See William Augustus Jones Jr., "Introduction," in *Out-standing Black Sermons*, ed. J. Alfred Smith Sr., 6–7.

5. Augustine, "Uses of Rhetoric," 280.

6. Smith, "Future of the Black Church," 75–76.

7. Ibid.

8. Ibid.

9. Deborah McGill-Jackson, "To Set at Liberty," 30–31.

10. This use of opposing ideas is also known as antithetical style, which incorporates contrasting ideas to amplify thought. Discussions of binary or antithetical contrasts as elements in rhetorical communication are found in Marvin Harris, *Culture, People, Nature: An Introduction to General Anthropology*, 4th ed. (New York: Harper and Row, 1985), 482; and David E. Aune, *The New Testament in Its Literary Environment* (Philadelphia: Westminster, 1987), 206.

11. L. Venchael Booth, "Are You Looking for Jesus," in *Outstanding Black Sermons*, ed. Walter B. Hoard, vol. 2 (Valley Forge, Pa.: Judson, 1979), 16.

12. Carolyn Ann Knight, "The Survival of the Unfit," in *Those Preachin' Women: Sermons by Black Women Preachers*, ed. Ella Pearson Mitchell, vol. 1 (Valley Forge, Pa.: Judson Press, 1985), 30–31.

13. As indicated in chapter 4, this use of disassociation reflects the statement of Buttrick that "Christian

preaching will also disassociate" or "distinguish Christian understandings from our common social attitudes," as well as show how "the ways and means of Christian love will be different." See David Buttrick, "Designing Moves," 342.

14. McGill-Jackson, "To Set at Liberty," 40.

15. See "Yield Not to Temptation," *Songs of Zion*, no. 62.

16. See Leotis Samuel Belk, "The Eyes of the Lord," in *Outstanding Black Sermons*, ed. J. Alfred Smith Sr., 9–14 (Valley Forge, Pa.: Judson, 1976), 11.

17. Ibid., 11–12.

18. See Buttrick, "Designing Moves," 342.

19. McGill-Jackson, "To Set at Liberty," 41.

20. See "Yield Not to Temptation," *Songs of Zion*, 62.

21. See Smith, "Future of the Black Church," 75.

22. See McGill-Jackson, "To Set at Liberty," 30–31.

23. See Booth, "Are You Looking for Jesus," 16.

24. See McGill-Jackson, "To Set at Liberty," 40.

25. See Belk, "Eyes of the Lord," 11.

26. See McGill-Jackson, "To Set at Liberty," 41.

27. Craig R. Dykstra, "Formative Power of the Congregation," 253.

28. Dykstra, "Formative Power of the Congregation," 259.

CHAPTER 6:
Faith, Hope, and the Promise of Salvation

1. This is part of the story found in the sermon by Otis Moss Jr., "Going from Disgrace to Dignity," in *Best Black Sermons*, ed. William M. Philpot (Valley Forge, Pa.: Judson, 1972), 56–57.

2. See Miller, "Empirical Theology," 165.

3. The words appear in the African American spiritual that was sung by the elders in the church of my childhood.

4. McGill-Jackson, "To Set at Liberty," 37.

5. Mieke Bal makes the point that textual analysis is not so much about the process of writing as it is about forming the conditions of the process of reception or the impact of the text on the reader. It seems to me that there is something similar that takes place in the sermon, particularly with reference to rhetoric that raises the hearers' consciousness of meanings of the text for their lives. That is, in the consciousness-raising process, worshipers are not simply invited into an analysis of what the message says or to consider answers to questions raised. Rather, the process into which worshipers are invited should somehow stimulate further thoughts and new questions. For the position of Bal, see Mieke Bal,

Narratology: Introduction to the Theory of Narrative, 2nd ed. (Toronto: Univ. of Toronto Press, 1997).

6. McGill-Jackson, "To Set at Liberty," 37–38.

7. Ibid., 38.

8. Ibid., 39.

9. See Ibid., 39–41.

10. See "Nothing but the Blood of Jesus," African American Heritage Hymnal, no. 262.

11. See "There Is Power in the Blood," African American Heritage Hymnal, no. 258.

12. See "How Can You Recognize a Child of God?" African American Heritage Hymnal, no. 266.

13. Versions of the spiritual appears in Anne Streaty Wimberly, The Church Family Sings: Songs, Ideas, and Activities for Use in Church School (Nashville: Abingdon, 1996), 58; Songs of Zion, no. 106.

14. See Washington, Conversations with God, 278.

15. See Ibid., 156.

16. See Ibid., 271.

17. Ibid.

18. Pollard, "Journey to Within," 39.

19. See Washington, Conversations with God, 203–4.

20. David Aune identifies this form of rhetoric as a teaching tool that was used in early Christian letters and homilies. See Aune, New

Testament in Its Literary Environment, 212.

21. Prathia Hall Wynn, "When the Hurts Do Not Heal," in Those Preaching Women: More Sermons by Black Women Preachers, ed. Ella Pearson Mitchell (Valley Forge, Pa.: Judson, 1988), 101.

22. The view of Ignatius appears in the context of the discussion in which Aune places the contrasting images style of rhetoric in "the two-ways tradition" found in early Christian letters and homilies. See Aune, New Testament in Its Literary Environment, 197.

23. See Washington, Conversations with God, 276.

24. Ella Pearson Mitchell, "Human Reclamation," in Those Preaching Women: African American Preachers Tackle Tough Questions, ed. Ella Pearson Mitchell, vol. 3 (Valley Forge, Pa.: Judson, 1996), 73.

25. Mitchell, "Human Reclamation," 74.

26. Ibid., 75.

27. Ibid., 76.

28. Ibid.

29. Ibid., 76–77.

30. Proctor, "Everybody Is God's Somebody," 26–27.

31. See "I Know It Was the Blood," African American Heritage Hymnal, no. 267.

32. See "He Looked Beyond My Fault," African American Heritage Hymnal, no. 249.

33. See "Balm in Gilead," *Songs of Zion*, no. 123.

34. See "Oh, It Is Jesus," *African American Heritage Hymnal*, no. 259.

35. See "Victory Is Mine," *African American Heritage Hymnal*, no. 489.

36. See "The Lord Is My Light," *African American Heritage Hymnal*, no. 160.

37. McGill-Jackson, "To Set at Liberty," 38.

38. Ibid., 37.

39. Stephen G. Ray Jr., *Do No Harm: Social Sin and Christian Responsibility* (Minneapolis: Fortress, 2003), 131.

40. See Washington, *Conversations with God*, 278.

41. See "Balm in Gilead," *Songs of Zion*, no. 123.

42. See Washington, *Conversations with God*, 278.

43. See Lovell, *Black Song: The Forge and the Flame*, 323.

CHAPTER 7:
Nurturing Faith and Hope through Baptism

1. James Mellon, ed., *Bullwhip Days, the Slaves Remember: An Oral History* (New York: Avon, 1988), 188–89.

2. The response emerged as part of a series of open discussions on the chapter of the book in classes at Interdenominational Theological Center.

3. Porter, "Nobody Knows Our Names," 82.

4. Meland makes the claim that the process of coming to appreciative consciousness entails an increasing receptivity that exposes more than what is immediately considered. See Bernard Eugene Meland, *Higher Education and the Human Spirit* (Chicago: Univ. of Chicago Press, 1953), 57.

5. Porter, "Nobody Knows Our Names," 87.

6. Mary Elizabeth Moore describes the phenomenological approach as that of helping persons to reflect on their stories and life situations, to uncover insights from what that experience discloses, and to decide on actions that the insights call forth. Her entire discussion of the uses of phenomenology in teaching appears in Mary Elizabeth Mullino Moore, *Teaching from the Heart: Theology and Educational Method* (Harrisburg, Pa.: Trinity, 1991, 1998), 104–30.

7. This statement appears in "Service of the Baptismal Covenant: Introduction," *The United Methodist Book of Worship* (Nashville: United Methodist Publishing House, 1992), 83.

8. Moore describes gestalt as "a theory of perception and learning based on the ways people organize

different phenomena into a unity greater than the sum of the parts." See Moore, *Teaching from the Heart*, 61.

9. See Charry, *By the Renewing of Your Minds*, 22.

10. See John A. Berntsen, "Christian Affections and the Catechumenate," *Worship* 52 (1978): 208.

11. Berntsen makes the point that emotions have a logic and conceptual determinacy. Moreover, emotions are not "wholly intelligible apart from thoughts, reasons, beliefs, and knowledge." See John A. Berntsen, "Christian Affections and the Catechumenate," in *Theological Perspectives on Christian Formation: A Reader on Theology and Christian Education*, ed. Jeff Astley, Leslie J. Francis, and Colin Crowder, 229–43 (Grand Rapids, Mich.: W. B. Eerdmans, 1996), 240.

12. Anderson and Foley, *Mighty Stories, Dangerous Rituals*, 74.

13. Foster reminds us that eventfull education, of which baptism is part, must include occasions for mutually critical reflection with others outside the boundaries of the event. This kind of reflection can be transformational as we discover more fully and live out the meanings we discover. This view is contained in: Foster, *Educating Congregations*, 48.

14. Berntsen, "Christian Affec-

tions and the Catechumenate," *Theological Perspectives on Christian Formation*, 231.

15. Ibid., 232.

16. A version of the spiritual is found in *African American Heritage Hymnal*, no. 676.

17. A version of the spiritual is found in *African American Heritage Hymnal*, no. 678.

CHAPTER 8:
Nurturing Faith and Hope through Holy Communion

1. James Evans Jr. identifies the Lord's Supper, or the eucharist, as basic in the life of the black church. See James H. Evans Jr., *We Have Been Believers: An African-American Systematic Theology* (Minneapolis: Fortress, 1992), 140.

2. References in the black church to Holy Communion as the Welcome Table is traceable to the slave era when white churches in the South and North routinely relegated black people to the backs, galleys, and standing spaces of white churches and would not allow them to take communion alongside white people. See Eugene D. Genovese, *Roll, Jordan, Roll: The World the Slaves Made* (New York: Vantage, 1976), 235; and Mellon, *Bullwhip Days*, 185.

3. The narrative is a testimony of an anonymous older adult.

4. See, for example, "The Great

Thanksgiving," in the Service of Word and Table, *The United Methodist Book of Worship* (Nashville: United Methodist Publishing House, 1992), 37.

5. See "Jesus Is Here Right Now," by Leon Roberts, published first by GIA Publications in 1986 and appearing currently in *African American Heritage Hymnal*, no. 684.

6. Craig Dykstra, "No Longer Strangers: The Church and Its Educational Ministry," in *Theological Perspectives in Christian Formation: A Reader on Theology and Christian Education*, ed. Jeff Astley, Leslie J. Francis, and Colin Crowder (Grand Rapids, Mich.: W. B. Eerdmans, 1996), 116.

7. Ella Pearson Mitchell, "The Welcome Table," in *Those Preaching Women: More Sermons by Black Women*, ed. Ella Pearson Mitchell, 81–87, vol. 2 (Valley Forge, Pa.: Judson, 1988).

8. Grey describes the central importance of positive self-esteem and the experience of "redemptive knowing" in the learning process in Mary C. Grey, "Feminist Images of Redemption in Education," in *Theological Perspectives on Christian Formation: A Reader on Theology and Christian Education*, ed. Jeff Astley, Leslie J. Francis, and Colin Crowder (Grand Rapids, Mich.: W. B. Eerdmans, 1996), 219, 221.

9. Stanley Hauerwas, "The Gesture of a Truthful Story," in *Theological Perspectives of Christian Formation: A Reader on Theology and Christian Education*, ed. Jeff Astley, Leslie J. Francis, and Colin Crowder, 97–105 (Grand Rapids, Mich.: W. B. Eerdmans, 1996); Stanley Hauerwas, *A Community of Character: Toward a Constructive Christian Social Ethic* (Notre Dame: Univ. of Notre Dame Press, 1981); Stanley Hauerwas, *The Peaceable Kingdom* (Notre Dame: Univ. of Notre Dame Press, 1983), 109–10.

10. Puckett reports a historical account of a black slave woman who entered a spiritual heaven and was nourished by a dinner with Jesus that consisted of turnip greens. See Newbell Puckett, *Folk Beliefs of the Southern Negro* (Chapel Hill: Univ. of North Carolina Press, 1996), 542.

11. See Dolan Hubbard, *The Sermon and the African American Literary Imagination* (Columbia Mo.: Univ. of Missouri Press, 1994), 132.

12. See "Plenty Good Room," *Songs of Zion*, no. 99.

13. Hauerwas, *Peaceable Kingdom*, 144.

14. Ibid.

15. This song by Andrae Crouch was first published by Manna Music, Inc., Burbank, California, 1996 and appears in *Songs of Zion*, no. 184.

16. Margie Lewter-Simmons,

"Our Spiritual Account," in *Those Preachin' Women: Sermons by Black Women Preachers*, ed. Ella Pearson Mitchell, (Valley Forge, Pa.: Judson, 1985), 114.

17. Lewter-Simmons, "Our Spiritual Account," 117.

18. Ibid.

19. The content of Ella Mitchell's sermon points to this essential function of nurture that takes place at the Welcome Table. See Mitchell, "Welcome Table," 85.

20. Samuel D. Proctor, "The Pastor as Teacher," in Samuel D. Proctor and Gardner C. Taylor, *We Have This Ministry: The Heart of the Pastor's Vocation* (Valley Forge, Pa.: Judson, 1996), 16.

21. Ibid.

22. Evans makes the point that, although Jesus' death was a concrete historical reality, the Lord's Supper "is the occasion for the celebration of Christ's contemporary with the faith." See Evans, *We Have Been Believers*, 140.

23. Robert L. Browning and Roy A. Reed, *The Sacraments in Religious Education and Liturgy: An Ecumenical Model* (Birmingham, Ala.: Religious Education Press, 1985), 179.

24. Anderson and Foley, *Mighty Stories, Dangerous Rituals*, 157.

25. Ibid.

CHAPTER 9:
Preaching as a Pathway to Nurture

1. Walker refers to preaching, praying, and singing as the essential trilogy in black worship. See Wyatt Tee Walker, *The Soul of Black Worship, A Trilogy: Preaching, Praying, Singing* (New York: Martin Luther King Fellows, 1984).

2. James H. Harris, *Pastoral Theology: A Black Church Perspective* (Minneapolis: Fortress, 1991), 56.

3. Thomas R. Swears, *Preaching to Head and Heart* (Nashville: Abingdon, 2000), 34–35.

4. Gardner Taylor, "The Pastor's Commission, " in Samuel D. Proctor and Gardner C. Taylor, *We Have This Ministry: The Heart of the Pastor's Vocation* (Valley Forge, Pa.: Judson, 1996), 19.

5. Olin P. Moyd, *The Sacred Art: Preaching and Theology in the African American Tradition* (Valley Forge, Pa.: Judson, 1995), 56.

6. See Thomas R. Swears, *Preaching to Head and Heart* (Nashville: Abingdon, 2000), 32–33.

7. See Victor Paul Furnish, "Theology and Ministry in the Pauline Letters," in *A Biblical Basis for Ministry*, ed. Earl E. Shelp and Ronald Sunderland (Philadelphia: Westminster, 1981), 109–11.

8. Gardner Taylor makes clear that some have drawn attention to the symmetry between the life of the

preacher and the preaching of the preacher. However, he goes on to point out that preachers confront the challenges of the world. Struggling with these challenges is very real. Yet, on the other hand, pastors are also called to be more than what they are—to exceed who they are. See Taylor, "Pastor's Commission," 8–11.

9. The superlative value of freedom in black churches dates back to the "Invisible Church" of the slaves. See C. Eric Lincoln and Lawrence H. Mamiya, *The Black Church in the African American Experience* (Durham: Duke Univ. Press, 1990), 5.

10. Reference to internal propheticism as a means of self-criticism appears in Dennis W. Wiley, "Black Theology, The Black Church and the African-American Community," in *Black Theology: A Documentary History*, ed. James H. Cone and Gayraud S. Wilmore, vol. 2, *1980–1992* (Maryknoll, N.Y.: Orbis, 1993), 130–34.

11. James Harris, *Preaching Liberation* (Minneapolis: Fortress, 1995), 56.

12. See Patricia Gould-Champ, "Unfinished Agenda," 77–78.

13. Ibid., 77.

14. Ibid., 73.

15. Ibid., 77.

16. Ibid., 75.

17. Ibid., 76.

18. Ibid., 77.

19. Samuel D. Proctor, "Relevant Religion," in *Outstanding Black Sermons, vol. 3*, ed. Milton E. Owens Jr. (Valley Forge, Pa.: Judson, 1982; repr., 1991), 58.

20. Delores Carpenter, "Bridging the Chasm," in *Out of Mighty Waters: Sermons by African American Disciples*, ed. Darryl M. Trimiew (St. Louis: Chalice, 1994), 14.

21. Magdalen Shelton, "Jesus, the Resurrector," in *Out of Mighty Waters: Sermons by African-American Disciples*, ed. Darryl M. Trimiew (St. Louis: Chalice, 1994), 69.

22. Ibid., 70.

23. Gould-Champ, "Unfinished Agenda," 79–80.

24. Harris indicates that uplift education typifies "the preaching tradition of stalwarts of the faith and giants of the church such as Bishop Joseph Johnson, the Rev. Jarenna [sic] Lee, Vernon Johns, Mordecai Johnson, Martin Luther King, Jr." See James Harris, *Preaching Liberation*, 12.

25. Ibid., 10.

26. Benjamin E. Mays, "What a Man Lives By," in *Best Black Sermons*, ed. William M. Philpot (Valley Forge, Pa.: Judson, 1972), 34–37.

27. See Anne Streaty Wimberly, *Soul Stories: African American Christian Education* (Nashville: Abingdon, 1994), 40–43.

28. James Harris, *Preaching Liberation*, 10.

29. Swears, *Preaching to Head and Heart*, 37.

30. See Swears, *Preaching to Head and Heart*, 37–38.

31. Ibid., 40.

32. Ibid., 41.

33. See Ibid., 43–44, 49.

34. See Ibid., 51–52, 56.

35. Ellen T. Charry, *By the Renewing of Your Minds*, 22.

36. Swears refers to a *theotokos*, or "God-bearer," as a description of the Catholic version of pastoral authority, which has to do with the pastor's role of leading others "more deeply into the mystery and pathos that surrounds life." See Swears, *Preaching to Head and Heart*, 53.

37. Michael I. N. Dash and Christine D. Chapman, *The Shape of Zion: Leadership and Life in Black Churches* (Cleveland: Pilgrim, 2003), 27.

38. Sanders makes the claim that our churches and preachers have forsaken the ancestral insistence on "love and kindness for each other in an unfriendly world" as a result of integration. From his perspective, there is need for repentance and deliverance that makes a prophecy more than simply "negative remarks about questionable lifestyles of people and nations." See Boykin Sanders, *Blowing the Trumpet in Open Court: Prophetic Judgment*

and Liberation (Trenton, N.J.: Africa World Press, 2002), 166–67, 172.

39. Dash and Chapman, *Shape of Zion*, 32–33.

CHAPTER 10:
Music Making as a Pathway to Nurture

1. The importance of black church music is discussed in W.E.B. DuBois, *The Souls of Black Folk* (New York: Washington Square, 1970), 206; Walker, *Soul of Black Worship*, 3, 45–85; Wyatt Tee Walker, *Somebody's Calling My Name: Black Sacred Music and Social Change* (Valley Forge, Pa.: Judson, 1982); Jon Michael Spencer, *Protest and Praise: Sacred Music in Black Religion* (Minneapolis: Fortress, 1990); Costen, *African American Christian Worship* (Nashville: Abingdon, 1993).

2. Westerhoff makes the point about the connection of cross-generational participation in worship to communicating faith by *being* the community of faith who offers the faith through the experience of its message. See John H. Westerhoff III, *Values for Tomorrow's Children: An Alternate Future for Education in the Church* (Philadelphia: Pilgrim Press, 1970), 29. Sandell also builds on this point in the resource: Elizabeth J. Sandell,

Including Children in Worship: A Planning Guide for Congregations (Minneapolis: Augsburg, 1991), 13.

3. See Westerhoff, *Will Our Children Have Faith?* 53–54; Sandell, *Including Children in Worship*, 13.

4. Sandell makes the point about the formation through worship in general of a foundation for future participation of children in the ministry of the church. See Sandell, *Including Children in Worship*, 14.

5. Zakkai describes the guidance of natural movement experiences through mention of "kinesthetic intelligence," which is activated through brief commands rather than having to explain everything before people move. However, my observations of and firsthand experiences of spontaneous bodily responses to music and Spirit-led movement in the black worshiping congregation are not guided in any fashion. Moreover, it seems to me that these responses and movements reflect the natural expression of what Zakkai calls "kinesthetic intelligence." See Jennifer Donohue Zakkai, *Dance as a Way of Knowing: Strategies for Teaching and Learning* (Los Angeles: The Galef Institute, 1997), 35.

6. Zakkai makes reference to a "built-in-movement vocabulary" and the importance of listening as well as stillness, including active stillness that is a highly energized

form of halted motion, and passive stillness, "in which all the muscles give into gravity and relax." See Zakkai, *Dance as a Way of Knowing*, 34.

7. See Urban T. Holmes III, *Ministry and Imagination* (New York: Seabury, 1976), 89.

8. Holmes raises the point about a language that promotes "inscape" or that helps people to see meanings behind words. Holmes also draws on Northrup Frye to state that imagination is something we *train* by saturating ourselves with the imaginative works of others. Moreover, he draws on Gerald Manley Hopkins to describe the quality of imaginative religious experience that promotes the convergence of phenomena into a unity around their source, which is God. See Holmes, *Ministry and Imagination*, 95–96, 105.

9. Astley draws attention to the implicit Christian educational role of worship that changes persons by promoting emotions, experiences, and attitudes that lie at the heart of Christian spirituality. See Astley, "The Role of Worship in Christian Learning," 244.

10. Berntsen describes the presence of emotions in the worshiping community as having logic that is expressed in emotion language. According to Berntsen, this language comprises a vocabulary that has

explanatory power in that it gives a *reason* for what is taking place. See Berntsen, "Christian Affections and the Catechumenate," 232.

11. Berntsen is very clear in his assertion that reason, belief, and knowledge cannot be separated from religious affectivity. See Berntsen, "Christian Affections and the Catechumenate," 231–33. Astley also concurs by making the claim that "All human acts are cognitive-affective; merely affective or merely cognitive acts do not exist." See Astley, "The Role of Worship in Christian Learning," 245.

12. See Holmes, *Ministry and Imagination*, 104.

13. Stephen Nachmanovitch, *Free Play: Improvisation in Life and Art* (New York: Jeremy P. Tarcher/ Putnam, 1990), 21–22.

14. See Lovell, *Black Song: The Forge and the Flame*, 323.

15. Nachmanovitch states that improvisation points to the importance of appreciating each moment, but he does not place his views in a religious framework. See Ibid., 24.

16. Astley, "Role of Worship in Christian Training," 247.

17. Ibid., 249–50.

CHAPTER 11:
Praying as a Pathway to Nurture

1. Prayer is identified as primary speech in Ann and Barry Ulanov, *Primary Speech: A Psychology of Prayer* (Atlanta: John Knox, 1982), 1.

2. Exact words to the gist of the prayer appearing here is found in Bowyer, Hart, and Meade, *Prayer in the Black Tradition*, 39.

3. Washington refers to prayer as "an oratory of hope" that addresses the distance between who we are and who we want to be. See Washington, *Conversations with God*, xxx.

4. Wyatt Tee Walker, *Soul of Black Worship*, 33.

5. Words to a prayer that presents this idea in specific terms are found in Washington, *Conversations with God*, 210.

6. Words to a prayer that presents this idea in specific terms are found in Ibid., 135.

7. See *African American Heritage Hymnal*, no. 451.

8. See "Kum ba Yah, My Lord," *Songs of Zion*, no. 139.

9. See "Lead Me, Guide Me," *African American Heritage Hymnal*, no. 474.

10. See "We Remember You," *African American Heritage Hymnal*, no. 683.

11. Washington, *Conversations with God*, xxxiii.

12. The words "Why have you forsaken me?" appear in Psalm 22:1; Mark 15:34; and Matthew 27:46.

13. Cully makes clear that people are taught ways of addressing God

that typically suggest God's love and kindness, while other teachings give voice to God's chastisement or rebuke. She contends that the ambivalence that comes from these conflicting "images" of God must be addressed in the presence of God so that God can be revealed. From her perspective, the spiritual life is impoverished if this is not done. See Iris V. Cully, *Education for Spiritual Growth* (San Francisco: Harper and Row, Publishers, 1984), 155.

14. See Washington, *Conversations with God*, 269–70.

15. Cully makes the point that prayers not only are means through which people can see nothing is hidden from God but also are avenues for transformation. See Cully, *Education for Spiritual Growth*, 155.

16. Thurman's prayer appears in Washington, *Conversations with God*, 218.

17. See "Give Me a Clean Heart," *Songs of Zion*, no. 182.

18. See "Lead Me, Guide Me," *African American Heritage Hymnal*, no. 474.

19. Ibid.

20. See Howard Thurman's prayer in Washington, *Conversations with God*, 218.

21. The prayer that incorporates a paraphrase of this pericope is found in Washington, *Conversations with God*, 33.

22. The prayer that incorporates this pericope is found in the song "Here Am I," *African American Heritage Hymnal*, no. 466.

23. See "Even Me," *African American Heritage Hymnal*, no. 457.

24. See Washington, *Conversations with God*, 211.

25. Ibid., xxxiv.

26. Ibid., 156.

27. See "Total Praise," *African American Heritage Hymnal*, no. 113.

28. Adrienne Rich in Washington, *Conversations with God*, xlvii.

29. Walker, *Soul of Black Worship*, 39.

30. See "Guide My Feet," *African American Heritage Hymnal*, no. 131.

31. See Washington, *Conversations with God*, xxxiii–xxxiv.

32. Dykstra makes three points in describing what is entailed in growing in faith. First, growth in faith requires persons' engagement in practices . . . in particular physical and material settings in the context of actual face-to-face interactions with us and with other people. Second, the practices must become one's own if they are to be actual actions of growing persons. Third, growth in faith is connoted by greater understanding, participation, and complexity of involvement, including carrying the practices out in broader arenas. See

Craig R. Dykstra, "No Longer
Strangers, 115.

33. Ibid.

34. See Jon Hendricks, "It's
about Time," in *Aging and the
Meaning of Time: A Multidisciplinary Exploration*, ed. Susan H.

McFadden and Robert C. Atchley,
(New York: Springer, 2001), 37–38.

35. See Anne E. Streaty
Wimberly, "Congregational Care in
a Wisdom-Seeking Age." *The
Journal of Pastoral Theology* 13, no.
1 (Spring 2003): 13.

BIBLIOGRAPHY

African American Heritage Hymnal. Chicago: GIA Publications, Inc., 2001.

Anderson, Herbert, and Edward Foley. *Mighty Stories, Dangerous Rituals: Weaving Together the Human and the Divine.* San Francisco: Jossey-Bass, 1998.

Andrews, Dale P. *Practical Theology for Black Churches: Bridging Black Theology and African American Folk Religion.* Louisville: Westminster John Knox, 2002.

Astley, Jeff, and Leslie J. Francis, eds. *A Reader on the Aims, Principles, and Philosophy of Christian Education.* Harrisburg, Pa.: Gracewing Books through Morehouse Publishing, 1994.

Astley, Jeff. "The Role of Worship in Christian Learning." *Theological Perspectives in Christian Formation: A Reader on Theology and Christian Education,* edited by Astley, Francis, and Crowder, 244–51.Grand Rapids, Mich.: W. B. Eerdmans, 1996.

Augustine. "The Uses of Rhetoric." In *The Company of Preachers: Wisdom on Preaching, Augustine to the Present,* edited by Richard Lischer, 277–92. Grand Rapids, Mich.: W. B. Eerdmans, 2002.

Aune, David E. *The New Testament in Its Literary Environment.* Philadelphia: Westminster, 1987.

Bal, Mieke. *Narratology: Introduction to the Theory of Narrative.* 2nd ed. Toronto: Univ. of Toronto Press, 1997.

Benson, Peter L., and Carolyn H. Eklin. *Effective Christian Education: A National Study of Protestant Congregations—Summary Report on Faith, Loyalty, and Congregational Life.* Minneapolis: Search Institute, 1990.

Berntsen, John A. "Christian Affections and the Catechumenate." In Astley, *Theological Perspectives on Christian Formation,* 229–43.

———. "Christian Affections and the Catechumenate." *Worship* 52 (1978).

Billingsley, Andrew. *Mighty Like a River: The Black Church and Social Reform*. New York: Oxford Univ. Press, 1999.

Bowyer, O. Richard, Betty L. Hart, and Charlotte A. Meade. *Prayer in the Black Tradition*. Nashville: Upper Room, 1986.

Braithwaite, Ronald L., and Sandra E. Taylor. *Health Issues in the Black Community*. San Francisco: Jossey-Bass, 2001.

Brown-Douglass, Kelly Delaine. "Reflections on the Second Assembly of EATWOT" [Ecumenical Association of Third World Theologians]. In *Black Theology: A Documentary History*, edited by James H. Cone and Gayraud S. Wilmore. Vol. 2, *1980–1992, 399–404*. Maryknoll, N.Y.: Orbis, 1998.

Browning, Robert L., and Roy A. Reed. *The Sacraments in Religious Education and Liturgy: An Ecumenical Model*. Birmingham, Ala.: Religious Education Press, 1985.

Butler, J. Donald. *Religious Education: The Foundations and Practice of Nurture*. New York: Harper and Row, 1962.

Buttrick, David. "Designing Moves." In *The Company of Preachers: Wisdom on Preaching, Augustine to the Present*, edited by Richard Lischer, 337–51. Grand Rapids, Mich.: W. B. Eerdmans, 2002.

Capps, Donald. *Living Stories: Pastoral Counseling in Congregational Context*. Minneapolis: Fortress, 1998.

Charry, Ellen T. *By the Renewing of Your Minds: The Pastoral Function of Christian Doctrine*. New York: Oxford Univ. Press, 1997.

Cone, James H., and Gayraud S. Wilmore, eds. *Black Theology: A Documentary History*, Vol. 2, *1980–1992*. Maryknoll, N.Y.: Orbis, 1998.

Cooper-Lewter, Nicholas C., and Henry H. Mitchell. *Soul Theology: The Heart of American Black Culture*. San Francisco: Harper and Row, 1986.

Costen, Melva Wilson. *African American Christian Worship*. Nashville: Abingdon, 1993.

Cully, Iris V. "Christian Education: Instruction or Nurture." In *Who Are We? The Quest for a Religious Education*, edited by John Westerhoff, 150–64. Birmingham, Ala.: Religious Education Press, 1978.

———. *Education for Spiritual Growth*. San Francisco: Harper and Row, 1984.

Dash, Michael I. N., and Christine D. Chapman. *The Shape of Zion: Leadership and Life in Black Churches*. Cleveland: Pilgrim Press, 2003.

Dash, Michael I. N., Jonathan Jackson, and Stephen C. Rasor. *Hidden Wholeness: An African American Spirituality for Individuals and Communities*. Cleveland: United Church Press, 1997.

DuBois, W.E.B. *The Souls of Black Folk.* New York: Washington Square, 1970.

Dykstra, Craig. "No Longer Strangers: The Church and Its Educational Ministry." In Astley, *Theological Perspectives in Christian Formation,* 106–118.

———. "The Formative Power of the Congregation." In Astley, *Theological Perspectives on Christian Formation,* 252–265.

Evans, James, Jr., *We Have Been Believers: An African-American Systematic Theology.* Minneapolis: Fortress, 1992.

Felder, Cain Hope, ed. *Stony the Road We Trod: African American Biblical Interpretation.* Minneapolis: Fortress, 1991.

Foster, Charles R. "Faith Community as a Guiding Image for Christian Education." In *Contemporary Approaches to Christian Education,* edited by Jack L. Seymour and Donald E. Miller, 53–71. Nashville: Abingdon, 1982.

———. *Educating Congregations: The Future of Christian Education.* Nashville: Abindgon, 1994.

Foster, Charles R., Ethel R. Johnson, and Grant S. Shockley. *Christian Education Journey of Black Americans Past, Present, Future.* Nashville: Discipleship Resources, 1985.

Furnish, Victor Paul. "Theology and Ministry in the Pauline Letters." In *A Biblical Basis for Ministry,* edited by Earl E. Shelp and Ronald Sunderland, 101–144. Philadelphia: Westminster, 1981.

Genovese, Eugene D. *Roll, Jordan, Roll: The World the Slaves Made.* New York: Vantage, 1976.

Goode, W. Wilson. *In Goode Faith.* Valley Forge, Pa.: Judson, 1992.

Grey, Mary C. "Feminist Images of Redemption in Education." In Astley, *Theological Perspectives on Christian Formation,* 216–226.

Hammond, Fred. *Radical for Christ: Pages of Life, Chapter 1.* Nashville: Brentwood-Benson Music Publishers, 1998.

Harris, James H. *Pastoral Theology: A Black Church Perspective.* Minneapolis: Fortress, 1991.

———. *Preaching Liberation.* Minneapolis: Fortress, 1995.

Harris, Maria. *Fashion Me a People: Curriculum in the Church.* Louisville: Westminister John Knox, 1989.

Harris, Marvin. *Culture, People, Nature: An Introduction to General Anthropology.* 4th ed. New York: Harper and Row, 1985.

Harvey, Louis Charles. "Black Gospel Music and Black Theology." *Journal of Religious Thought* 43, no. 2 (Fall–Winter 1986–87).

Hauerwas, Stanley. *A Community of Character: Toward a Constructive Christian Social Ethic.* Notre Dame: Univ. of Notre Dame Press, 1981.

———. "The Gesture of a Truthful Story." In Astley, *Theological Perspectives on Christian Formation*, 97–105.

———. *The Peaceable Kingdom.* Notre Dame: Univ. of Notre Dame Press, 1983.

Hendricks, Jon. "It's about Time." In *Aging and the Meaning of Time: A Multidisciplinary Exploration*, edited by Susan H. McFadden and Robert C. Atchley, 21–50. . New York: Springer, 2001.

Holmes, Urban T., III. *Ministry and Imagination.* New York: Seabury, 1976.

Hoyt, Thomas, Jr. "Interpreting Biblical Scholarship for the Black Church Tradition." In *Stony the Road We Trod: African American Biblical Interpretation*, edited by Cain Hope Felder, 17–39. Minneapolis: Fortress, 1991.

Hubbard, Dolan. *The Sermon and the African American Literary Imagination.* Columbia, Mo.: Univ. of Missouri Press, 1994.

Hull, John M., and others. "Critical Openness in Christian Nurture." In *A Reader on the Aims, Principles, and Philosophy of Christian Education*, edited by Jeff Astley and Leslie J. Francis, 251–75. Harrisburg, Pa.: Gracewing Books through Morehouse Publishing, 1994.

Johnson, Ethel, and Charles Foster. "Aims of Christian Education for United Methodists from the Perspective of the Black Religious Experience." In *Christian Education Journey of Black Americans, Past, Present, Future*, edited by Charles R. Foster, Ethel R. Johnson, Grant S. Shockley. Nashville: Discipleship Resources, 1985.

Jones, B., and others. "Good Times." *WOW Gospel 2000: The Year's 30 Top Gospel Artists and Songs.* Franklin, Tenn.: Brentwood-Benson Music Publishers, 2000.

Jones, Kirk Byron, "An Interview with Gardner Taylor." *The African American Pulpit* 2, no. 3 (Summer 1999): 87–92.

Jones, Major J. *The Color of God: The Concept of God in Afro-American Thought.* Macon, Ga.: Mercer Univ. Press, 1987.

Jones, William Augustus, Jr. "Introduction." In *Outstanding Black Sermons*, edited by J. Alfred Smith Sr., 6–7. Valley Forge, Pa.: Judson, 1976.

LaRue, Cleophus J. *The Heart of Black Preaching.* Louisville: Westminster John Knox, 2000.

Lee, James Michael. *Religious Education in the Third Millennium.* Birmingham. Ala.: Religious Education Press, 2000.

Lift Every Voice and Sing II: An African American Hymnal. New York: Church Hymnal Corporation, 1993.

Lincoln, C. Eric. "Introduction." In *Mighty Like a River: The Black Church and Social Reform*, by Andrew Billingsley, xix–xxiv. New York: Oxford Univ. Press, 1999.

———, and Lawrence H. Mamiya. *The Black Church in the African American Experience*. Durham: Duke Univ. Press, 1990.

Lischer, Richard, ed. *The Company of Preachers: Wisdom on Preaching, Augustine to the Present*. Grand Rapids, Mich.: W. B. Eerdmans, 2002.

Lovell, John, Jr. *Black Song: The Forge and the Flame, The Story of How the Afro-American Spiritual Was Hammered Out*. New York: Macmillan, 1972.

Maguire, Jack. *Creative Storytelling*. New York: McGraw-Hill, 1985.

McFague, Sallie. *Models of God: Theology for an Ecological Nuclear Age*. Philadelphia: Fortress, 1987.

Meland, Bernard Eugene. *Higher Education and the Human Spirit*. Chicago: Univ. of Chicago Press, 1953.

Mellon, James. *Bullwhip Days, The Slaves Remember: An Oral History*. New York: Avon, 1988.

Miller, Randolph Crump. "Empirical Theology and Religious Education." In *Theologies of Religious Education*, edited by Randolph Crump Miller, 148–171. Birmingham, Ala.: Religious Education Press, 1995.

Mitchell, Ella Pearson. *Those Preachin' Women: Sermons by Black Women Preachers*. Valley Forge, Pa.: Judson, 1985.

———. *Those Preaching Women: More Sermons by Black Women Preachers*. Vol. 2. Valley Forge, Pa.: Judson, 1988.

———. *Those Preaching Women: African American Preachers Tackle Tough Questions*. Vol. 3. Valley Forge, Pa.: Judson, 1996.

Moore, Mary Elizabeth Mullino. *Teaching from the Heart: Theology and Educational Method*. Harrisburg, Pa.: Trinity, 1991.

Moyd, Olin P. *The Sacred Art: Preaching and Theology in the African American Tradition*. Valley Forge, Pa.: Judson, 1995.

Murphy, James J. *Rhetoric in the Middle Ages: A History of Rhetorical Theology from Saint Augustine to the Renaissance*. Berkeley: Univ. of California Press, 1974.

Nachmanovitch, Stephen. *Free Play: Improvisation in Life and Art*. New York: Jeremy P. Tarcher/Putnam, 1990.

Proctor, Samuel D. *Preaching about Crises in the Community.* Philadelphia: Westminster, 1988.

———. "The Pastor as Teacher." In *We Have This Ministry: The Heart of the Pastor's Vocation,* by Samuel D. Proctor and Gardner C. Taylor, 13–30. Valley Forge, Pa.: Judson, 1996.

Puckett, Newbell. *Folk Beliefs of the Southern Negro.* Chapel Hill: Univ. of North Carolina Press, 1996.

Ray, Stephen G., Jr. *Do No Harm: Social Sin and Christian Responsibility.* Minneapolis: Fortress, 2003.

Reagon, Bernice Johnson. *We'll Understand It Better By and By.* Washington, D.C.: Smithsonian Institute, 1992.

Roehlkepartain, Eugene C. *The Teaching Church: Moving Christian Education to Center Stage.* Nashville: Abingdon, 1993.

Sandell, Elizabeth J. *Including Children in Worship: A Planning Guide for Congregations.* Minneapolis: Augsburg, 1991.

Sanders, Boykin. *Blowing the Trumpet in Open Court: Prophetic Judgment and Liberation.* Trenton, N.J.: Africa World Press, 2002.

Seymour, Jack L., and Donald E. Miller, eds. *Contemporary Approaches to Christian Education.* Nashville: Abingdon, 1982.

Seymour, Jack, Margaret Ann Crain, and Joseph V. Crockett. *Educating Christians: The Intersection of Meaning, Learning, and Vocation.* Nashville: Abingdon, 1993.

Snyder, Ross. "Toward Foundations of a Discipline of Religious Education." *Religious Education* 62 (September–October 1967).

Songs of Zion. Supplemental Worship Resources 12. Nashville: Abingdon, 1981.

Spencer, Jon Michael. *Protest and Praise: Sacred Music in Black Religion.* Minneapolis: Fortress, 1990.

Stewart, Carlyle Fielding, III. *African American Church Growth: 12 Principles of Prophetic Ministry.* Nashville: Abingdon, 1994.

Swears, Thomas R. *Preaching to Head and Heart.* Nashville: Abingdon, 2000.

Tarasar, Constance. "Orthodox Theology and Religious Education." In *Theologies of Religious Education,* edited by Randolph Crump Miller, 83–120. Birmingham: Religious Education Press, 1995.

Taylor, Gardner. "The Pastor's Commission." In *We Have This Ministry: The Heart of the Pastor's Vocation,* by Samuel D. Proctor and Gardner C. Taylor, 1–30. Valley Forge, Pa.: Judson, 1996.

Thurman, Howard. *Deep Is the Hunger.* New York: Harper, 1951. Reprint, Richmond, Ind.: Friends United, n.d.

United Methodist Church. "Service of the Baptismal Covenant: Introduction." *The United Methodist Book of Worship, 81–84* Nashville: United Methodist Publishing House, 1992.

United Methodist Church. "The Great Thanksgiving." In the Service of Word and Table, *The United Methodist Book of Worship*, 38–38. Nashville: United Methodist Publishing House, 1992.

Trimiew, Darryl M. *Out of Mighty Waters: Sermons by African-American Disciples.* St. Louis: Chalice, 1994.

Ulanov, Ann, and Barry Ulanov. *Primary Speech: A Psychology of Prayer.* Atlanta: John Knox, 1982.

Walker, Wyatt Tee. *Somebody's Calling My Name: Black Sacred Music and Social Change.* Valley Forge, Pa.: Judson, 1982.

———. *The Soul of Black Worship, a Trilogy: Preaching, Praying, Singing.* New York: Martin Luther King Fellows, 1984.

Walls, Nee-C, Da'dra Crawford, Steve Crawford, and Mary Tiller. "The Call." *Wow Gospel 1998: The Year's Top Gospel Artists and Songs.* Franklin, Tenn.: Brentwood-Benson Music Publishing Company, 1998.

Washington, James Melvin. *Conversations with God: Two Centuries of Prayers by African Americans.* New York: HarperCollins, 1994.

Washington, Joseph R., Jr. *Black Religion: The Negro and Christianity in the United States.* Boston: Beacon, 1964.

West, Cornel. *The Cornel West Reader.* New York: Basic Civitas, 1999.

Westerhoff, John H., III. *Values for Tomorrow's Children: An Alternate Future for Education in the Church.* Philadelphia: Pilgrim, 1970.

———, ed. *Who Are We? The Quest for a Religious Education.* Birmingham, Ala.: Religious Education, 1978.

———. *Will Our Children Have Faith?* New York: Seabury, 1983.

White, David F., and Frank Rogers. "Existentialist Theology and Religious Education." In *Theologies of Religious Education*, edited by Randolph Crump Miller, 172–96. Birmingham: Religious Education Press, 1995.

White, Michael. *Re-Authoring Lives: Interviews & Essays.* Adelaide, South Australia: Dulwich Centre Publications, 1995.

Wiley, Dennis W. "Black Theology, The Black Church and the African-American Community." In *Black Theology: A Documentary History*, edited by

James H. Cone and Gayraud S. Wilmore, 130–34.. Vol. 2, 1980–1992. Maryknoll, N.Y.: Orbis, 1980.

Wimberly, Anne E. Streaty. "A Black Christian Pedagogy of Hope: Religious Education in Black Perspective." In *Religious Education in the Third Millennium*, edited by James Michael Lee, 155–78. Birmingham, Ala.: Religious Education Press, 2000.

———. "Congregational Care in a Wisdom-Seeking Age." *The Journal of Pastoral Theology* 13, no. 1 (Spring 2003): 13–24.

———. *Soul Stories: African American Christian Education.* Nashville: Abingdon, 1994.

———. *The Church Family Sings: Songs, Ideas, and Activities for Use in Church School.* Nashville: Abingdon, 1996.

———. "The Faith Community as Listener in the Era of Cyberspace." *The Journal of the Interdenominational Theological Center* 25, no. 2 (Fall 1997).

Yes, Lord! Church of God in Christ Hymnal. Memphis, Tenn.: Church of God in Christ Publishing Board, 1982.

Zakkai, Jennifer Donohue. *Dance as a Way of Knowing: Strategies for Teaching and Learning.* Los Angeles: Galef Institute, 1997.

SERMONS CITED

Belk, Leotis Samuel. "The Eyes of the Lord." In *Outstanding Black Sermons*, edited by J. Alfred Smith Sr. Valley Forge, Pa.: Judson, 1976.

Bellinger, Mary Ann. "Upright but *Not* Uptight." In *Those Preachin' Women: Sermons by Black Women Preachers, edited by* Ella Pearson Mitchell. Valley Forge, Pa.: Judson, 1985.

Belt, Cynthia. "Who Is Your Primary-Care Physician?" *The African American Pulpit* 2, no. 4 (Fall, 1999): 9–13.

Black-Griffith, Karen. "So We Rebuilt the Wall." In *Those Preaching Women: African American Preachers Tackle Tough Questions*, edited by Ella Pearson Mitchell Vol. 3. Valley Forge, Pa.: Judson, 1996.

Booker, Marjorie Leeper. "A Prescription for Humility." In *Those Preachin' Women: Sermons by Black Women Preachers*, edited by Ella Pearson Mitchell. Valley Forge, Pa.: Judson, 1985.

Booth, L. Venchael. "Are You Looking for Jesus?" In *Outstanding Black Sermons*, edited by Walter B. Hoard. Vol. 2. Valley Forge, Pa.: Judson, 1979.

Bowman, Gail E. "The Elder Brother, the Coins, and Those Other Ninety-Nine Sheep." *The African American Pulpit* 4 no. 2 (Spring 2001): 44–48.

Brown, Nan. "The Mind of the Insecure." In *Those Preachin' Women: Sermons by Black Women Preachers*, edited by Ella Pearson Mitchell. Valley Forge, Pa.: Judson, 1985.

Brown, Teresa L. Fry. "Breathing Lessons." *The African American Pulpit* 2, no. 3 (Summer 1999): 8–14.

———, "Just Preach." Millennium issue, *African American Pulpit* 3, no. 2 (Spring 2000): 59–64.

Brown, Walter M., Jr. "Are We Merely Gazing?" *The African American Pulpit* 2, no. 4 (Fall 1999): 14–18.

Bryant, John R. "Don't Give Up." Millennium issue, *The African American Pulpit* 3, no. 2 (Spring 2000): 150–53.

Carpenter, Delores. "Bridging the Chasm." In *Out of Mighty Waters: Sermons by African American Disciples*, edited by Darryl M. Trimiew. St. Louis: Chalice, 1994.

Cook, Suzanne D. Johnson. "Look for Your Miracle." *The African American Pulpit* 2, no. 4 (Fall 1999): 19–24.

Cuff, Elliott. "A Great Gulf Fixed." *The African American Pulpit* 2, no. 3 (Summer 1999): 21–27.

Delk, Yvonne V. "Singing the Lord's Song." In *Those Preachin' Women: Sermons by Black Women Preachers*, edited by Ella Pearson Mitchell. Valley Forge, Pa.: Judson, 1985.

Gould-Champ, Patricia. "An Unfinished Agenda." In *Those Preaching Women: More Sermons by Black Women Preachers*, edited by Ella Pearson Mitchell. Vol. 2. Valley Forge, Pa.: Judson, 1988.

Grant, Jacqueline. "On Containing God." *The African American Pulpit* 3, no. 3 (Summer 2000): 24–31.

Jones, Kirk Byron. "An Interview with Gardner Taylor." *The African American Pulpit* 2, no. 3 (Summer 1999): 87–92.

King, Martin Luther, Jr. "Three Dimensions of a Complete Life." In *Best Black Sermons*, edited by William M. Philpot. Valley Forge, Pa.: Judson, 1972.

Knight, Carolyn Ann. "If the Worst Should Come." Millennium issue, *African American Pulpit*. 3, no. 2 (Spring 2000): 84–91.

———. "The Survival of the Unfit." In *Those Preachin' Women: Sermons by Black Women Preachers*, edited by Ella Pearson Mitchell. Vol. 1. Valley Forge, Pa.: Judson, 1985.

———. "You've Got the Power." *African American Pulpit* 4, no. 2 (Spring 2001): 69–73.

Lewter-Simmons, Margie. "Our Spiritual Account." In *Those Preachin' Women: Sermons by Black Women Preachers*, edited by Ella Pearson Mitchell. Valley Forge, Pa.: Judson, 1985.

Mays, Benjamin E. "What a Man Lives By." In *Best Black Sermons,* edited by William M. Philpot. Valley Forge, Pa.: Judson, 1972.

McGill-Jackson, Deborah. "To Set at Liberty." In *Those Preachin' Women: Sermons by Black Women Preachers*, edited by Ella Pearson Mitchell. Valley Forge, Pa.: Judson, 1985.

McKinney, Samuel B. "The Hot Winds of Change." In *Best Black Sermons,* edited by William M. Philpot. Valley Forge, Pa.: Judson, 1971.

Mills-Morton, Clara. "The Blessings and Burdens of the Divinely Chosen." In *Those Preachin' Women: Sermons by Black Women Preachers,* edited by Ella Pearson Mitchell. Valley Forge, Pa.: Judson, 1985.

Mitchell, Ella Pearson. "Human Reclamation." In *Those Preaching Women: African American Preachers Tackle Tough Questions,* edited by Ella Pearson Mitchell. Vol. 3. Valley Forge, Pa.: Judson, 1996.

———. "The Welcome Table." In *Those Preaching Women: More Sermons by Black Women Preachers,* edited by Ella Pearson Mitchell. Vol. 2. Valley Forge, Pa.: Judson, 1988.

Mitchell, Henry H. "The Christmas Plunge." *The African American Pulpit* 3, no. 1 (Winter 1999–2000): 37–41.

Moss, Otis, Jr. "Going from Disgrace to Dignity." In *Best Black Sermons,* edited by William M. Philpot. Valley Forge, Pa.: Judson, 1972.

Perkins, James C. "The Burden of the Lord: The Need for a Prophetic Voice." *The African American Pulpit* 2, no. 4 (Fall 1999): 47–51.

Pollard, Alton B., III. "Journey to Within." *The African American Pulpit* 2, no. 3 (Summer 1999): 35–41.

Porter, John R. "Nobody Knows Our Name." In *Outstanding Black Sermons,* edited by Walter B. Hoard. Vol. 2. Valley Forge, Pa.: Judson, 1979.

Proctor, Samuel D. "A Nation under God." In *Outstanding Black Sermons,* edited by Walter B. Hoard. Vol. 2. Valley Forge, Pa.: Judson, 1979.

———. "Everybody Is God's Somebody." In *Sermons from the Black Pulpit,* by Samuel D. Proctor and William D. Watley. Valley Forge, Pa.: Judson, 1984.

———. "Finding Our Margin of Freedom." In *Sermons from the Black Pulpit,* by Samuel D. Proctor and William D. Watley. Valley Forge, Pa.: Judson, 1984.

———. "Relevant Religion." In *Outstanding Black Sermons,* edited by Milton E. Owens Jr. Vol. 3. Valley Forge, Pa.: Judson, 1982.

———. "The Recovery of Human Compassion." In *Sermons from the Black Pulpit.* Valley Forge, Pa.: Judson, 1984.

Proctor, Samuel D., and William D. Watley. *Sermons from the Black Pulpit.* Valley Forge, Pa.: Judson, 1984.

Riddick, Leon C. "This Is the Life." In *Outstanding Black Sermons,* edited by Walter B. Hoard. Vol. 2. Valley Forge, Pa.: Judson, 1989.

Rowe, J. Esther. "Living in the Paradox." *The African American Pulpit* 2, no. 3 (Summer 1999): 56–63.

Sampson, Frederick G., II. "In This Moment, at This Dawn." *The African American Pulpit* 4, no. 3 (Summer 2001–2002): 104–7.

———. "The Death of Hope." *The African American Pulpit* 5, no. 1 (Winter 2001).

Shelton, Magdalen. "Jesus, the Resurrector." In *Out of Mighty Waters: Sermons by African-American Disciples*, edited by Darryl M. Trimiew. St. Louis: Chalice, 1994.

Smith, J. Alfred, Sr., "The Future of the Black Church." In *Outstanding Black Sermons,* edited by J. Alfred Smith, Sr. Valley Forge, Pa.: Judson, 1976.

Thomas, Walter S. "Leadership for the New Millennium." Millennium issue, *The African American Pulpit* 3, no. 2 (Spring 2000): 171–78.

Walters, Kenneth, Sr. "Would You Repeat That, Please?" *The African American Pulpit* 3, no. 3 (Summer 2000): 63–67.

Watley, William. "Growth and the New Millennium." Millennium issue, *The African American Pulpit* 3, no. 2 (Spring 2000): 179–86.

Wiggs, Richard. "Try and Try Again." *The African American Pulpit* 3, no. 3 (Summer 2000): 75–80.

Wills, Richard. "From Mundane to Marvelous." *The African American Pulpit* 3, no. 1 (Winter 1999): 66–71.

Wright, Jeremiah, Jr. "What Makes You So Strong," *Sermons of Joy and Strength from Jeremiah A. Wright, Jr.* Valley Forge, Pa.: Judson, 1993.

Wynn, Prathia Hall. "When the Hurts Do Not Heal." In *Those Preaching Women: More Sermons by Black Women Preachers*, edited by Ella Pearson Mitchell. Vol. 2. Valley Forge, Pa.: Judson, 1988.

RELATED TITLES FROM THE PILGRIM PRESS

BODACIOUS WOMANIST WISDOM
Linda H. Hollies

Hollies takes a look at the "bodaciousness" of women of color through stories of biblical women such as Queen Esther, Mary, the "bent over woman" in Luke 13, and other unnamed biblical women.
ISBN 0-8298-1529-5/Paper/144 pages/$18.00

THE MARK OF ZION
Congregational Life in Black Churches
Stephen C. Rasor and Michael I. N. Dash
Foreword by Carl S. Dudley

The companion book to *The Shape of Zion: Leadership and Life in Black Churches, The Mark of Zion* is the only Gallup-supported national sample of black religiosity. Takes a look at African American congregational life in the 21st century.
ISBN 0-8298-1576-7/Paper/144 pages/$16.00

MARTIN LUTHER KING IN THE AFRICAN AMERICAN PREACHING TRADITION
Valentino Lassiter

Lassiter shows how King—in his sermons which expressed determination in the struggle for justice and freedom—exemplified the African American preaching style begun in the early 1600s by slave preachers.
ISBN 0-8298-1433-7/Paper/128 pages/$14.00

METHODOLOGIES OF BLACK THEOLOGY
Frederick L. Ware

Ware provides an outstanding classification and criticism of perspectives in the academic study, interpretation, and construction of black theology in the U.S. from 1969 to the present.
ISBN 0-8298-1484-1/Paper/192 pages/$20.00

PLENTY GOOD ROOM
Women Versus Male Power in the Black Church
Marcia Y. Riggs

Riggs discusses African American church life as a case study for ethical reflection about sexual ethics and clergy ethics—the prevailing silence about sexuality in black churches and sexuality as a taboo in the Christian tradition.
ISBN 0-8298-1508-2/Paper/176 pages/$20.00

RECLAIMING THE SPIRITUALS
New Possibilities for African American Christian Education
Yolanda Y. Smith

The author encourages and aids African American churches in reclaiming their full heritage as Africans, African Americans, and Christians—their triple heritage—while emphasizing and illuminating the central role of the spirituals.
ISBN 0-8298-1551-1/Paper/192 pages/$22.00

THE SHAPE OF ZION
Leadership and Life in Black Churches
Christine Chapman and Michael I. N. Dash
Foreword by Lawrence H. Mamiya

A practical and functional resource providing a public profile of the organizational backbone of historically black congregations. The companion book to *The Mark of Zion: Congregational Life in Black Churches.*
ISBN 0-8298-1491-4/Paper/208 pages/$19.00

TROUBLE DON'T LAST ALWAYS
Emancipatory Hope among African American Adolescents
Evelyn L. Parker

A critical examination of African American adolescent spirituality that offers congregations a new theological framework for ministry. ISBN 0-8298-1540-6/Paper/176 pages/$19.00

TRUMPET IN ZION
Worship Resources
(Years A, B, and C)
Linda H. Hollies

Addresses God in the voice, verbiage, and expression of African Americans in worship. Lectionary-based resource.

Trumpet in Zion, Year A
ISBN 0-8298-1410-8/Paper/224 pages$14.00

Trumpet in Zion, Year B
ISBN 0-8298-1477-9/Paper/224 pages/$14.00

Trumpet in Zion, Year C
ISBN 0-8298-1558-9/Paper/224 pages$14.00

To order these or any other books from The Pilgrim Press, call or write to:
The Pilgrim Press
700 Prospect Avenue East
Cleveland, OH 44115-1100

Phone orders: 800.537.3394 (M-F, 8:30am-4:30pm ET)
Fax orders: 216.736.2206
Please include shipping charges of $5.00 for the first book and 75¢ for each additional book.
Or order from our Web site at www.thepilgrimpress.com.
Prices subject to change without notice.

264.0089
W757

110892